THE ULTIMATE
BAD BOYs

D1390406

THE ULTIMATE

Bad Boys

STAN FISCHLER

W

Warwick Publishing

Toronto   Los Angeles

www.warwickgp.com

We acknowledge the financial support of the Government of Canada through the Book Publishing Industry Development Program for our publishing activities.

ISBN 1-894020-35-9

Published by Warwick Publishing Inc.
388 King Street, West, Suite 111, Toronto, ON M5V 1K2
1300 North Alexandria Avenue, Los Angeles, California 90027

Distributed by Firefly Books Ltd.
3680 Victoria Park Avenue, Willowdale, ON M2H 3K1

Photographs: Dan Hamilton, Vantage Point Studios
Design: mercer digital design/Kimberley Young
Research Editors: Dan Saraceni, David Kolb, Amy Spencer

Printed in Canada

CONTENTS

THE ULTIMATE ALL-TIME HOCKEY FIGHTERS LIST

THE CURRENT CHAMPION — TONY TWIST

PROBERT, KOCUR, DOMI & MCSORLEY — KAYO KINGS OF THE DECADE

PROFESSOR PUNCH'S ALL-TIME HITTERS HALL OF FAME

30-SECOND THIRD DEGREE

BLASTS FROM THE PAST

To Jim McKenzie, an honest enforcer who always will be remembered for visiting my son, Simon, at Columbia Presbyterian Hospital while he awaited a heart transplant.

And to Tie Domi, who cared enough to write and phone Simon in his hours of need.

And to all the other maligned but honest sluggers who add mustard to our favorite game.

Acknowledgments

Each previous edition of the *Bad Boys* series was accompanied by a deserving list of credits for those who helped make the editions possible. The latest work is no exception.

For starters, we would like to acknowledge and commend the expertise of three who have made a scholarly work out of hockey-fight watching. Randall S. Chadwick, Joe Lozito and David Singer, each his own way, treat hockey fights with scientific precision. We are not only grateful for their contribution but laud them for their meticulous treatment of the subject. And, of course, we thank them for their participation.

In many cases, NHL public relations departments were of singular assistance in connecting us with players. From us to them, special kudos to John Rosasco, Rob Koch, Greg Post, Rob Scichili, Damon Zier, Mike Altieri, Ken Arnold, Karen Davis, Rick Minch, Mike Levine, Jeff Altstadter, Devin Smith and Larry Kelly.

Instrumental in writing this was the work of the Fischler Hockey Service correspondents, who sacrificed their free time to delve into the minds of hockey's toughest customers: Joel Bergman, Kevin Hubbard, Jeff O'Rourke, Rick Sorci, Christina Oh, Mike Wray, Bob Matuszak, Jim Ramsey, Lee Callans, Sean Farrell, Rick Middleton, Diane Gerace, John Duncan, Pete Scierka, Mary McCarthy, Alan Goldfarb, Thomas Losier, Mark Losier, Ron Spence and our in-house crew: G.P. Aroldi, Christina Attardo, Thomas Berk, Michael Casey, Eric Marin, Edward Salib, Dan Saraceni, Jonathan Scherzer, Darren Seigel and Amy Spencer. Plus good pal, Mark Topaz, who knows as much about hockey as anyone.

And, as always, the gang at Warwick Publishing: Nick Pitt and Kimberley Young for their patience and cooperation.

Introduction

Sometime in the 22nd century, it is possible that the National Hockey League will abolish fighting.

Possible, but not probable.

Fighting has been part of the woof and warp of Canada's national game since the invention of artificial ice.

In the deathless words of Tie Domi, "If there was no fighting, hockey wouldn't be as popular as it is now. People pay to see it. Why change it?"

That is precisely how we feel about it after a lifetime of covering the NHL. Some of the most interesting, arresting and downright exciting moments have come from such colossal battles as Gordie Howe vs. Lou Fontinato, Rocket Richard vs. Bob Dill and Bill Ezinicki vs. Ted Lindsay.

As we approach the next century, the pugilistic beat goes on despite the critics. What's more, the job of enforcer has become one of the best-paid in sports. And if you don't believe it, ask such heavyweights as Marty McSorley, Bob Probert and Rich Pilon.

If fighting didn't pay, owners wouldn't be so tickled to have a Darren Langdon or a Donald Brashear in their line-up.

What's more, the enforcers are among the most intriguing people you'll find. They treat their difficult assignments with grace and honesty.

We hope that you enjoy their stories and our tales of the tough guys in this volume.

Stan Fischler
New York, N.Y.

THE PlaYErs

Ken Belanger

When I was old enough and mature enough to see who
Cam Neely was, I tried to model myself after him.

For more than a decade, Mick Vukota had been the prime enforcer on the New York Islanders. But in January 1996 general manager Don Maloney executed a major trade with the Toronto Maple Leafs which would somewhat change the fistic picture at Nassau Coliseum.

In a complex deal that saw Kirk Muller come to Long Island, the Leafs also included a large, young forward who had established impressive credentials in the American Hockey League as both a fighter and a goal scorer.

He scored a goal in the 1996 AHL All-Star Game and also was considered one of the more promising power forwards in The A. Some even believed that his long-term future suggested the second coming of Cam Neely.

Like Neely, Belanger's career has been riddled with injuries but hardly goals. Like Neely, Belanger can handle his dukes with a 6-4, 225-pound fuselage to go with his armament.

Late in the 1996-97 season — after being recalled from the minors — Belanger battered Paul Laus of the Florida Panthers on one night and in the next game Ken waxed the Philadelphia Flyers Scott Daniels.

"Belanger's fights didn't actually win games," noted Colin Stephenson in the New York Daily News, "but they did give his teammates room to do what they had to do."

In other bouts, Belanger has taken on Stu Grimson, whom he bloodied in a pre-season fight, and Rudy Poeschek, who got the edge on Ken at the start but who lost the second half of the tilt to the Islander.

"I'm still learning," Belanger admitted. "One of the things I've learned is that the commitment has to be there every day. Also, that it takes a while to learn how to be motivated and prepared for every game and practice.

"I try to turn a negative — for example, when I was sent down to the minors — into a positive. It was hard at first but now I'm better prepared for an NHL career."

One hockey fight analyst rated Belanger "the toughest Islander since Ken Baumgartner," who was dealt away from Long Island in 1992. Whether he is or not is a moot point. But there is nothing moot about Belanger's view of his job.

"I understand my role," he explained. "I have to protect my teammates. If the other team takes cheap shots, I have to be there. I'm also getting more confident in my ability as a fighter as well as somebody who can put points up on the board."

Belanger was the Hartford Whalers' Seventh Round selection, 153rd over-all, in the 1992 Entry Draft. He was traded to Toronto for the Maple Leafs' Ninth Round Choice (Matt Ball) in the 1994 Entry Draft on March 18, 1994.

Although he played three games with Toronto, Belanger spent most of his time with St. John's, Toronto's American League affiliate. He had scored 16 goals and 14 assists for 30 points in 40 AHL games with St. John's before he was acquired by the Islanders in the Kirk Muller deal.

Following an Islanders scrimmage at Nassau Coliseum, Belanger expounded on his life and times in a question-and-answer session with Fischler Hockey Service correspondent Dan Saraceni.

SARACENI: When did you start playing hockey?
BELANGER: I grew up in Sault Ste. Marie, Ontario and when I was two years old I got my first pair of skates. By the time I was four, I was playing league hockey with my dad coaching me. Somewhere back home there's a video of one of the first times I actually put on skates. I was pushing a chair on the ice.

DS: How involved was your family in hockey?
KB: My brother also played hockey and my sister was into dancing. Both my parents were working — dad in a steel plant and mom at Sears — and we were a close family. My mom sacrificed a lot of her time coming to the rinks where my brother and I were playing. We were playing every single weekend. When I was eight I started playing travel hockey and was out-of-town every weekend. It was difficult for my parents — travel-wise and money-wise — but they backed us both.

DS: When did you start thinking seriously about a hockey career?
KB: I always wanted to play hockey but the dream about becoming a National Leaguer didn't come until I was sixteen-years-old; actually when I was drafted. No question, hockey was important to me but it wasn't as if I was eating, sleep-ing and breathing it when I was going through high school. I wasn't like some of the other guys who would play hockey during the summer. I always took my summers off and enjoyed the cottage and family life. Being from a smaller town, I didn't focus that closely on Junior hockey and that stuff. We didn't know about the NHL Draft at all. There were no NHL teams around and Toronto was eight hours away. But after I was drafted, the hockey reality set in and I began to take a career more seriously.

DS: In those days who was your favorite player?

KB: It was Wayne Gretzky because he was the greatest player in the world. But when I got old enough and mature enough to see who Cam Neely was, I got interested in him. Cam played the same style as me and anyone who knows anything about hockey knows that a player who can play two ways has one of the toughest jobs in the world of sports. And I'd like to be a player like Neely.

DS: When did you start playing an intimidating style of hockey?

KB: In my first year of Juniors. In fact it happened in training camp but was nothing that I had planned in advance. As a rule, I don't like to fight and it's a tough job to do. It's difficult for me to do if I don't get mad out on the ice. But in my first year of Junior, it just happened. I got into a couple of fights and did well. It was just something natural that happened and it went on from there. But at that training camp, there were some over-age guys — and I was running around — and one of them came after me. I was scared and didn't know what to do but it was over with before I knew it.

DS: Which coaches molded your style of play?

KB: I played Junior for Brian Kilrea (in Ottawa) and he was one of those coaches who either liked you or hated you. In his mind, I was a longshot going into training camp. I was a Fifth Round pick but I went in and played hard and Kilrea kicked me around all year. The thing was Brian gave me a chance to play and I owe him a lot.

DS: But then you got traded to Guelph and became a teammate of Todd Bertuzzi.

KB: I was traded half-way through the year which made it different; I mean going from one division to another. But I found it a good experience. In Guelph we did a lot less travelling. I had known Bertuzzi for several years. We had always played against each other. He's from Sudbury and played a year above me in the league so I knew him from way back.

DS: Your first NHL training camp was with Hartford. What was it like?

KB: It was good. I was eighteen-years-old and pretty scared going in because of the older, experienced faces all around me. I looked across the dressing room and saw guys who were thirty-years-old and some even looked as if they were the same age as my parents and I was just a kid. It was intimidating because I didn't know anybody and there were fifty of us fighting for a spot. It was, however, a good experience for me except that I sprained my ankle. Then the second year I went there, I got a pinched nerve in my neck. Altogether, I played one exhibition game.

DS: How did you feel sitting across from a Pat Verbeek and John Cullen?

KB: After watching the veterans for a while, I realized that to them, this was all a job. They go to work and don't look around the dressing room at all. When you're a kid you do look around. Later, when I was in the Toronto dressing room, it was a bit different with Doug Gilmour and Felix Potvin being there. But after a while, I figured that I did what I did to get up to their level so, to me, everyone was on the same page.

DS: Where did you play your first NHL game?

KB: It was Maple Leaf Gardens in Toronto and, for me, it was a great experience. Any kid who wanted to be a hockey player and who grew up in the province of Ontario will tell you that it's always a dream to put on a Toronto uniform and skate out onto the ice at the Gardens. Unfortunately, my parents couldn't be there because there wasn't enough notice from the time I got word that I was being called up and the time of the game. In a situation like that, when a minor leaguer gets called up, he doesn't even know whether or not he's going to be playing with the big team. There was really no time for them to see me in Toronto because the Leafs sent me right back to St. John's in the American Hockey League.

DS: When you became an Islander you brought a reputation as an enforcer to the NHL. How did that play into your mind when you showed up on Long Island?

KB: When I first got to Nassau Coliseum, they told me they wanted me to play hard but they never specified they wanted me to "just go out and fight." It's no secret that if you're a big kid like me and you go out and play hard, some guys will go after you and things are going to happen. My thinking was to play hard for the Islanders, finish my checks and look after my team.

DS: How does playing with a tough fellow such as a Rich Pilon mold your game or drive you?

KB: I respect Rich. As a matter of fact, I respect any older guy who plays in the NHL. But the truth is, I mold myself now to play my own style and that differs from Pilon's because he's a defenseman and I'm a forward. What I try to do is go out every night and make my own name, not to follow someone else.

DS: Even though you have been considered a fourth-liner, you have played on the first line with Ziggy Palffy and Robert Reichel. What was that like?

KB: I would like to see more of that (Laughs). But when you come down to it, playing me on a first line is tough on the coaches. A guy like me is not a First Round pick and I didn't sign a million-dollar ticket. I'm basically a plugger, a fourth-line guy. Some players stay in that role for their entire career and it's difficult. Players such as that don't get a lot of ice time and if things are going bad in the game, the coach will throw that fourth-liner in to change the game. If he doesn't, then he doesn't get another shift. It's hard for us but it's hard for the coaches as well. They're under pressure from the owners to play the million-dollar players.

DS: Is there a selection process to fighting? How do you know you're about to get into a fight?
KB: I just go by the tempo of the game. If something dirty happens, I want to go out there and let the other team know that that's not going to happen again. I'm still young and I'm still learning a lot about fighting; when to fight, what's the right time and when not to fight.

DS: Who is the toughest guy you ever went up against?
KB: Between Rudy Poeschek and Stu Grimson.

DS: You've played with another tough, young guy named Steve Webb. What is your relationship with him?
KB: Steve's a good guy. I played in the minors with him and in Junior hockey against him. He plays hard but he has been in one of those fringe positions where a team can carry only so many players and that has made it difficult for him. I was in his position for a few years. It took me two-and-a-half years in the minors to battle my way to the NHL. And even now it's still a battle to keep my spot.

DS: What does it take to keep that spot?
KB: I have to keep things simple. When the coach calls me to go out on the ice, I have to keep the puck out of our end. I have to try not to have our line scored against and I have to work hard every day. If the coach sees me working hard, he won't have any complaints.

DS: Mike Milbury, your boss on the Island, was a famous tough guy. Does playing for him help?
KB: Now he's more into the professional aspect of it. He knows as well as I do that he's going to play the players that make the big money. I think that draws a line when you're a coach or a general manager.

DS: How important is it for a team or an individual player to establish a physical presence?
KB: That's probably the biggest factor in The Game. If a big team runs a smaller team, you know that nine times out of ten, the bigger team will probably win by playing physical enough. As a big player, I know that I have to

establish myself. I have to be making hits and making room for myself so that the opposition is going to have a hard game when I'm on the ice. But I'm not just going to come out and run around and hit guys.

DS: How does a smaller, skilled player like Ziggy Palffy relate to you?
KB: We might be sitting next to each other on the bench and he'll turn to me and say, "This guy out there wants to beat me up. Can you help me?" Ziggy and the other guys on the team have the respect for me to know that I'm going to be there to help them. I'm not going to let someone run around and hit them. If a player like Ziggy knows that, he can have the confidence to play hard.

DS: Does a bigger team, such as the Philadelphia Flyers, have an advantage on a smaller team with, perhaps, more goal-scorers?
KB: Definitely. If the bigger team finishes all its checks, even if the smaller team finishes all its checks, the smaller team will be worn down.

DS: Does the home crowd get you going?
KB: Definitely. Whether I score a goal or make a big hit, I like to hear the crowd. The best adrenaline rush I get is to hear the crowd cheering. When the crowd is with them, the guys are really up.

DS: How much can a big hit affect a game?
KB: It's huge. The big hit gives the guys on the bench and the crowd some energy. It's like a chain reaction and everyone gets pumped up.

Jeff Beukeboom

When refereeing is done properly, nobody talks about it.
But when a ref makes a mistake, everyone talks about it.

At the time that Jeff Beukeboom was drafted by Edmonton in 1983 — the Oilers First Choice, 19th overall — Glen Sather's sextet had just been beaten by the New York Islanders in four straight games.

Beukeboom was to be part of the Oilers' new wave defense. Huge (6-5, 225 pounds), Jeff was an Ontario farm boy whose size was intimidating alone.

When he chose to throw his weight around, Beukeboom could devastate an opponent; but in order to do so, he had to learn the ways of big-league hockey and that would take time.

In the eyes of Edmonton's high command, it simply took too long for him to flower into the player they had hoped to develop. On November 12, 1991 Sather dealt Beukeboom to the New York Rangers for David Shaw.

As a Ranger, Beukeboom amassed the confidence required to be an effective regular backliner. When New York won its first Stanley Cup since 1940 in 1994, Beukeboom played in 22 playoff games and totalled six assists and 50 penalty minutes.

For the most part, however, Jeff played his position without fuss and fanfare but with the appreciation of the coaching staff and teammates.

"With a defenseman, when he plays well, you don't notice him," said goalie Mike Richter. "I often would say to myself, 'I guess Jeff had a good game because nothing exciting happened.' What I meant was that he did all the hard-working things that often go unnoticed but are so important."

Or, as a *New York Daily News* headline once proclaimed, BEUKE IS SOLID AS AN OAK. It was well put.

Under the coaching of Mike Keenan in 1993-94, Beukeboom flowered as never before. "He played so well positionally," Keenan remembered. "Jeff added a physical presence and strength to the blue line. He worked extremely well at protecting Brian Leetch — and I don't mean in terms of intimidation. I mean in terms of taking the physical workload off Brian. He made the big hits and developed a great mix between the two that year."

When necessary, Beukeboom could handle his dukes. Once, when Troy Crowder was hammering teammate Darren Langdon while the latter was being restrained by officials, Jeff threw punches from the New York bench at Crowder.

"I'd do the same thing all over again," defended Beukeboom. "I don't mind a tough game but what Crowder did (hitting Langdon while Darren was being held) was not right."

Were there any doubts about Jeff's value to the Rangers, they were eliminated in 1996 when the Broadway Blueshirts inked him to a four-year contract worth more than $8 million.

"After that," said Beukeboom, "there were occasions when I kept thinking that I had to live up to the contract. I would try not to think of it but it would always be at the back of my mind. I always wanted to prove that I was worth what they were paying me."

Through the 1997-98 season — Jeff's seventh in New York — he had played virtually all that time with Leetch as his defense partner.

Never a Norris Trophy candidate, the man called "Beuke" epitomizes that big, hard-hitter of the 1990s. Or, as former coach Colin Campbell once noted, "There aren't too many Jeff Beukebooms around."

Following a Rangers scrimmage at their Playland Ice Rink facility in Rye, New York, Beukeboom participated in a question-and-answer period with Fischler Hockey Service correspondent Ira Gitler. Their dialogue follows:

GITLER: How did you get involved in hockey?
BEUKEBOOM: I was born in the town of Ajax, Ontario but when I was only a month old, the family moved to Lindsay, Ontario. I followed the steps of older brothers who started playing minor hockey. I did what most Canadian boys did when they were young, play as much hockey as possible.

IG: Were you always big for your age?
JB: Definitely. I always was one of the bigger guys on every hockey team I played on: if not one of the biggest players in that particular league. But with that size came a certain awkwardness and that stayed with me through Juniors until I was almost a pro.

IG: How did your game develop?
JB: When I was young and played physical, I always got a lot of penalties so lots of times I played non-physical. But when I was sixteen, I played for a team in Newmarket, Ontario and my coach there got me to play more physical, more aggressive. It was the same thing in Juniors. I went to Sault Ste. Marie, Ontario and played for Terry Crisp. By that time I recognized that I wasn't by any means going to be a finesse player. My number one asset was my size and I had to take advantage of it if I was going to make it to the NHL.

IG: How rough was it in Junior hockey?

JB: They play very aggressively on the Junior level. Granted, it can also be very skilled but it's also rough and because of that the Juniors make a good stepping-stone to the pros. In my case, I was playing in rough competition from the age of sixteen on up. It became part of my game and I learned that fairly quick and played it that way for the rest of my career, amateur and pro.

IG: Did you have much success before turning pro?

JB: I was fortunate in that I played on some great Junior teams with some terrific teammates. In my last year in the Ontario Hockey League, we went to the Memorial Cup round and I also played in the World Junior tournament which was held in Finland and we won a Gold Medal there.

IG: Who were some of the big-leaguers you played with in amateur hockey?

JB: In my first year there was Rick Tocchet and John Vanbiesbrouck. Beezer was the goalie for Sault Ste. Marie. In my last year Derek King, who later moved up to the New York Islanders, was a teammate. Also, I played with Bob Probert and Rob Zamuner.

IG: Who helped you along the way?

JB: My brother played pro in the minors for six years before me. The knowledge I got from him was invaluable for me. He paved the way for me. My brother was a role model and so was my uncle. He didn't start playing organized hockey until he was eighteen-years-old and yet he still made it to the pros. Mentally, that left a lot of doors open to me. I looked at what he did and said to myself that there's room for advancement. Plus, Terry Crisp helped in Juniors and when I got to Edmonton, Glen Sather and John Muckler. Glen did a lot for my attitude; learning how to carry myself and learning how to be a good — and then better — pro.

IG: What else did Sather do for you?

JB: I've been fortunate to have played on four championship teams and Glen had a lot to do with that. He pointed out that every spoke was important to the wheel. On top of that, I was lucky to have as teammates in Edmonton such models as Mark Messier and Wayne Gretzky.

IG: How tough was that Oiler team?

JB: We had some fairly tough guys. When I came to the NHL, I was tested as a defenseman first and then as a tough player second. Some tough guys checked me out and discovered what I was all about. But on the Oilers we had enough rough players that other teams didn't "test" us that much. Remember, we had fellows like Marty McSorley and Dave Semenko, among others. There was a back-up system on the Oilers.

IG: How tough have you found fighting in terms of your overall game?

JB: Whenever I was challenged, I accepted the challenge and moved on. I never found the fighting to be the toughest aspect of hockey. To me the major challenge always has been playing against top skill players such as Mario Lemieux and Jaromir Jagr; against the NHL's best offensive performers. The challenge of winning battles against artists such as those, that was the toughest part of the entire defense business.

IG: What other challenges have you faced as a pro?

JB: By far the most important goals for me were to improve my mobility and my skating. To this day, I still work on that challenge and I have to continue to do so in order to maintain the level to which I'm accustomed.

IG: Can you think of any memorable fights in which you were involved?

JB: One night when we were playing the Detroit Red Wings, I fought Randy McKay (before he was traded to the New Jersey Devils.) That fight took place in the first period and then later in the game I went toe-to-toe with Bob Probert, who everyone knows has been one of the toughest fighters of the past dozen years.

IG: How did you feel after those bouts?

JB: That was funny. Once the game was over and we were sitting in the dressing room, one of my teammates piped up, "Okay, guys, what do we want to do after we get dressed?" Well, I was so exhausted — man, I had never been so exhausted in my life — from those fights I couldn't even get off the lockerroom bench. That proved to me how tiring those bouts can be.

IG: What's your opinion about the growth of head injuries from elbowing and high sticks as well as the chopping on gloves?

JB: It's not as if this stuff didn't happen in the past. Ten years ago when a player had a concussion, he was told to take a few days off and then come back. Nowadays doctors realize that it could be a lot more serious. Concussions have to be monitored. The game is changing. In the past if someone hit somebody deliberately in the head, the whole team would go after him. Now the league goes after him. Whether this is a better system or not, I don't know.

IG: In your estimation, what is the most important aspect of the game?

JB: The team concept. That's what people love about hockey. They like the fact that in our sport, everybody contributes. Take the case of the Rangers. Wayne Gretzky, obviously, is a big part of the team. We all know that. But you take a player who gets less publicity; such as a Darren Langdon. He's also a big part of the team but in a different way. You could say the same thing for any NHL club but only the names are different.

IG: What aspect does the media play in terms of influencing opinion about hard-hitting, injuries and that?

JB: As far as injuries are concerned, they get a lot of attention because there is so much press these days; there's much more coverage of the game from so many different angles; television, radio, the print guys. With all that media, every fan knows more about what's going on; which isn't a bad thing. Hey, hockey is a business and everyone in the business is trying to get his piece of the pie including the media. They have their job to do and they do it.

IG: Has there been a rise in illegal stickwork since you came to the NHL?

JB: Nowadays, kids who are learning hockey have full equipment. They figure they can't get hurt when they are so well-protected. When they get to Junior hockey or collegiate hockey they wear either half-shields or full shields. That plays a part in the attitudes about sticks. But in the NHL, I have found that stickwork is down because players simply don't want to lose money from what could happen by keeping the sticks up. Players are very valuable properties these days and the league should want to protect them as well.

IG: How do you feel about the NHL and the job it has done in terms of protecting players?

JB: The league has done the best job it can do under the circumstances. It's not an easy solution. The same thing holds for refereeing. That's a thankless job. When it's done properly, no one talks about it. Where there's a mistake, everyone talks about it. With all the media watching, everybody — referees included — is under the microscope. Everyone sees it on SportsCenter or MSG Network or on Fox Sports.

IG: Give me final thoughts on toughness and playing in the NHL.

JB: Rough play is always going to be part of the game. But the game has changed in recent years and that change has been significant. Players who have that (enforcers) role in today's game also must be able to play and to have a vital role on their team. They can't be there just to fight. Nowadays, most of that type of player can play the game, not just fight.

IG: What about toughness and the playoffs?

JB: In the playoffs the intensity and physical play goes up about three to four notches compared to the regular season. It's often a business of survival and the teams that survive and punish the other team the most usually are the ones that succeed. Other than goaltending, it is the one factor most people overlook.

Donald Brashear

*I'm a smart fighter. I take my time. I like to take control
of the guy before I land some punches.*

They said it couldn't be done.

They said that Donald Brashear simply was not good enough to play in the National Hockey League.

That was in 1993, shortly after the Montreal Canadiens had won The Stanley Cup.

Brashear had just completed his first full year of professional hockey. He was a left wing on the Habs' Fredericton farm team in the American Hockey League. He was big (6-2, 220 pounds) and rough and even scored eleven goals in 76 AHL games. But NHL calibre? Who would have believed it?

Yet only one year out of the Junior ranks (Verdun), there was Donald, enjoying a 14-game tryout with the Habs and — wonder of wonders — scoring a pair of goals and another two assists while he was at it. P.S. He added 34 penalty minutes.

Questions still were raised about the Bedford, Indiana native by the Canadiens general staff. But by 1995-96 Brashear had cleared all his minor league hurdles and was a big-leaguer to stay. He played in 67 games and totalled 223 minutes but Donald was not exactly a happy camper.

"I never felt I was part of the team in Montreal," said Brashear. "I'd only get two shifts a game and watch the rest of it from the bench. I felt more like a spectator than part of the team."

On November 13, 1996, Brashear, an African-American, was traded to Vancouver for Jassen Cullimore. His response was more than the Canucks high command ever imagined. He recorded eight goals and five assists for a career-high 13 points and finished second on the team — and sixth in the NHL — with a career-high 245 penalty minutes.

Former teammate — and fellow enforcer — Gino Odjick remembered how Brashear proved to be an immediate tonic the moment he donned a Vancouver uniform. "Donald gave everyone some breathing room," said Odjick. "He also surprised a lot of people with his toughness."

Another teammate, Scott Walker, recalled that he was impressed with Brashear's offensive skills as much as he was with his two-fisted prowess. "Donald knows when and when not to fight," said Walker. "He can be productive without dropping his gloves."

An episode during the 1997-98 season magnified Walker's point. The Canucks were trailing Colorado with less than a minute remaining in the game. Of all things, Vancouver had Brashear on the ice with those designated to score the tying goal.

And who should score in the dying seconds but Donald, himself, who followed his red light with a stirring victory dance worthy of Pavel Bure.

"Donald can be a force," added teammate and captain Mark Messier. "He's in the mold of Bob Probert the way he can influence a game. He skates well and has pretty good hands."

Brashear felt that his move from Montreal to Vancouver was a liberation of sorts. Like so many enforcers, there was a part of him that insisted he could play the game better than some critics believed.

"I want to be more than just one of the tough guys of the NHL," Brashear asserted. "I'll fight, but I want to be more complete like Cam Neely or Rick Tocchet."

Although he was born in Indiana, Brashear moved to Quebec when still a youth and learned his hockey in the colder climate. However, he still is an American citizen and in 1997 was invited to play for Team USA at the World Championships in Finland.

"I was surprised when they asked me," said Brashear. "Playing on a team like that is for the stars."

Not that Brashear is a star, but he certainly has become an NHL force.

"When he came into the league," noted Walker, "everyone wanted to fight Donald. Now people are more choosy. Wary, if you will."

Yes, Brashear will take on anyone at anytime but he has learned there are more important things to do apart from throwing upper cuts. In an interview with Fischler Hockey Service reporter Ron Spence, Brashear revealed his thoughts about the business of hockey playing and hockey fighting. The following oral history was drawn from that one-on-one.

How would I describe my style?

I'm an aggressive player. I try to get things going during the game. Once the puck is dropped, I'm out there throwing bodychecks and getting some flow going. When that kind of play happens, there's always a chance of a fight.

My fighting technique? I'm a smart fighter. I take my time and like to take control of the opponent before I land some punches. I don't think I'm the toughest guy, or the guy who takes the most punches. I have to be careful and take the punches at the right place. I think out there when I'm fighting. I take my time.

My upper body is my strength. I work out all the time. When I'm in a fight, I need good balance and strength. Some have it and some don't. I have pretty good balance on my skates and natural strength.

When I was a kid learning hockey, my idol was Cam Neely. He was one of the NHL's top power forwards and even though he was a good fighter, I didn't idolize him so much for his fighting. At the time I wasn't looking for fighters to be my heroes. I was idolizing good players — complete players.

I found that the best thing that could happen to me as a pro was the ability to get enough ice time to develop my skills. That's what happened when I played in Fredericton. The coach gave me the chance to get out there and, maybe, make some mistakes but most of all to get the experience. Playing first line, second line, power play and defensive play. I had a lot of chances and that's how I improved.

It was the same thing when I was invited to play for Team USA in the World Championships. I went out there as a confident player. I knew it was about hockey not about fighting and everything. It was a chance for me to show I could play and it proved to be a good time for me, career-wise.

Let's face it, fighting still is part of my game and I can never think that I'm not obliged to fight. But sometimes I won't feel like it at all, but still I'll have to get things going. Or, get the respect of some of my opponents who may be hitting our smaller players.

Meanwhile, I'm always trying to improve my skills. I want to have better hands; I want to be able to see the play better and make better plays; and make them faster. I want to develop the quickness that comes natural to the better players.

It's the same with playing the piano, which I am learning and which I like to do. I wouldn't say that I am a pianist but I am learning to play the piano. Like in hockey, I have to practice to be a good pianist. The more I practice, the better I get. If I stop practicing, then I won't be as good.

I learned all about the benefits of practice when I began playing hockey. Quebec City was where I learned the game. I started when I was eight years old and worked my way from there. I was raised in a foster family and my parents had three boys who were playing hockey.

Compared to the other kids with whom I played, I was a big guy. I could skate and shoot hard and was scoring a lot of goals when I was young. Pretty soon, I was playing against fellows who were bigger and better than me. I was somewhere in between on the skill scale; never the worst but never the best. I always wanted to be the best and, if nothing else, I worked my butt off trying to reach the top.

The tough part of my game didn't develop until I reached the Bantam level. That's when bodychecking comes into play although fighting isn't allowed in some leagues. Actually, the fights really start in Juniors. It's not that anyone specifically tells you to go out and fight but all of a sudden you're out there and start hitting and the next thing you know some guy wants to fight you.

In my case, I did well in my first fight so I tried again and again and realized that I could do it well. I got more and more confidence whenever I dropped my gloves. There were players in Junior who I fought down there and continued fighting once I got to the NHL. Sandy McCarthy was one. When I was playing Junior for Longueuil (near Montreal) he was playing at Laval. I wound up fighting him almost every game. It was more about respect than anything else. Plus, Laval had a pretty tough team and they kept saying that Longueuil wasn't very tough. People were coming to see me and Sandy fight more than anything.

Not that I wanted to be considered a goon; I didn't. To me "goon" means someone who scraps but can't play hockey. I didn't like that word. What I wanted was to be respected as a good hockey player who worked on his skills but who tried to keep fighting as he went along.

The trouble was, when I started scoring goals, I began thinking I didn't want to fight anymore. The reality was different. You have to keep doing it and that's what kept me going. And that's why I still think I can play in the NHL for a long time.

In my last year of Juniors — with Verdun — I reached 283 penalty minutes over 65 games, more than I ever had before. Then, I got into the pros with Fredericton in 1992-93 where the guys were a little bigger and a notch faster than Juniors. I had 261 penalty minutes in my first year pro and then got my break with Montreal a year later.

Jacques Demers was coaching the Canadiens at the time and had come off a Cup-winning year in the Spring of 1993. Demers gave me a chance to play when he thought there was the right opportunity for me on the ice.

In other words, when the Habs had injuries, Jacques would put me on the third line. Once in a while he actually put me on the first line although we knew that that really wasn't the place for me. The thing was, at least he gave me a chance and that meant that I had an opportunity to improve with the experience.

I got along well with Demers but the club hit an awful slump at the start of the 1995-96 season. Demers got fired less than a month into the new year and was replaced by Mario Tremblay. All of a sudden, we're confronted with a totally new and different coaching style. I played the rest of the season with Tremblay and ten games into 1996-97 before I got traded to Vancouver.

With Tremblay, I wasn't getting much ice time. When that happens, it's harder to come off the bench and fight. When you play regularly, you're warm and you can respond to incidents on the ice. You're in the game. But the other way around, you get cold on the bench and feel a bit helpless just because you're sitting there.

But when it comes to scraps, it doesn't matter whether you're in the American League or the National League. New guys come up and they want to set their territory and determine who is going to be the toughest.

AHL guys battle really hard to work their way to the NHL. Once you get to The Show, it's really the top guys fighting against each other.

When I got to the NHL and started hitting the tough guys, I got the standard response: "Hey, you're not gonna play around with me." Or, "We're gonna go!" That's how it starts.

The first NHL battle that sticks out in my mind took place in my rookie year with Montreal. We were playing the Red Wings and I was playing what I felt was a good game. I had a goal and an assist and was hitting guys around. Bob Probert got on my back real quick and the next thing I knew, I was in a fight with him. Wow! Was I ever nervous.

Bear in mind that at the time, Probert was considered the toughest guy in the NHL. I was kind of shaking a bit because I wanted to do good. As tough a fighter as Probert was, he still was a guy I didn't want to lose to even though it was my first fight.

What kind of fight was it?

Well, I wouldn't exactly call it a very big tilt or anything like that. I was so nervous that my legs were shaking. I lost my balance as we squared off and just fell. Probert landed a punch or two and that was the end of it. That happened to me in my first few fights; I was falling at the start because I was so nervous. What I learned was that successful hockey fighting is all about confidence. It's all in the head.

A lot of times when I was with Montreal, there were scraps on the ice but I was riding the bench just wishing that I could be out there. I was always thinking, "If only I could get out there."

That all changed once I got to Vancouver. All of a sudden I got respect and I got respect because I had the chance to get out there and have more ice time. I wanted to show the coach, "I'm the tough guy and I can play and I'm gonna help this team."

And I did. I scored eight goals in that first year with the Canucks; way more than I ever got with the Habs. I was fighting more aggressively and really wanted to win my fights. I wanted to be respected as one of the toughest guys. I wanted my Vancouver teammates to know that I was going to drop the gloves for them and would kick ass.

The more I fought, the more word got around about how I was doing. Other fighters watch the games on television and one player talks to another. They talked about Donald Brashear and I began to get respect. It didn't take much time, I just had to do it.

Is fighting necessary? Bob Probert had said that fighting creates space, but for an individual like myself, it depends on which team I'm playing against.

For instance, if I'm playing on a Cup-winning team like Detroit was in 1997 and 1998 there was not much hitting. Those guys know that if they get on you quick, you lose your senses. If you play the tough teams and you beat up their tough guys, they just leave you alone. I knew that when I played against skill teams like Detroit and Pittsburgh — with Jaromir Jagr — those guys were right on my ass. But they won't finish their checks all the time so I'll sometimes be able to make a move. When I play the tough teams, I feel I get more space.

The general feeling is not to fight at the end of a shift because you're tired, but if the guy on the other team forces the issue then I have no choice but to go with him. That happened to me once against Bob Probert. He got me at the end of a shift and I said, "Why did you get me then?" He came right back and said, "Remember that last fight we had in Montreal? That's why I did it. You did it to me one time and now I'm doing it to you."

It's all about respect but there's also a lot of smarts involved. I consider myself a smart fighter. Sometimes I won't go right away. I'd rather wait for the next shift and get the job done well. When I'm tired, I just go out there and hold on to the other guy. In a situation like that, I can't afford to make a mistake because that mistake can cost me.

Another mistake is letting the yapping, little guys get under my skin. That type will never fight but what they try to do is goad me into taking penalties. Those are the guys who bug me and are the hardest to take. Every once in a while you'll see a tough guy grab one of those little guys and pound him. I know I'll snap every once in a while and that will happen.

It happened to me once in Junior hockey. A little guy was bugging me, putting his hands in my face. I just snapped and started punching him around. You don't gain any respect doing that but you do gain respect from this one guy. After that, I knew that he would stay away from me.

Fights can produce interesting reactions. I can remember an exhibition game against Edmonton when I beat up a couple of guys in one game. After that, I got a lot of respect. I could skate around the rink with the puck and had a lot of time to do things. I scored two goals that game.

I learned from other tough guys. When I arrived in Vancouver, Gino Odjick, my new teammate, already had had six years in the league. Gino was always known as one of the toughest guys and I looked up to him to learn when to go and when not to go. Actually, I learned that Gino and I are different types of fighters. What I mean is that he'll go any time with anybody. He'll just go. I like to watch how the game is going. I like to stay on the ice.

When I was playing for the Canadiens, I felt as if I was fighting for nothing. That's why I fought the way I did there, holding on; I had no purpose. In Vancouver, I found that I had a purpose. Sometimes I was just mad and sometimes I just wanted to get respect for the guys. Sometimes it was just to get things going. In Vancouver, I have always had a reason. In Montreal, I never did.

But when I watched Gino, I said to myself, "If he can be one of the toughest guys in the NHL, I can be one of the toughest guys, too." Having him as a teammate with the Canucks really helped me, especially when we were on the same line. We got a lot of respect as a unit. Had I been by myself it would have been different.

Someone in my shoes has to know when to get involved. Here's a good example: Vancouver has a skill player like Pavel Bure. If somebody runs Pavel, I have to jump right on his ass! If it happens to be a tough guy that runs Pavel, I'll just take him and we'll fight. Otherwise, I'll just say, "Hey, leave Number Ten alone, otherwise you and I are going to go. Or, I'll crosscheck you in the face. Or take your legs out."

One of the things that has changed strategy is the "instigator" rule. I have to be more careful. I can drop a guy and start punching him and pounding him but if he doesn't drop his gloves, I'll be kicked out of the game.

Outsiders who look at players like me often have misconceptions. The usual image that enforcers have is of being very mean, nasty people. But when I'm not on the ice, I'm not a mean person. I like everybody — the fans, everything about hockey. On the other hand, there are times when I won't feel like talking to anybody. When that happens, some people might consider me mean.

Because of my background — I did not grow up with my real parents — I have had some problems with communication. I kept everything inside. It was hard. If I had a problem, I had to solve it myself. I was always taking the hard way and still do sometimes. Because of my childhood, I had a tendency to do things the wrong way.

What I learned since coming to Vancouver is that you play for your teammates, you live for your teammates and you have to think about your teammates all the time. You don't win anything by yourself. You can score a hundred goals in a season but the team might not go anywhere.

I know that racism can happen in hockey. It happens, but I kind of pretend that I don't hear it or anything. It might happen because I might piss off somebody on the other team. Sometimes someone on the opposition might try to make me lose my focus on the game, make me lose my head. Those things happen although it doesn't happen that much.

A long time ago my parents and my brothers would tell me, "Hey, you're going to have to take it sometimes because you're going to find that some bigger guy is going to kick your ass." As a result, I learned control as a fighter. I am a control guy. Sometimes an opponent will bug me and I won't always go. I try to control myself and my emotions and always in the best interests of the team. The best interests of the team is primary.

Eric Cairns

When I win against a tough guy I feel really good.
I might be better at it than he was just that one time.

One thing about Eric Cairns is certain: you can't miss him. His physical presence commands attention. He stands 6-6, 230 pounds. An inch taller than Jeff Beukeboom, Cairns has been the New York Rangers' biggest player. In two seasons with the Broadway Blueshirts, the Oakville, Ontario native has nearly logged as many minutes in the penalty box as he has minutes played. If nothing else, Cairns thrives on the physical aspect of the game.

Fights early in his career frequently left Cairns at the receiving end, but he is still a gamer. Summer boxing lessons, the desire to succeed, and a teammate named Darren Langdon have helped the 24 year-old do more than just survive in the world of NHL tough guys.

In addition to his skating, Cairns has also strived to improve his fighting since he entered the league. He is a well-conditioned athlete who works hard to stay strong and ready. Cairns can be found lingering on the ice after practice or sweating it out in the weight room.

Cairns chatted with Fischler Hockey Service reporter Christina Attardo after practice at Rye Playland, the Rangers' practice facility, to determine where he has been and where his fists might take him.

Christina Attardo: When did you start skating?
Eric Cairns: I was four years old. My dad got me skates. I started playing organized hockey when I was five in my hometown, Oakville, Ontario, which is near Toronto. My dad played Junior A and he gave me a stick for Christmas, so I started playing. I rooted for the Edmonton Oilers. I used to have a Wayne Gretzky jersey. I loved it when they came on TV and I used to stay up all night to watch them. To me, a Ranger practice is definitely the biggest dream anybody could ever live; playing with the person that you idolized and watched your whole life [Gretzky]. It's the best feeling every day for me to see him and talk to him.

CA: When was your first fight?

EC: When I was about ten or eleven, I had one. Then a couple of years after that I got into another one. I don't remember who it was with. I was probably screwing around and got pissed off at something.

CA: Have you always been a fighter?

EC: Not always. I used to like to score goals. I had a few points here and there, but nothing special. Then I realized at my size I've got to play a physical game and protect my players. I came to that thinking in Junior B where guys got a little bigger and stronger and it was more expected.

CA: Was it your role to be a fighter before you started playing professionally?

EC: I've always been kind of a little spazzy, but I never thought I'd be fighting as part of my living. But it's the way to play in this league and I have to do it.

CA: When did you start to develop your physical game? Do you feel that is what got you to this level?

EC: In Major Bantam I got more physical and into a few fights here and there. I would get in trouble with my coach for doing it. If I wasn't as tall and as big, I don't think I would be here. But God gave me the chance to be this tall, so I might as well take advantage of it. At the beginning of Grade Nine I stood 5-10 and, at the end of Grade Nine, I was 6-4. I grew quite a bit and then I started putting on more weight. When I was 17, I started filling out. In fact, I'm still filling out — hopefully not much more. It helped me out a lot, gave me more confidence in myself, and I feel stronger on the ice.

CA: Do you ever have fears going out on the ice?

EC: Not really. I don't fear anyone. It's more that I fear making a bad mistake in a game and the puck ending up in my net. I'd love to score some goals. That may come or it may not come. If you let things flow the way it goes and if you work hard on some different skills it could happen. You never know. I'd definitely like to do a little bit more than to just be a tough, physical defenseman.

CA: Have you ever had a confrontation with a fan?

EC: Twice in Junior hockey. One time I was walking off the ice — I had a real bad game — and a fan was screaming at me and I swung my stick at him. I missed, but I think he was pretty upset by it. He told my coach and then my coach rushed down to the lockerroom and gave me hell. Another time, we were in North Bay during the OHL finals. There's short glass there and this fan was hanging over the glass yelling at the guys. I was skating around and I skated pretty close to him. I didn't even think about it. He punched me in the face, so

I turned around and dropped my gloves, grabbed him, and started punching him. Then I saw about ten sticks come over top of me. It was all of my teammates hitting him with their sticks. The guy actually got pretty beat up. He looked like he was a little woozy. This all happened during warm-up and the police ended up escorting him out of the game.

CA: Do you think fighting is glorified in hockey?
EC: I don't think it's necessarily glorified. Fighting is needed in the league to protect the smaller players. We're a bunch of men out there playing a physical game and tempers flare. If it happens, it happens. And if they show it on TV, big deal. The fans like it, too.

CA: How do you actually get into a fight?
EC: Usually something will happen out there. A player will throw a strong check or someone will take a cheap shot at your smaller player. When there's another so-called-tough-guy on the ice, he has to go out there and stick up for his teammate. You know something is going to happen if the guy comes over to you. Usually I ask the guy if he wants to go. I don't like to throw cheap shots, so if he wants to go, then he'll fight. That's the way it usually starts.

CA: Would you say protection is your driving force behind a fight?
EC: Mostly protecting. If we're down a goal or two or three — if we're getting killed a little bit and you want to get the team going — there's another reason. You try and get the team going by pumping up your enthusiasm by getting into a fight. Win or lose, you know you're out there battling for your team. You're making a statement to both your team and to the other team that we're not going to take this and we want to get things moving in our direction. Our guys respond really well. They're all behind you. Whatever happens, they give you a pat on the back. That's the main thing, as long as you know that everyone is behind you and what you're doing.

CA: Is fighting ever more than a team issue for you?
EC: Sometimes if a guy says something to me that I don't like or maybe gives me a stick in the face or a spear then I would approach him. I always fight for my team, but I also get angry at things like that against me personally.

CA: What is the biggest misconception about you and other fighters?
EC: I guess that we're not nice guys off the ice. We're looked at basically just as goons, but we're really pretty normal, nice guys off the ice. On the ice, we play mean because that's the way we have to play.

CA: Do you employ any strategy when you are going into a fight?

EC: I have a couple. I'm learning more watching Langer (Darren Langdon). He's unbelievable the way he swings around. You've got to have a strategy. If you just go in there swinging that isn't going to work, especially in this league where everybody competes harder in every way. I'm a tall guy and I have really long arms, so I like to hold the guy off with my arms, throw with my right, and try to watch where he's going to come and throw one back at me. I try to not stick my face in the middle of it. When he switches to his left hand, I'll try and tie it up and throw with my left hand.

CA: What do you consider to be fighting smart?
EC: Sticking up for a teammate and trying to get everything going for my team is a good thing. I realize I'm not always going to win. I have to try and dodge punches and try not to take a big one. That's basically what I do. I try to tie up his arm and not leave myself open for a big punch, just swing back and try to hit him.

CA: Do you really have time to think about all that?
EC: It just happens. I think about it before the game, before it might happen. Just a little bit. It gets my nerves going. When I'm in there, I've got to react fast and do the right things in order to be one of the best.

CA: How do you feel when you lose?
EC: Bad, but I know it's going to happen eventually. Just as long as everyone knows I'm out there fighting for my team. That's the main thing. Everyone is going to lose a fight at one time or another. Obviously, I'm mad at myself when it happens, but there's nothing I can do if a guy hits me on the chin and I go down. Or if I get a little cut on my nose and it looks like I lost — I might not have, but that's the way it goes. That's the way it works sometimes. When I win obviously I'm a lot happier. I feel like I did something really good for the team and when I win against a tough guy I feel really good. I might be better at it than he was just that one time.

CA: Do you feel there is more dimension to your game? Or is that the type of player you perceive yourself as — strictly a fighter?
EC: I feel like there's a little bit more to me defensively in moving the puck out of my end, hitting, and such. But I don't mind the fighting label. It earns respect around the league, but it doesn't mean I have to go out and do it every game. If it happens, though, they know I'm going to be there for my team to do it.

CA: How did the fighting elements of your game develop?
EC: In my first year of Junior I fought a lot. I wasn't really that good a fighter — just a power puncher. I won some and lost some. In my second year I

wasn't as good as in my first year. I lost confidence in a couple of bad fights. In my third year, I did well again. When I came to the minors I took it slow at first and gained a lot of confidence and got better. Over the past two years I started taking boxing lessons and that helped.

CA: Do you work on your footwork?
EC: I've been doing that for a long time. After every practice I work on it to get better. They make me do it and I want to do it. I work on power, quickness, and acceleration. Every day it is a learning experience.

CA: Does your personality on the ice reflect your personality off it?
EC: Not at all. I'm a totally different person on the ice than I am off the ice. I like to be really focused on the ice and that's where I try to leave any aggression. Off ice, I like to relax, take things easy, and have a lot of fun. I don't have a bad temper unless something happens that gives me a bad temper. It's not tough for me to relax away from the rink. I'm able to leave what's on the ice on the ice. Off the ice, I just try to forget about hockey.

CA: Describe your most memorable NHL fights.
EC: I had a pretty good one with Lyle Odelein in exhibition two years ago and another with Grant Marshall and couple of other guys from Dallas. I remember against Scott Thornton he got me with a pretty good shot and I ended up falling down. I had two with Mick Vukota. He's very tough and we had a pretty good fight. Marshall was definitely a good one. We went back and forth and he hit me with a pretty good punch. I thought I had a pretty good fight with Donald Brashear in 1997-98. Those are tough guys and I held my own against them, so they're memorable for me that way.

CA: You also fought Stu Grimson.
EC: It wasn't so much a fight — we both fell down. I didn't see it, but he hit Alex Kovalev at the end of the game. I heard our bench yelling. Stu is really tough and I respect him a lot, but I had to go over and do something. The game was pretty lopsided.

CA: You were vulnerable. You went down and he really could have let you have it.
EC: Yeah, he was really good about it. We both fell down and I got into a bad position and I didn't know he had backed off a little bit. I got up and I thought we were going to go at it again, but the referee ended up getting in between us.

CA: Do you remember the first player you fought in the NHL?
EC: Mike Peluso, when he was with New Jersey, in exhibition. It was a pretty

good fight — he throws lefts — but we ended up both falling down in the end.

CA: I have heard a lot of stories about fights in training camp, players trying to prove themselves. Did you find yourself doing that when you came into the league?

EC: They don't really allow fighting in the Rangers camp, but two years ago I came in and I fought Shane Churla. It ended up that we became friends and teammates, which was really good. But I felt like I had to do something out there to try and make the team. He was the right guy to go after.

CA: Who is the best fighter in the NHL?

EC: Anyone on any given night can be the best. There are guys like (Tony) Twist, Darren Langdon, Grimson, (Sandy) McCarthy who are all really, really tough guys. I have a lot of respect for them. Also, Matt Johnson. They're all tough.

CA: How would rate yourself as a fighter?

EC: I've got a lot to learn. But I've gotten better and I'll improve again by taking more boxing lessons. I should learn a few more things from watching Darren Langdon fight. I watch him and get pointers. Talking with him has helped me.

Kris Draper

I've had some fights and I don't think there is anything wrong with it. You have a fight, you go in the box for five minutes and that's it."

When does a good guy become a "Bad Boy"?

When his name is Kris Draper.

With the singular exception of Claude Lemieux, both friend and foe regard Draper with the admiration usually reserved for such redoubtables as Ron Francis and Adam Graves.

He is Mister Grit and certainly not Monsieur Dirty — as in Monsieur Lemeiux.

Yet, because of one fateful incident in the 1996 Colorado-Detroit playoff, Draper emerged as the centerpiece of an endless Red Wings-Avalanche war that has continued through 1998.

Lemieux's blindside collision with Draper is being analyzed to this day. As in, how dirty was it? Or was it dirty at all?

Obviously the Red Wings thought so and sought retribution for two years thereafter.

As for Draper, he recuperated from the blow, got himself stitched up and asked when he could go back in to play. He was finished, but his good friend Darren McCarty handled Lemieux in their first re-match. Lemieux has yet to apologize.

Draper is a naturally fast skater. The longer he remained with the Wings, the more fans took a liking to him. Coach Scott Bowman designated Kris for big face-offs late in games and he has evolved as one of the Wings best penalty killers. Along with Joey Kocur and Kirk Maltby, Draper has also become one of the elite NHL checkers. Known as the "Grind Line," the trio propelled the Wings to two consecutive Stanley Cups. Draper's overtime goal in Game Two of the 1998 Cup Finals all but sealed the series, a sweep over the Washington Capitals. Draper also scored an overtime winner against the Blackhawks in the 1995 play-off, proving even checkers come through in the clutch.

Red Wings trainer John Wharton summed up the feisty, red-head thusly: "You don't need to look at statistics to see if Kris is on his game. Look at his face. He's had more stitches to his face than any other guy in the room." More than 200 stitches to be exact, but who's counting? Certainly not Kris.

Draper, himself, is less interested in apologies than he is simply playing his game. He is a throwback who never stops relishing the fact that he is playing in the National Hockey League.

When Draper originally learned that he had been picked up on waivers by the Detroit Red Wings on June 30, 1993, he asked, "For what?" The answer was, "One dollar!" Draper has been paying dividends ever since. Plucked by Winnipeg in the Third Round of the 1989 Entry Draft, Kris has climbed the mountain twice as a Stanley Cup champion. Call him "Drapes" or "Nailz" (as his teammates call him), it is clear that he has the heart of a champion.

Kris trekked an unusual route to the NHL. Instead of playing Junior hockey, he found his way to the Canadian National Team following his drafting by the Jets. He credits the experience on the National Team with teaching him defensive hockey. He played against Viacheslav Fetisov and the KLM line as a 19 year-old and he took those experiences with him to Winnipeg.

Upon his arrival in Detroit, Kris knew that the Wings were more talented than the Jets, so he took an assignment to Adirondack. He played well in the minors and later that year was elevated to the big club. His first game was against the Blackhawks. The Wings were shut out by Eddie Belfour 4-0. Kris came into the locker room after the game and hit the bike to get the bad thoughts out of his head. Bryan Murray, then the Wings coach, came in to tell Kris that he was staying for awhile. Kris finished the year with 5 goals, 8 assists for 13 points, and he was plus 11. He knew that on a team with Steve Yzerman and Sergei Fedorov, that if he was going to stay he had to work his butt off every shift. That is what he has been doing for five years now.

Over the course of two days in December of 1997, The Fischler Report's Detroit correspondent, Jim Ramsey, talked with Draper at Joe Louis Arena as he nursed a thumb injury.

Jim Ramsey: Tell me about your mom and dad. What did they do?
Kris Draper: My mom calls herself a domestic engineer. She's a housewife and my dad is in the medical supply business. He is a territory manager in Toronto and works with seven or eight of the major hospitals in Toronto.

JR: Any brothers or sisters?
KD: Two sisters. One is older and she is a teacher in Toronto, and one is younger and is studying to be a teacher.

JR: Tell me about where you grew up.
KD: I grew up in the eastern part of Toronto, in a little town called Westhill. I was pretty fortunate as my house was at the end of a road and there was a big pond that would freeze over. My dad was able to turn it into a nice little ice

rink. I had the luxury of having a rink at the side of my house. At two, my mom strapped a pair of skates on me and a buddy down the road, and I just started skating from there. All day all I ever wanted to do was to skate.

Then I started playing organized hockey when I was four years old. Most of my childhood and my life has been centered around hockey. I was very fortunate to have two parents who supported me in the game. My sisters were great. They came and watched my games. They were never envious of my situation although I was the only boy and playing hockey. With the success I've had and the team's had, they've shared it with me. They were here the night we won the Cup and were in the dressing room. My sister, who is married, and her husband were there and they came to the party with us and my little sister was there. My girlfriend, who is now my fiancee, was there with her brother. I had a whole bunch of buddies and my parents were down, my uncle and aunt. I am very family oriented and I am very lucky to be surrounded by some great people. They were my number one fans when things weren't going so well, and now that they are going good, they're still my number one fans.

JR: What kind of kid were you?

KD: A little bit of a trouble maker. I think obviously the red hair can say something like that. I was a trouble maker, but I always respected adults and kind of knew when to draw the line. I would push it as far as I could, and then I would say it's time to back off. I was never a great student. My dad grew up playing hockey, and he did everything I did. I was lucky to have a father like him, who wasn't only a father, but also a friend. He said, "Listen, you have to go to school. You are always going to have time for hockey, but when it's time to go to school, go to school."

He was not expecting straight A's because he knew he wasn't going to get them. He just wanted me to be an average student, and if I was going to commit myself to playing hockey, then he expected me to excel at it. He was very supportive and understanding of the situation I was in. If school wasn't going very well, then he would punish me by taking away hockey because he knew that it was my passion. Obviously, that was something I didn't like, and he didn't like to have to do.

He's a dad who loved going to the rink and watching his son play, as did my mom, but he was a disciplinarian. He felt if I was getting away with a few things, that he had to step in and discipline me and the best way to do that was through hockey.

JR: What do you remember about your first equipment?

KD: Bobby Orr skates and Bobby Orr Victoriaville hockey stick. When I first started playing organized hockey, my dad came home with Bobby Orr skates and I thought that was the greatest thing. I was four years old and probably didn't know who Bobby Orr was at the time. All I knew was that these skates were awesome. The one thing my dad said was that when I put these skates on I was going to skate like Bobby Orr. That's when I started finding out who Bobby Orr was and how great he was. It's funny, you know how you cut sticks down and put them in your sliding door, well that Victoriaville was there for a long time. Like when I was in my teens, we still had that stick

JR: When did you first start playing organized hockey?
KD: Four years old. Scarborough had a league, and my buddy and I went out and they took us in the league. We were playing against five and six year olds. We went out and played and that was the one thing that I always looked forward to, I always enjoyed playing hockey. I loved putting the equipment on, and I loved going out there and skating. Even now I go out, and I still have that passion for the game. I'm 26 years old and I love coming to the rink and being around the guys. Some guys come to the rink, put their time in and leave. I'm one of those guys who likes to stick around. It's such a fun game with such a great bunch of guys.

JR: Who were the biggest influences in your life?
KD: My parents were, for sure. I have a great relationship with my parents. They are my parents, but they are also my friends and I am proud to say that. When I was playing in the Winnipeg organization and things were going rough, I was down in Moncton, they were my biggest supporters. They believed in me.

This summer when we had the Stanley Cup, I was able to have it for a couple of days and to bring it in to their house where I grew up and to be able to give them something back; to see my dad carrying it around. He was such a big part of it: there was a time when I thought he won it. As much fun as I had with it, I still say my greatest moment was giving it to my dad and letting him have fun with it. It's funny, he went down into the basement and put on a Red Wing Draper 33 jersey and the Cup is sitting out in the back yard. He comes out, lifts it over his head and starts doing a victory lap around the yard. He is a fun guy and to see his excitement made everything worthwhile.

JR: Talking about mom, she went through something this year when you had a fight with Darcy Tucker in Montreal. Tell me about that.
KD: Their seats were at the opposite end of the rink from where this started and all of a sudden they saw it. It started in the center of the ice, and my dad says, "Here he goes." Everyone is standing up and my mom gets up and goes out into the concourse. She didn't come back for the rest of the game. Remember now, this fight happened about six minutes into the game. She had a tough time with it, but she's getting back into it now. She loves coming to Joe Louis. And she's doing much better now. She grimaces if I'm going to get hit. Let's just say she isn't someone I would enjoy watching a hockey game with.

JR: Did you have a favorite team growing up? How about a favorite player?

KD: Growing up in Toronto, it was the Maple Leafs. It was great on Saturday night when my dad would take me down to the Gardens. We'd get a bite to eat, see the game and come home. You wouldn't have thought there could be a better night. A friend of mine who I grew up with, Billy Carroll, went and played for the New York Islanders and I kind of started liking them. I was someone who loved following teams who won. It was jumping on the bandwagon, sure, but it was also great to see them win all those Cups.

My favorite player was Bryan Trottier. The thing I loved about him was that he was a two-way center. He could do it in the offensive and defensive end, and if I could be like any player I would like to be like him. I also liked when Steve Yzerman came into the league in the early eighties. I liked watching him play too.

JR: You played in the OHL for the Ottawa 67's. Tell me about playing in the OHL and the Canadian World Junior Teams.

KD: I did what no one else had ever done before. After my midget year I went to the Olympic team as a 17 and 18 year old, and played my first year of Juniors as a 19 year old. When I was with the Olympic team, we were playing against teams that were much better than us and all we concentrated on was defense. I had a great chance to go into Juniors and play for coach Brian Kilrea, who had a great reputation for working with the players. He told me right away, "Listen Kris, we know you can play in your own end, it's time for you to go out and put up some offensive numbers and prove to people you can score some goals." So I went from one spectrum to the other in hockey. It was a great experience. We lost in the Finals to the Oshawa Generals, who went on to the Memorial Cup. We took them to seven games. It was a great time and learning experience. To have the chance to go out every night and score a couple of goals, play two minutes on the power play, things I had never had the opportunity to do before.

It's funny because I was just looking back home at a picture of our World Junior team that won the Gold medal back in 1991. There are three guys from that team who are playing in the NHL right now. It was an unbelievable hockey team: Marty LaPointe, Mike Sillinger, Greg Johnson and myself have all played here in Detroit. Felix Potvin and Trevor Kidd were the goalies, Scott Niedermayer was one of the defensemen, Chris Simon, the Chief, was one of my linemates. It was a great team.

JR: When did you first realize that you had the talent to play in the NHL?

KD: When I went to my first training camp with Winnipeg. It was in Saskatoon. I had a two-week camp with the World Juniors, a one-week camp with the 67's and then I flew out to the Winnipeg camp. I just thought I would be there for 10 days to two weeks, and I was looking forward to having a great year in Junior hockey. All of a sudden, training camp went longer and longer.

I was calling the guys back in Ottawa and telling them I should be back soon.

Sure enough, training camp ends and I remember talking to a friend of the family, who was also a scout for Winnipeg, a guy named Paul Henry. I said, "Paul, what's going on? I've been around here for a while now." He said, "Kris, if you keep doing what you've been doing, you're going to stick with this hockey club for the season opener." Here I was going to training camp not even thinking about making the Winnipeg Jets. Just going there and having a good camp so they would remember me, and then having a good year in Juniors, hopefully, as a 20 year old playing. Then, sure enough, Mike Smith and Bob Murdoch called me into their office and told me that I had made the hockey club and would be starting against Toronto on October 4th. I was thinking, "Holy Jumpin," and I rushed out to call my dad. I told him "You'll never guess what's going on. I made the Jets." Right then is when I realized I might be able to play in the NHL. As a 19 year old things went great, and then as a 20 and 21 year old things started to fall apart quickly. I didn't lose confidence in myself. I thought to myself I was the same person and player that I was and things could still happen for me. I went down to the minors to learn, and then I got a break with the Detroit Red Wings. I never would have thought that I would be here and have done what I have done: being a Stanley Cup Champion. It was frustrating for a couple of years, but I never lost hope and I never gave up on myself.

JR: When you were picked up off waivers by Detroit for $1.00, what were your feelings?
KD: To tell you the truth about that, I didn't know anything about it until the playoffs, and I was already in Detroit. Detroit was playing San Jose in the playoffs and that's when it started coming out. Bryan Murray came up and said, "You were picked up for a dollar." I asked him if that was a true story and he said, "Yes." When I first came to Detroit nothing had to happen, but as soon as you play in an NHL game, there must be some type of transaction. So to make it easy, Winnipeg said, "Just give us a buck."

JR: Tell me what happened during the Stanley Cup celebration at Joe Louis Arena with Red Wings' owner Mike Ilitch.
KD: I was in a tough situation because I was going to speak following Kevin Hodson, and he had everyone in stitches. I was just sitting there thinking, "What can I do?" As I got up on stage, I was thinking that last summer I was lying in a hospital with my mouth wired shut, and a year later I'm standing on a stage before 20,000 people celebrating with the Stanley Cup sitting right in front of me. I said that Mr. Ilitch took a big gamble on me and had to break the bank to get me, spending a whole dollar. It would be my pleasure to give him back the dollar. I reached in my back pocket, pulled out a dollar and

handed it to Mr. Ilitch. He stood up laughing and took the dollar, gave me a big hug, and shook my hand. It was a spur of the moment thing.

JR: Tell me about your first fight in the NHL.

KD: It was during that first game in Winnipeg against Toronto. There was a scrum and I didn't know who it was, but I cross-checked a guy in the back. When he turned around it was Drake Berehowsky. Well, the sticks went down and the gloves came off and we were just swinging away. After the linesman broke it up and we were on our way to the penalty box, I remember 20,000 people standing and screaming and I thought this wasn't bad at all. After that game my dad came up and said, "What got into you?" and I said I didn't know.

JR: Why was it so hard to repeat as Champions?

KD: I'd say because there are so many great teams right now. I think that is a credit to our sport. You look around and there are no dynasties being built. Every year there are five or six teams that have a legitimate chance at winning the Stanley Cup. The exciting thing about it is that things have to fall into place for that one special team. We had that last year, and that's why I think it's so hard to repeat as Champions.

JR: You are one of the best and fastest skaters in the NHL. What did you do to become this good?

KD: I just love to skate. After practice or after a bad game the coaches will always skate us. I never took that as punishment, I just had a smile on my face and kept skating.

JR: Do you take the game home with you?

KD: A couple of times I did, but I've been lucky. I don't have kids or the family around, so I can normally put in enough time in the weight room riding the bike to get it out of my system. There are times — I mean we are only human — that we have a bad day at the office. You take a lot of pride in your performance, and when you have a bad game you take it personally. We have a lot to be thankful for, so there is no reason to dwell on it. You just get ready to do better tomorrow.

JR: Tell me everything that you remember about that tragic night in Colorado when Claude Lemieux hit you from behind and hurt you so badly.

KD: I remember the puck was coming up along the boards and Joe Sakic was coming at me. I was concerned that I got the puck past him. I kind of chipped it, and my momentum kind of turned me a little bit and put me in a very vulnerable position. All of a sudden I got absolutely blind-sided. I didn't know what had hit me or anything. I went right down and knew I had lost my helmet. I was on my hands and knees trying to get up, but John Wharton, our trainer (It happened in front of our bench, and he was on the ice immediately) said, "Drapes are you all right?" I said, "Yeah, let's get up," and he said, "No, take your time." I was just kind of sitting there, and he had a towel over my face. When he moved it, I looked down and there was just a pool of blood. I wasn't sure where I was cut. Everything was kind of numb.

John put the towel back and helped me up, and we started skating off the ice. Keith Primeau came over to help me off the ice, and just before I stepped off the ice was when I lost consciousness. The next thing I knew I was on the medical table. I looked up and the doctors were sewing me up. I knew I had been hit, but I had been cut before and had gone back out to play the remainder of the game, and that's what I thought would happen this time. I was really light-headed when I sat up and just kind of looked at the doctors and asked if they were done. I guess with all the freezing they had done I couldn't feel the entire right side of my face. I was thinking a couple of stitches and I would be right back out there.

The doctor looked at me and said, "Kris you're done for the night, and you're done for the year." I said, "What happened to me?" Doctor Finley walked me over to the mirror, and I saw what had happened. A lot of people saw the pictures of me right after the game, and how swollen everything was and the scars that I had, especially with my jaw being off set, and I was like "Wow!" I asked what had happened, and they said "Claude Lemieux had hit you from behind and you caught the top of the boards." Doctor Collon was saying, "You are very lucky," and I'm looking in the mirror thinking I'm lucky. He said, "Can you imagine what could have happened and how close it was where the outcome could have been much different?" That scares you! You play the game hard and most players know where to draw the line! That obviously wasn't the case in this instance. I didn't have the puck, and I was in a very vulnerable position. It wasn't like I had a scoring chance. I was completely out of the play. I just remember going in and out of consciousness a couple of times. It scares you when you keep blacking out, and the doctors were very concerned with that.

At first they were thinking they should get me to a hospital, but the first thing I was thinking was I wanted to stay with the team and travel home with them. I didn't want to be spending any time in Colorado right then. I remember the reactions of all my teammates on the plane ride home. It hit home because they knew it could very easily have been one of them. A guy like Dino Ciccarelli, who has played for so many years in the league, as hard as he plays game in and game out said he had never seen anything like that before, especially the way things had swollen up. The jaw, the eye, my nose was broken, you name it, and on the right side of my face it was broken. John Wharton was just great through this entire episode. I knew the one thing I had to do was to call my girlfriend and my family and let them know what had happened. They were pretty shook up with the whole thing. I just told them I had to go to the hospital, and I went to Henry Ford.

The people at the hospital were great. They were waiting on me when I got there. We started doing treatment immediately. I had to undergo Cat Scans, MRI's and every test they could think of. I spent the entire night, until about 8:00 A.M. the next morning, undergoing tests. I was absolutely exhausted. I spent the entire day sleeping. The entire team came in the next day to see how I was doing. The timing of this was pretty tough, because at the end of the year you usually do things with everyone. They were having a retirement party for Mike Ramsey.

I had a trip planned with Chris Osgood and was going to play golf with Darren McCarty, stuff like that. The next day I was scheduled for surgery, and that was the day my parents came down. I went in and the operation took about three hours to set my jaw and wire it shut. They had to reset my nose and put a titanium plate in my upper maxilla. There was a lot of nerve damage. To this day, it is still numb up through the upper teeth. I was in the hospital for about six days and had to live on a liquid diet. Everything had to be through a straw.

That was the worst part. My girlfriend was a saint! Everything went through a blender. That went on for a month. I dropped 18 pounds not being able to eat or work out. That was a tough summer. With as long as the season went, it was probably July before I could do anything. I had two months to try to get back in shape. Usually you go back in to a gym after about two weeks and you haven't lost that much and you can make good progress. I was starting over from Square One and it became pretty frustrating. I had to ease back into everything because I didn't have much strength. I couldn't lift much weight, and I came into camp pretty lean. I was in decent shape, but I was still not able to build up my muscle mass. It took about four months to get myself back into playing shape.

JR: Darren McCarty has extracted some revenge twice now. When I asked him if it was over, he said "It's never over." How do you feel?

KD: That entire issue did not have to happen. I've never met Lemieux, and I don't ever want to meet him. The way he handled it just shows the kind of person that he is. There are a lot of players who took my side, including some of his teammates. My parents were watching the game and they are very superstitious. My dad used to watch the games downstairs and my mom upstairs. My dad was on his way upstairs to get a drink or something to eat when it happened and all he heard was my mom scream. She saw it all happen and it was pretty tough for them not knowing how their son was.

JR: The media and the fans didn't think the NHL handled this very well and the punishment did not fit the crime. Most felt he should have been suspended for the rest of the playoffs.

KD: Yeah! Absolutely! It was two games, and they are trying to magnify Stanley Cup games. The league had the opportunity to send a message that if you are going to hit from behind, there is going to be a very heavy penalty as your punishment. The league didn't do that. I mean, two games and a $1,000 fine, for what I had to go through that entire summer? I mean, please. I was very disappointed with Mr. Bettman and Mr.Burke. To this day, the one thing I can't understand is Dale Hunter's hit on Pierre Turgeon and all that happened was Pierre separated his shoulder, fortunately for him. Look at the two hits and Hunter ended up getting suspended for 21 games. I don't understand the reasoning behind that in comparison. That's the one thing I've always said. If I was Dale Hunter I would want all my money back when Lemieux only had to pay $1,000. My hit, compared to what Turgeon had to go through, and he didn't even miss a series. I wouldn't have been able to play for four months. That's what I don't understand about what those two guys were thinking about.

JR: Ken Dryden said he would like to ban fighting from the game. How do you feel?

KD: I'm not a fighter, but I've had a couple of fights and I don't think there is anything wrong with it. You have a fight, you go in the box for five minutes and that's it. I think it's part of hockey and it always has been. I mean Ken Dryden says this and he has Tie Domi and goes out and signs Kris King as a free agent. You realize you'll win with players like that. Most of the fighters are character players, and you need character players to be successful in this league. Fighters fight each other, they don't pick on smaller players. I mean Sandy McCarthy isn't going to be tapping me on the shoulder for 60 minutes.

They are there to protect their players, and everyone realizes that. The tough guys are the greatest guys in the locker room. They are colorful, they always have great things to say, they are always positive and all they are concerned about is the welfare of the team. The fans love it, and it is a great tool, also. Obviously, in a close game, things are not going to happen. You can use it as a motivation factor, you can use it to make a statement and it brings 20,000 fans right to their feet. It doesn't matter who is fighting, whether it's a team's toughest player or their scrappiest, the fans want to see it and they get excited about it.

JR: You have had over 200 stitches in your face. Why don't you wear a shield?

KD: I don't know. I don't see myself as a player who wears a shield, and that is nothing against players who do wear shields. We have the right to choose. And I choose not to wear one. I wore one in Junior and with the Olympic team, and I enjoy playing without one. I am very fortunate. I've had a lot of stitches, and I touch wood that nothing serious has happened to me. Every time I go out as a player, I see myself as a guy who just goes out and plays. I don't know why but I've never considered wearing a visor.

JR: I'll give you some tough guy names and you tell me what pops into your head.

JR: Tie Domi.

KD: Tie: character, especially on the ice. He'll do anything to help his team win. It's amazing that a guy his size can hang in there. You have to have a lot of respect for that guy.

JR: Darren McCarty.

KD: Great guy to have on your team; the ultimate team player. He turned himself into a very good two-way hockey player. I think that's a credit to Mac the way he has been able to change his style. He used to just want to go out and fight every game, knowing that if you do, it can catch up to you. This is the first year he has been asked to kill penalties. He and I were killing them together, and he just gets better every day. He can throw them with the best, but is learning when to do it at the right time and that's what I think makes a good fighter.

JR: Joe Kocur.

KD: Once again, a great guy to have on your team. I remember when we traded for Joey, Scotty put Joey, Kirk Maltby (Malts), and myself together and not really knowing what to expect of Joey as a hockey player. I knew he was as tough as they come, and the rumor was that he had one of the hardest punches in the league. But to play with him, I never knew he was as good a hockey player as he is. So tough down low on the puck, and so strong along the boards. He's a great linemate to play with.

JR: Bob Probert.

KD: I'll never forget the fight he had with Marty McSorley in this building. I had just got called up and I saw that fight and I was like, "Wow!" That was one of the best fights I have ever seen. Both guys knocked down and both guys got right back up. It was entertaining. It must have lasted for three or four minutes.

JR: Stu Grimson.

KD: I could not believe how intellectual he is. To be a tough guy and be that smart is very impressive. Just like all the other guys — he will do anything for his teammates.

JR: How would you like to be remembered after you hang up the skates?

KD: As a guy who, game in and game out, gave 100%. The one thing that I love the most in this game is the playoffs; how each game, each shift is so important. In the playoffs I try to be the toughest S.O.B. to play against. I get the opportunity to play against the other teams' top lines, and, if I can get those guys off their game, then we have a better chance to win. I just want to be known as a fierce competitor. That's why I take my name being considered for the Olympic team as recognition that I am doing some good things in this league.

Adam Foote

I fight when I have to for my teammates. I do play a hard game;
I try to hit everything that moves.

Adam Foote makes a statement few other big-leaguers can deliver: he played for a Stanley Cup-winning team during its very first year in the city.

The franchise is the Colorado Avalanche and in 1995-96 Foote was a cornerstone defenseman in front of goalie Patrick Roy as the transplanted Quebec Nordiques defeated the Florida Panthers in four straight games to annex Lord Stanley's silverware.

Colorado won, in part, because of Foote's bedrock backlining that has become recognized by Denver's hockey fans. During the 1998 Colorado-Edmonton playoff, *Denver Post* sportswriter Adrian Dater noted that Foote was any number of synonyms for the word "warrior."

"He battled." noted Dater, "He hit while he battled. For a defensive defenseman, he did it all. The Avalanche's most bruising defenseman, was a punishing force."

Foote's fighting ability transcends bodychecking and moves into the world of fisticuffs with ease. His battles with Detroit's Brendan Shanahan have been just short of epic.

"This Foote-Shanahan story line is a case of elite players appearing to rub each other the wrong way, again and again, in the on-ice course of a bitter team rival," said Terry Frei of the *Denver Post.*

"We match up against each other a lot," Shanahan said. "The way both of us play, things like that are going to happen."

Foote: "It's a reflection of respect for each other. If I don't go hard on him, he's going to make me look bad. Vice versa. He's an honest player and we'll probably go at it again."

Foote has attempted to better control his emotions as he reached veteran status. Occasionally, he'll stand up in the dressing room to pump up his teammates. "Like everyone in there, everyone gets his chance or his time. Sometimes, it's a good idea to say something. Sometimes it's not."

During an interview at Brooklyn's, a Denver sports grill, with Fischler Hockey Service correspondent Christina Oh, Foote provided insights into his business. The question-and-answer session follows.

Christina Oh: Tell me about growing up in Toronto.

Adam Foote: We lived in Toronto, near the beaches, until I was three and then we moved to Scarborough, and to Whitby when I was six. My dad's a policeman in Toronto. He's been a policeman there for close to 30 years. My mom worked in a bakery in a grocery store for 20 years.

C.O.: Did you want to be policeman like your dad?

A.F.: Not necessarily a policeman, but rather undercover work. But I'm just kidding. It's a tough job. I always just thought I had a chance to play hockey.

C.O.: When did you start playing hockey as a kid?

A.F.: I started skating when I was three and I ended up going into figure skating. My dad wanted us to go into figure skating. He wanted to play when he was 18 or 19 and broke a leg, tried again two years later, and broke another one, so he wanted his kids to learn how to skate.

C.O.: What was your favorite team growing up?

A.F.: Toronto Maple Leafs. I was really into it at a young age. When I started, Darryl Sittler was there, Ian Turnbull, Borje Salming, Mike Palmateer. Going back to Maple Leaf Gardens gives me chills. It's an old place with a lot of character. I just remember, when I was young if I had a nap, I got to stay up two periods to watch the game. Any of the Leafs were my favorite players, Lanny McDonald, Greg Terrion, Rick Vaive.

C.O.: Were you always tough as a little kid?

A.F.: I don't know if I was tough. I was always small until I reached my first year of Junior. The summer before junior, I grew two inches and put on 20 pounds. I was always a gritty kid. I wasn't a goon or a fighter but I had to be gritty to play because I wasn't big.

C.O.: Any memorable fights in the Juniors?

A.F.: I remember my first one was in my third game against the North Bay Centennials and it was against Shawn Antoski. I had no idea they called him the "Killer," I dropped the gloves and I hit him with one solid punch. His helmet fell off and I thought, "Whoa! That's not so bad. I was lucky he didn't kill me!" Because I was a rookie, the referee said, "What are you doing?! That guy's a killer!" So I said, "Oh. I'm glad you didn't tell me that before the play or I probably would have gotten killed!" Antoski probably won't remember I fought him. I was never an enforcer. My last year, though, my fights were very limited. Ted Nolan was my coach and he didn't want me to fight much.

C.O.: How about your other coaches early on?

A.F.: I was lucky, I had a coach that I felt was really good. My coach at Whitby taught us how to skate. He was with us every year; very, very strict and I think that discipline helped me there. I moved on and I was fortunate to have Ted Nolan for three years. He was disciplined, but in a different way. You didn't want to upset Ted Nolan. He was such a good person and he was so honest with you that you wanted to be honest and give your all for him.

C.O.: How was your rookie year with the Quebec Nordiques?

A.F.: I was more of a hitter. I just went out there and played hard defense, hit a lot of guys. I was in maybe five or six fights that year. I just tried to hit every-thing that moved and the coach liked it. When I came up, they wanted me to work on my defensive game. So I just worked on playing tough in the corners, showing them I could do that part of the game, too. There's more of a posi-tional game in the NHL. In Juniors, I was more of a free-skating offensive defenseman. Then in Quebec, they put the reins on me. You had your job and everyone else had their own jobs. You could tell the difference for sure.

C.O.: What is the relationship between a defenseman and a goalie? Patrick Roy has said many times that you are his favorite defenseman.

A.F.: Patty and I are roommates and there's another guy who's helped my game. When he came over to Colorado, it seemed like my game blossomed. You have to have a great relationship with your goaltender. It's something that Patrick taught the Colorado defensemen. The reason we won the Cup that year was because we knew to communicate well and to know what your goal-tender wanted you to do. You have to be on the same page with your goal-tender and we are. I know exactly what he wants me to do in pretty much every situation except those flukey ones.

C.O.: Do you remember your first NHL fight?

A.F.: It was against Adam Burt. It was a pretty good fight. I did all right, although I broke my thumb in it.

C.O.: Who was the toughest guy you ever fought?

A.F.: I dropped gloves with Bob Probert last year in the playoffs. I had to because he hit Peter Forsberg. I tried to hold Probert but he's so tough and so powerful. Probert is the toughest guy I got into a confrontation with. The toughest guy in the league today is Tony Twist. I've never fought him, though. I wouldn't call myself a fighter. I fight when I have to for my teammates and play a hard game. I try to hit everything that moves. I wouldn't call myself an enforcer or a top fighter in the league. I think fighting is a part of the game. It will always be here and it should be. It keeps the game respectable and honest. It stops guys from being dirty and the fans like it. The guys that do it have respect for each other and know when they have to do it.

C.O.: How did you feel when Claude Lemieux and Darren McCarty dropped gloves three seconds into the game in Detroit back on March 26, 1997?
A.F.: I thought it was good for Lemieux because of all the heat he was taking. He gained respect from his own teammates. Lemieux had to do it at that time. I think the media and the fans enjoyed it more than anything. The rivalry is always good for the game. You have two great teams that had to fight against each other to make it to the Stanley Cup. That's how the rivalry started and in the playoffs it seems you do anything to win.

C.O.: What was the best fight you've ever seen?
A.F.: I've seen a lot of good fights. The guy I like watching fight the most is Adam Deadmarsh. He's very quick and, pound for pound, he's really good at what he does.

C.O.: Are you friends with anyone off the ice that you've fought with?
A.F.: Owen Nolan. He and I are almost the same personality. We fought in training camp but were roommates, too. So we would fight and then go home and watch a movie and laugh about it. I've seen guys fight and then end up at a restaurant talking to the guy they fought with. I think that's the special part about hockey: the respect I think players have for each other as people. It makes hockey players special the way they are. They leave it on the ice.

C.O.: What about your relationship with Brendan Shanahan?
A.F.: This summer I was at a charity event with him and we got along just fine. We played in the World Cup together and we got along fine there, too. We've got the same agent. We play against each other so much, we're always matched against each other, then things happen. We're both physical players.

C.O.: So you don't consider yourself a "bad boy" of hockey?
A.F.: I'm a physical player. I'll do what it takes to win and I'll show up for my teammates, but I wouldn't call myself an enforcer, not even close. I respect the guys that do it. It's probably one of the toughest jobs in the league to get out, come off the bench, and fight. I'm not a dirty player, either. I'll hit, but if someone's dirty to someone on my team, I'll try to get them back. I have to play hard to be successful. Usually when I'm playing against top lines, you have to get under their skin. If it's necessary to win, I'll get under a guy's skin to get him off his game. Maybe that's a "bad boy." I don't want to get involved with Bob Probert every night, but if he hits one of my teammates, I have to.

Matt Johnson

If you get intimidated, that is when you are going to lose the fight.

The renaissance of the Los Angeles Kings in 1997-98 was a result of the blending of several components, big and small. One of the biggest — at least size-wise — was 6-5, 230-pound left wing Matt Johnson.

Kings marketing experts seized on Johnson's popularity by featuring him in a series of television and radio commercials. The Welland, Ontario native did a voice-over to slow-motion action of him hitting opponents with a pair of gloves finally falling to the ice. Johnson then clearly articulated the message: "I didn't make the team because I can score. I'm not the fastest skater, nor the most graceful passer."

True enough, but his belligerence made as much of an impact on the opposition as some of the Kings' top scorers. When Matt was on the ice, the enemy was more careful and, in many cases, more nervous. For, if nothing else, Johnson can fight.

Since making his National Hockey League debut in 1994-95, he has fought the likes of Gino Odjick, Darren Langdon, Jim McKenzie, Todd Ewen, Ken Baumgartner and Stu Grimson. Matt's running feud with Donald Brashear turned any Vancouver-Los Angeles game into a potential war and Philadelphians will long remember Johnson's bristling bout with Daniel Lacroix.

A product of the respected Peterborough Petes Ontario Hockey League organization, Johnson led the Junior club in penalty minutes with 233 (third highest total in the OHL) during the 1993-94 season. Within a year, he was in the NHL, enjoying a 14-game stint with Los Angeles in 1994-95. Amassing 102 penalty minutes in that brief debut, Matt averaged more than seven penalty minutes per game! Few NHL rookies could ever make that statement.

But it wasn't until 1996-97 that he clicked on all big-league cylinders. He played in 52 games, collected 194 penalty minutes, and that was enough for Matt to lead the team.

"There's a part of me that each night I have to tame," Johnson once explained. "I can't run around crazy and fight everybody. I've done that, and it can be a lot of fun. But it gets old fast."

His Kings coach, Larry Robinson, once was one of the biggest players in the NHL. Occasionally, Robinson was called upon to fight. During the 1976

Stanley Cup Finals, Robinson tamed Philadelphia Flyers goon Dave Schultz and, from that point, Montreal won the Stanley Cup. Robinson understands Johnson's role and Johnson understands his role, top to bottom.

"I take my job very seriously, " he asserted. "I realize how important it is if you can intimidate and get in somebody's face. No one likes playing against guys who do that. I know I can help our better players. If I do my job, they'll have more chances to do things. When I help them, I really love it."

Robinson: "Matt has to bang people around. He's got to have everybody looking for him when he's on the ice. "

Away from the rink, Johnson is like so many of his brethren in the enforcement business. He is described by teammates as quiet, shy, mild-mannered and mellow. "He gets his aggression out on the ice," explained teammate Sean O'Donnell.

Johnson was the perfect gentleman during an interview with Fischler Hockey Service correspondent Lee Callans. The pair chatted about Matt and his profession after a Kings practice at Great Western Forum in Inglewood, California. The oral history that follows was taken from that session.

For a guy who made it all the way to the NHL, I have to admit that I got a late start in the game. I actually didn't start playing organized hockey until I was ten years old. That's fairly late for a Canadian kid who reached the top at the age of twenty. It was ten years from the time I began in an organized league to when I came to Los Angeles.

I was lucky in one way; I had cousins who lived nearby and who were about the same age as me. When the ponds would freeze over, we would go out and fool around with the puck. Even though they weren't organized, the games were good and, most important, I grew to love hockey right there in the outdoors.

Size always was on my side. I was a big kid and was always the biggest on every team I played for right up to the Kings — until Steve McKenna (6-8, 247 pounds) came along. I had two younger brothers and a sister who was a year older and we did a lot of fighting when we were about eight, nine and ten years old, but then it got a bit lopsided and my dad had to step in.

My parents both were very supportive of me once they realized that I was dead serious about hockey. They would get me up at five in the morning when I had to go to the early practices and they sacrificed in every imaginable way to keep me on skates and further my career when it became evident that I wanted to do something with this hockey business.

The seriousness of hockey began for me when I joined an organized league and stuck with it, which I did. When I was twelve years old, I had graduated to the Peewee level and that's where I got into my first hockey fight.

Here's how it happened: a player on the other team ran into our goalie — or tripped into our goalie — during a tournament game.

It was a weird scene for a couple of reasons. Number one: the fellow who dumped our goalie was a friend of mine even though he played for the other team. Number two: our fathers were sitting next to each other in the stands, watching the game. Anyway, we dropped the gloves and fought. The funny thing was that while we were fighting, our dads were just sitting there talking. To me, that was kind of strange.

My fighting couldn't have had a negative effect on my game because the fact is that I kept moving up and up the hockey ladder. Eventually, I reached the Bantam section and, from there, moved on to Junior B, which is pretty organized hockey where I come from in Ontario. I must have been half-decent in Junior B because it only took a year and I was drafted into the Ontario Hockey League and played for Peterborough, which is a team with a long history and is highly-regarded in Junior hockey circles — and the NHL, for that matter.

Before I even got to Peterborough, I knew my role. As a fifteen-year-old in Junior B, I had something like 240 penalty minutes in 50 games. Plus, I was playing against all twenty-year-olds when I moved up. Peterborough knew what it wanted when I was drafted. They wanted toughness. The Petes had been pushed around the year before and management wanted to put a stop to that.

There was no question that my job was to help fulfill their needs in that area and, in so doing, I helped prepare myself for what eventually would be my job in the NHL; provided I made it all the way to The Show.

The way things turned out, the Juniors were — for me, at least — the best route I could have taken to the top.

Here's why: the schedule is a good example. We were on the ice every day once the season started so there was no end of practicing. On top of that, the competition was keen. As a sixteen-year-old, I couldn't have found a better situation to develop. Besides, I knew by that time what I wanted out of life and I knew what was required of me so all that remained was for me to do it. That meant being on the ice as much as possible.

It all paid off. After my second year in Peterborough (1993-94), I was drafted by the Kings in the Second Round, thirty-third overall. Was that ever exciting! Here I am drafted by L.A. and they already have players like Wayne Gretzky and Rob Blake in the lineup. The thought of actually being in the same dressing room with them kind of blew me away. Once I sat back and thought about what had happened at the Draft, I made up my mind that I would give myself the best possible chance to make the big team.

The first order of business was to make a good impression at training camp. When it actually came down to show up, I thought that I had made myself ready. The trouble was, I got drafted in June 1994 and once it came to October there was that NHL lockout. Instead of starting the season, I had to sit around and wait, and hope, and pray that it would be settled in time for us to get in at least part of the year.

Fortunately, the lockout ended in time for them to at least get half a season in and I was lucky enough to be kept with the Kings. For sure, I did not want to go back to Juniors anymore. Even getting a little bit of playing time in the NHL was better than returning to Peterborough.

The most amazing thing about coming to Los Angeles in the first place was that Gretzky still was there — and the captain — and he took me under his wing. I stayed with him during training camp and, let me say, that was something I'll someday tell my children and, later, even tell my grandchildren. It was awesome — and funny. Like, when I would phone home, my friends and family wouldn't even ask me whether I was going to make the team. Their first question always was, "How is Wayne Gretzky?"

In a sense, the lockout was a blessing for me. I had had problems with my knee and while we were sitting out, waiting for a settlement, I had my knee scoped arthroscopically. The recuperation laid me up for a good part of the time but I remained in Los Angeles and, at least, got to know the city. As it happened, they did send me back to Peterborough for fourteen games until the lockout was settled; then I returned to California to stay.

I loved being with the Kings. Right off the bat, I got friendly with Marty McSorley who, long ago, had established quite a reputation around the NHL as an enforcer. Apparently, Marty saw me as someone who was a lot the way he had been when he broke into the league. He was a sensitive enough individual to understand that I needed some guidance, so he took me under his wing and gave me pointers about going about things. Believe me, I appreciated what he did a whole lot. I had always respected McSorley from afar and had followed his career going back to his early days in the league. He had started his career as someone with limitations but developed into a good all-round performer who could play either defense or up front and do it either way with toughness. I saw him as more than just a fighter and that's precisely the way I hoped to eventually see myself.

Marty helped cure me of my inexperience. I was a kid, just running around. It wasn't so much that I was taking stupid penalties but I would do things that weren't necessary. Part of it was inexperience and part of it was just wanting to be in the middle of things.

"Settle down and just play the game," Marty would say.

He helped me pick my spots. He knew all the opponents and knew how they fought. Better still, he let me pick his brain. Before a game, I would ask him, "How is so-and-so? Does he punch lefty?" Questions like that, and he would give me guidance, although he wasn't the only King who helped out.

We also had some other tough skaters. Rick Tocchet was one and Troy Crowder another. Both had been around and knew the other fighters. Both of them gave me good advice but a lot of what I learned came from plain, old experience.

I got that right away. It was an exhibition game and the enforcer on the other side was none other than Stu Grimson, who by that time had the nickname of Grim Reaper. Before the game even started, I knew that he and I would be face to face. I figured that I had to try him on for size just because it would be a good test to see how I would make out against one of the truly strong men of the NHL.

Hey, if I couldn't stand my ground with Grimson, it would mean that I would have to take a bit more time making it at the top. Once the game started, it was inevitable that we would go and we did — not once but twice. It was a good test. I hung in there both times and the Kings people who saw it must have been a little impressed by the way I handled the role.

There were plenty of fights after that but I wouldn't call any single one "my most memorable fight."

To me, fights are fights and anything can happen in a fight. I don't even understand what "a most memorable fight" really means.

What I do know — and what I learned along the way — is that I can't let myself get intimidated by anyone on the other side of the ice. If I get intimidated in advance, that is the time I will lose a fight. I can't let that happen and no one should let that happen.

When I first came up to the Kings, I wanted to fight the good ones like Bob Probert and Tony Twist just to get a name for myself. Now I find that it's more a case of Matt Johnson doing his job and doing it well. If I have to stick up for a teammate, you can be sure that I'm going to do that. Or, on the other hand, if I have to awaken my team, I'll do what I can that way.

If you check the rosters, you'll find that there are plenty of good fighters around, enough so that it's difficult to actually pick four or five who are "the best fighters in the league." Many do it and do it well; so well that on any given night, one of them will look like the best. Then, there are fellows who have been around a while who don't fight quite as much as they once did but who still are at the top of the "best fighters" list.

I know that Bob Probert is still there and so is Tony Twist. Chris Simon, Sandy McCarthy and Tie Domi — all those guys are there as well. And in our division Vancouver had Gino Odjick — before he got traded to the Islanders — and Donald Brashear. When the Canucks had both of them in the lineup against us, I had a lot of "fun" with that!

There's still plenty of fighting in the NHL but there's no question that the enforcer's role has changed. Things are different than they were ten years ago. At that time, a player like Probert could win a fight and you knew that his team would win its hockey game.

Nowadays, an enforcer may win a fight but the most he's likely to do is change the momentum of the game a little bit or put the game on hold. The way it is now someone like me has to be able to play the game and not hurt my team when I'm on the ice.

Here's a good example: during the 1997-98 season, I would be put out on a shift and the first things that came to mind were, "Who am I gonna run? Who am I gonna hit?" My problem — especially in the eyes of the coaches — was "Matt isn't thinking about playing." The result was that they sat me down and said straight out, "You're not going to play if you're gonna do that."

The experience taught me a lesson and the lesson was, "Go out and work on your skills." Which is exactly what I did. Not long afterward, I was back in the lineup, playing every night and more effective than before. Granted, I felt weird not fighting for four or five games. It was almost as if I was copping out but if there are no fighters out there, that means there are no fights out there so there's no sense in throwing them.

Once I stopped obsessing about the fights, I began to feel better about myself. I realized that being a well-rounded player is the goal I should be striving for because it would be better for me as a big-leaguer. It would be better for my career and certainly provide me with longevity. I came to realize that what was going to keep me in the NHL was my playing. I knew that, sooner or later, there would be another tough guy coming along. Doesn't matter who it is — Matt Johnson or Bob Probert or Tony Twist — what I had to do was establish myself as a player first and then some team, somewhere in the NHL would want me.

Which is not to say that I would stop fighting. If it happens, it happens although I'm not the type who goes around chirping, yapping, starting something with his mouth. That's not my way. I really don't say much. If I think it's time to go, I'll tell my counterpart on the other side, "Hey, we gotta go. It's time. Let's do it!"

If I think a guy is taking too many liberties, I'll let him know. I'll say something like, "Watch it!" Or, "Keep your shit down." Or, "Keep your stick down." You hear a lot about trash talk and my experience has taught me that some skilled players can be intimidated by warning them, "I'm gonna run you over."

There's nothing like experience to improve your fighting ability. Working on balance is important and for that I'll train in the summer and hit the bag and use other boxing techniques. I also make sure to lift weights so my strength is there.

Hockey fighting is a special category of boxing all into itself. It's not like boxing in a ring — like and Ali versus Frazier — and it's not like plain streetfighting. And it certainly isn't like wrestling. It's a unique kind of fighting because of the ice, the skates, the gloves and whatever.

That's why balance on the ice is so important. A lot of times I'll try to throw a big punch — a haymaker — and balance really comes into play when that happens. If I happen to connect, it could end the fight right then and there. And if I miss it also could end the fight right then and there!

My style is not to throw a million punches. But what I do is try to throw them fast and as hard as I can. If they hit, they hit; if they don't, they don't. I try to use my strength, speed and reach and overpower opponents.

A fighter like Marty McSorley likes a long fight. The longer it goes, the better Marty usually makes out. Once Marty left the Kings, and went to the Sharks, I didn't go out of my way to fight him. For that to happen, something on the ice would really have to provoke me. We still play hard against each other and it's not that I wouldn't fight him. After all, what happens happens. It's all business out there.

If there's one thing about fighting that's important to me it is that it be fair. I don't believe in cheap shots and stuff like that. Anyone who indulges in cheap shots will get it back sooner or later. What goes around, comes around. Guys who respect their opposites tend to get more respect from the other side.

Not that I haven't had my problems. In February 1997 I was suspended for four games after an altercation with Andrei Nazarov who was with San Jose. If he had not been injured the way he was after that, I don't think there would have been a suspension. But the fact that he did get his jaw broken meant that the league had to do something. I knew that they would suspend me for a while. That's part of the game. I accepted it and paid my dues for it.

On the one hand fights are part of the game but, on the other hand, I never really want to see a guy get hurt. I want my opposite to be able to play and earn his check but the bottom line still is that hockey is a physical game. Every year players are getting hurt. It happens. Injuries are not something I relish seeing but they do happen.

Me, I've been fortunate. I haven't suffered any major injuries from fighting, just cuts and bruises and maybe a banged-up knuckle or two.

What am I like away from the rink?

Well, I don't go around hitting people. I ride my Harley and have a good time.

Daniel Lacroix

I was taught to stand up for my teammates.

Daniel Lacroix has been standing up for his teammates for more than a decade.

A Montreal native who played Junior hockey in Granby, Quebec, the French-Canadian center has the arsenal to do so. At 6-2, 205 pounds, he is well-endowed to handle his dukes as opponents in the International and American Leagues learned soon enough.

Originally drafted by the New York Rangers in 1987 (31st overall), Lacroix alternately played for Binghamton, New York, the Boston Bruins and Rangers again before being signed as a free agent by the Flyers on July 15, 1996.

During the 1996-97 season Lacroix played in 74 games, scored seven goals and one assist while totalling 163 penalty minutes. A year later, he played in 55 games, with one goal and four assists and 118 penalty minutes.

Although he was not a regular, Lacroix allowed that he was comfortable with his role. "I make a contribution," he asserted.

To put it mildly.

When the Philadelphians required muscle, Lacroix was ready, willing and able. A case in point was a game on March 3, 1998 against the New York Islanders.

Isles defenseman Rich Pilon delivered a low hit to Flyers ace John LeClair. In the eyes of Philly followers, the Islander went for LeClair's knees. Lacroix roared to the boards in retaliation, cross-checked Pilon high about the neck, and tried to fight him.

"Pilon rolled into a ball to protect himself," commented Tim Panaccio of the *Philadelphia Inquirer*.

Lacroix was assessed a double-minor penalty and was suspended for three games by the NHL, which also fined him $1,000. "Some of the guys offered to pay my fine," Lacroix recalled. "I don't want to take money from players. At the same time, if someone does something for me and for the team like that, I understand."

The smiling enforcer elaborated on his profession following a Flyers scrimmage at their practice rink in Voorhees, New Jersey. Fischler Hockey Service correspondent Diane Gerace interviewed Lacroix from where this oral history evolved.

I've been the same type of player since my minor hockey days in the Province of Quebec. I always felt that I had to bring a little bit more of an edge to my game. I've always had to play that way to be successful. Others with more talent didn't have to do that but I had to compensate.

I had two older brothers who played a little hockey but they never wanted me to play with them. They considered me too young. When they needed somebody to play goal, then they'd stick me in the nets. My job was to carry the sticks and the net on my back. And, of course, they did what older brothers always do; they beat up the youngster in this case, me! I got the worst of it because I was the little kid who wouldn't go away.

In school, math wasn't my big thing but I compensated there, too, becoming good at drawing and photography. I would do caricatures of my teachers and would draw cartoon strips. I found what I liked and pursued those hobbies although hockey was tops on my list.

It all jelled for me in Junior hockey at Granby. That's where I found my niche. I was one of the younger guys when I got there so in that situation I had to make an impact in order to break into the lineup. There are several ways of doing that. If you don't score that many goals then you have to find an alternative. Playing aggressive and dropping the gloves is one of those ways.

Several of my opponents from amateur hockey are in the NHL playing the same style of hockey they did then and some are my teammates. Luke Richardson is a good example. He became my teammate on the Flyers in 1997-98 yet I remembered going up against him in minor hockey. He was a rough, tough kid. I also played against Tie Domi in a summer hockey tournament; another tough kid.

My first fight was in Midget hockey. One of the players hit one of my friends really bad. The tough guy was stocky and went around stirring things up, abusing the younger kids. I went in and got one for my buddy. I dropped the guy!

Why did I do it? We had been told to stand up for our teammates. If someone touched our goalie, we had to jump in. If there was a scrum, I was there. This philosophy was embedded in me at an early age. Teammates appreciate when players like myself stick up for them. I got respect and felt good about myself because I did something positive for my team. I could feel it from the rest of the guys.

Not that it always turned out positive. Once in Juniors, I was getting ready to get into a scrum and was all fired up for the fight. Suddenly, my belt broke and my pants dropped to my knees. There I am ready to fight and look around and see the linesmen laughing and my opponent grinning and my own teammates having a roar. I looked down and saw my pants had fallen off. We all got a good chuckle out of that. When I reached the Major Junior level, I was very fortunate because we had a strong team in Granby. Some of our skill players included Pierre Turgeon and Eric Desjardins but I had to make an impression another way although not necessarily fighting.

After I turned pro with the Rangers, they sent me to their American League farm team in Binghamton. Talk about a team of tough guys, we had Rudy Poeschek, Tie Domi, Denny Vial, Pete Fiorentino and Mark Janssens. I was seventh in line when it came to toughness.

It was funny because when we would play another team, the opposition would look at our lineup — very intimidating — and decide that they would rather fight me than Domi or Vial or Poeschek.

Tougher, physical players must also be responsible defensively as well as sharp on the bench and good in the lockerroom. I learned that I had to accept my role in order to eventually be a good fourth-line player in the NHL.

I also knew that there were a lot of fourth-liners who also were skilled guys. A good example of that is Randy McKay of the New Jersey Devils. He was a skilled player working a fourth line, doing what he was asked to do. After a number of years, he became almost a star, moving up to the top line.

My first NHL fight was against Lyle Odelein. He was playing defense for the Montreal Canadiens and I was with Boston. Frankly, it wasn't much of a bout because we were both holding on most of the time.

Some enforcers make a study of the opposition. I find that I pay attention to the other club but I don't put any pressure on myself. I just make myself aware of who they have.

Some people who get to know me are surprised that I still do art work. For instance, I do some of my own Christmas cards and caricatures of some of my teammates. We have a long season and the distractions help. My teammates seem to appreciate the drawings I do on the blackboard. Sometimes I come into the room before anyone else, pick a subject and put it on the board.

I'm also into photography. That's a medium I like because it's more direct. I'm not a patient guy so for me drawing and doodling is easier because I do it quick and get it over with. I don't have patience to do paintings. When it comes to photography, all I have to do is look at the lights, shadows and snap! My favorite subjects are my two kids.

When I was in the minors, we had a game in Salt Lake City. I went to a local store and rented a camera and took it to the Utah Jazz basketball game that night with the intentions of shooting the game.

I sneaked into the arena and wound up at the side of the court. But I got a lot of heat from the players over that because we had a game the next night. It made me realize that if I was going to play hockey, I wasn't going to travel with the camera and be a tourist. I had to take this game seriously. Since then, I tend to leave my camera at home.

I'm considered a tough guy but if there's one thing I've learned it's that a tough guy all by himself on a team is not going to do his club that much good if he's alone. If the group as a unit is tough — and plays that way — and surrounds itself with a couple of guys who can handle themselves, that makes for a better situation.

It's funny; my three-year-old recently started skating. Last winter we had him at the Flyers Christmas party and was on the ice. He dropped his gloves for the first time. He's a hyperactive type of kid and we're trying to contain him.

Now I have to tell the baby-sitter to turn off the hockey games because I think he's watching too much of Dan Kordic. I want him to stick to basic hockey.

Denny Lambert

When the Ottawa Senators upset the favored New Jersey Devils in the 1998 opening Stanley Cup playoff round, one of the most unlikely heroes was a chunky left wing who previously had been a pro hockey bedouin. Denny Lambert had bounced from San Diego to Anaheim and finally Baltimore before actually finding a home in Canada's capital city.

At age 27, the native of Wawa, Ontario had once and for all established himself as the Senators resident bodyguard. He was assigned the role of protector and spacemaker for the club's more artistic forwards and Denny responded with an élan that few others in the National Hockey League could boast. Enthusiasm is as much a part and parcel of his makeup as his helmet and stick.

"I try to make space so others can go about their work," Lambert explained. "If the opposition tries to push around our skill players, I come in and take care of things. I'm there to take pressure off them and make some room. I'm going to get space but I don't want to be a knucklehead in the process."

During the Ottawa-New Jersey playoff Lambert was more than a pest-enforcer. He turned into an occasional offensive threat and a reasonable two-way player.

"There was a reason," asserted coach Jacques Martin. "Denny worked on improving his game. During the summer of 1997 he worked hard with a good program. He dropped some weight and that, in turn, improved his skating. I give him a lot of credit for the way he has improved himself."

Not that Lambert has forgotten how to fight. Far from it. During the 1996-97 season — his first with Ottawa — he totalled 217 penalty minutes over 80 games. In 1993-94, skating for San Diego in the International League, he hit an all-time high of 314 PIM.

"There have been times when I got so carried away that I forgot what was happening with the puck," said Lambert. "I would lose my perspective."

What he has never lost is his enthusiasm. Lambert virtually bubbles as he criss-crosses the rink and his *joie de vivre* clearly spills over to his teammates. If he can chip in a goal or two in critical moments — as he did in the 1998 playoffs — all the better but Denny has no illusions about his job description.

"They don't want me to be a twenty-five goal-scorer," he said. "That's not my role. I have to be the player they want me to be. I have to be physical and make the other team pay the price."

Lambert was plucked from Ottawa by the Nashville Predators at the 1998 Expansion Draft.

Bad Boys

During an after-practice interview with Fischler Hockey Service reporter Rick Middleton at Kanata, Ontario, Lambert provided insights into his character and background. The following oral history was produced from that conversation.

✦ ✦ ✦

I come from Wawa, Ontario and if you're wondering what Wawa means, it's Indian for "goose." My family lived in the town, which has about five-thousand people. My father was a millright in the steel plant there. My mom worked as a guard at the penitentiary in Kingston, Ontario.

There were three other kids in the family. The oldest was my sister, Kim. The middle one was Rochelle and the youngest of us is my brother, Danny, although everyone calls him Tiggers.

When I was growing up there, Wawa was a very tight community where everyone knew everyone else. I had a lot of fun there as a kid and still have lots of friends back home. When I return there in the summer and take a walk to go shopping with my dad, it takes about a half an hour just for him to get a loaf of bread because he knows everybody and there's so much time needed to chat with all the folks. We have a very friendly community.

It also was hockey-friendly. By that I mean playing it — starting as a kid — was fun. I should point out here and now that my parents never pushed me into the game. They supported me, yes, but pushed me, no. There's a big difference.

As much fun as it was, hockey always was a challenge for me; a challenge to learn the game and a challenge to get better at it and make all the teams that were there to make on my way toward my ultimate goal, which was to be a professional hockey player.

What made the challenge so much more difficult was my ability; or lack of same. I was never the most skilled player on my teams and was always the guy getting the last cuts off teams. But the key was that I never gave up. Never! The result was that I was able to play on the Peewee level and progressed from there. Not that it was easy. I had my ups and downs but got to Sault Ste. Marie, Ontario where I got cut from one team but made another and eventually made it with the Soo team in the Ontario Hockey League, which is as high as it gets in the Junior ranks.

Halfway through my first year, Ted Nolan came in as our coach and what an experience that was for me. Teddy was unbelievable. I mean, a great motivator and a guy who knew the game inside out. After all, he had played at so many levels and knew so much. He was what I call "a player's coach." By that I mean, he knew exactly when to let the boys out and go have a few beers but he also knew when to tighten his fist. As a result, a coach like that is going to get a solid effort from his players. We knew that if we worked hard for Teddy, he would reward us.

Besides, Nolan likes a tough game and I had been playing tough hockey ever since I remember. I have a short temper; always did growing up. I grew up with Chris Simon and he had the same kind of temper as me — short! If somebody hit me the wrong way, I'd say, "Screw you. You're not going to do this to me." And then I would do something about it. I found that that was a good way to get rid of some anger. That, or hit the heavy punching bag!

But no coach ever pushed me into a fight and I thank God that the "tap on the shoulder" never was felt nor the words "Go out!" On the other hand, I learned the way I had to play in order to stay on those teams. I knew full well that I had to play physical. I learned that when I turned pro with San Diego in 1991-92, I had to drop my gloves if I was going to stay at that level.

I played in games where I had two shifts and probably two fights. That was when I was trying to make a name for myself; trying to show them that, hey, Denny Lambert will do the fighting. When I was breaking in as a pro, I would fight, claw, bite, whatever it was to stay in the lineup. I would basically do anything.

It became clear that I was a third or fourth-line hitter. I was to run around, try to get something going for the team, for the goal-scorers. Obviously, it meant throwing off the gloves and duking it out with the one on the other team who was the policeman.

The "rule" is pretty simple: if the fellow on the other club starts taking liberties, I say, "Hey, don't be hitting anybody else or we're going to go." That was defined for me in Junior hockey. Fighting was going to be part of my game and if not fighting then banging somebody, or hitting someone in the face or trying to do something to agitate the other side. I see a lot of Ted Nolan in me.

His influence was profound and it centered on one theme — don't quit!

Here's one incident I'll never forget: we were having a practice and he had us in sort of a race. I knew that I had no chance of beating some of the really good skaters on the team and I was getting tired so I finally gave up and started skating backwards. When Nolan saw me do that, he threw his whistle down and started screaming: "Don't you ever quit! Don't anybody ever quit on this hockey team again like Denny did just now!"

Later on he called me into his room and I sat there crying. I was devastated but I finally realized that he was just trying to make a point. In retrospect, he certainly did make the point. From that point onward, I never gave up. I realized then and there that there are ways of overcoming obstacles such as not being a great skater.

So I was very fortunate to have played for Ted Nolan. The other way I was lucky was that Teddy recommended that I get an agent and he was friends with a guy from Rochester named Steve Bartlett. Steve had helped Teddy quite a bit so I figured that if he was good enough for Ted Nolan, he would be good enough for Denny Lambert.

Steve made a lot of calls around — whatever agents do — and I wound up going to a Buffalo camp at Sabreland. I spent a week there with all the

Buffalo rookies and even played in a rookie game against the Toronto Maple Leafs rookies. Next thing I know all the "big boys" are arriving. How do I know? I looked in the parking lot and saw all the Mitsubishi 3000 GTs and the Hummers and all that big, expensive stuff. That was the tip-off that the big camp had started. And, by the way, I never did skate with the big guys.

But I sure was impressed. Like, "Wow! Look at the cars they're driving. Look how big they are. Look at all the guys I've been idolizing and watching on TV." Right away, I knew that I wanted to be one of them. And I tried. I had hoped to make the Sabres roster but I didn't and they sent me to San Diego of the IHL where the hockey was a lot more open but there also was fighting.

I can remember my first IHL bout; it was against a player named Kevin Edwards. It took me eight games in the IHL before I actually started throwing them and Edwards was a good match because he was a feisty guy; reminiscent of Kevin Dineen who was in the NHL at the time. In other words, he was a fighter. At first, I was scared, a bit intimidated, I admit. Think about it, this was my first fight in the pros and when that happens it's almost automatic that you're going to be scared. But once the fists started to go, I got over my fright and I did really well against him. After that, I fought more and more. I knew that now I could handle myself on this level and not worry about being intimidated the way I had been before I actually fought Edwards.

My coach in San Diego was Don Waddell and I have to say that he never told me to go out and fight anybody. I just did it and loved it when I fought. I piled up the penalty minutes in San Diego and finally got my break in 1994-95 when Anaheim signed me as a free agent. The bigger break was Ottawa took me aboard as a free agent in 1996.

In my first two seasons as a Senator, the club made the playoffs twice. That's not bad. It's been fun and, of course, there have been the tough moments. I've won some fights and I've lost some. I remember one with Jeff Beukeboom of the Rangers. Now there is a BIG man. We had two bouts in one game. He got the upper hand in the first fight and after I shook off the aftereffects and sat in the penalty box, I really wanted to prove that I wasn't scared of him — or anybody, for that matter. The initial fight was in the first period so it took me until the third period to even get my courage up to get at him again. Now it was near the end of the game and I said to myself, "I'm gonna show them that I don't care who it is and whether I get beaten up or not, I'm gonna fight." I have to admit that it took me a bit of digging down inside to go out and try to fight someone who had clobbered me only about an hour earlier. Brother, what a chore that was because he is just so huge. Not a great fighter, but huge. Anyway, I did it the second time and survived to tell the tale.

On some nights I'm just not ready to fight but there's no choice. I can remember and incident in Miami. We were playing the Panthers and this was right at the beginning of the game. As a matter of fact, it was the very first shift.

The Panthers had a tough defenseman by the name of Paul Laus and he's on the ice and I'm on the ice and this first shift was like a cold shift. I was just trying to get myself warm but it just wasn't there. Meanwhile, Laus comes flying over at me and yells, "Let's get her going here!" Before I could do anything, he dropped his gloves, grabbed the stick out of my hands and started throwing. I definitely was not ready for that fight.

Nothing against Laus. Paul is a good, tough guy. He knew that I would accept the challenge. There are so many guys who are tough — and smart. Kelly Chase is right up there. He'll hold you, hit you, although he's not that big. He goes with the big boys and does well because he's a very smart fighter.

On the other hand, Laus is pure power. He usually likes to throw a couple of straight hooks to the face or helmet and then he comes up with an uppercut. He catches a lot of guys with that uppercut of his.

No, I haven't fought Eric Lindros although he would probably scrape my butt. I wouldn't bat an eye to fight him. He's so dirty. He's got a club in his hand and he just swings that thing around. Granted, he's a great player and I'm impressed with his skills and the way he plays the game with so much emotion. But the way he swings that stick around, he's going to hurt somebody one of these days. He'll swing and hit you. He's so strong. In fact, I don't know if he knows his own strength. If he hits you in the wrist where you have no protection, he'll break your wrist. He swings his stick a little too much and doesn't back it up all the time.

Then, you have the Ulf Samuelsson type. In the corner he always has a glove in your face, trying to rub your nose and water your eyes or do something. He's just dirty. He's always trying to somehow hit you in the face or come up with the stick and glove and hit you an uppercut. A dirty player; that's the way he plays.

Or Darius Kasparaitis. He's pretty dirty. He gets you when you're not expecting it. Then, all of a sudden, he'll come up and hit you. When that happens, you think, "Geez, where did that come from?" He plays a hard, dirty role but he's not much of a fighter.

There have been a lot of complaints about Bryan Marchment. Dirty hits, low blows to the knees. Submarine hits. He gets great open-ice hits but a lot of them are dirty. When you play against Marchment, you have to know he's out there and there's a chance that he'll hurt you.

Darren Langdon

*Most tough guys are very honest and that's the way I like to be.
I don't like cheap-shots or anything like that. I don't see too
many tough guys cheap-shotting anybody.*

Ever since he graduated to the New York Rangers from the American Hockey League, Darren Langdon has turned heads — in more ways than one — with his deceptive size and style.

More of a cruiser than a battleship, Langdon nevertheless has held his own with some of the National Hockey League's foremost heavyweights and rarely has lost a bout in the bigs. A prime reason for his success is Darren's ability to withstand the hardest blows early in the fight, retain his stamina and then counterattack while the fatigued foe helplessly covers up.

No better example of that was a one-on-one between oversized New York Islanders defenseman Zdeno Chara and Langdon during an exhibition game at Nassau Coliseum in the autumn of 1997. The tallest player in the league, Chara stung Langdon with a series of long jabs at the outset and appeared en route to a decisive victory. But Darren absorbed the blows with little after-effect and retaliated with a flurry of uppercuts and jabs that left his opponent urging linesmen interference.

One of the few Newfoundlanders to make his way to the NHL, Langdon was signed as a free agent by the Rangers on August 16, 1993 in what was one of the wisest moves general manager Neil Smith ever made. He spent the 1993-94 season with Binghamton in the AHL, totalling 327 penalty minutes. It not only earned him attention but a look-see during the lockout-abbreviated 1994-95 season with the Rangers.

The 18 games didn't exactly clinch a berth but Smith and coach Colin Campbell realized that they had a diamond-in-the-rough. He spent only one more game in the minors — during 1995-95 — and has been a Ranger ever since. A fighter himself during his playing days, Campbell believed that Langdon could become an effective force in time.

"Darren's challenge," said Campbell, "was to move his game to the next notch. He had to get the puck into scoring position and get maybe 20 assists and perhaps even 13 to 14 goals." He was far from that in his first full big-league season, 1996-97, but there was no question that Langdon was improving. By

November 1997, Campbell was calling Darren the "first star all year long."

The ultimate reward was being placed on a line with Wayne Gretzky. "When Darren goes out there," Campbell explained, "something happens. He has as much talent in his whole body as three-quarters of our guys have in their pinkies."

Langdon has made no bones about his being torn between trying to be a skill player and his role as an enforcer. Yes, he would like his points but, no, he does not want to forget his roots. Sometimes it can be confusing.

"If I look at a game and say, 'Geez, I might try to carry the puck a bit here,' and then all hell breaks loose and I'm back at Square One. As a result, I try to keep it simple. I figure that if I do the simple things right, I'll be all right. Simple to me is getting the puck deep, cycling and doing whatever it takes to stay in the NHL.

"I'm tickled to be in the Show. When you grow up in Newfoundland, as I did, you never think about making the NHL. As a matter of fact, I didn't even think about playing this role. All I ever wanted to do was play hockey like I thought it should be played; the way Mark Messier did his job and never backed down from anybody."

Darren certainly has not backed down, having fought such stalwarts as Stu Grimson, Bob Probert and Tie Domi. In an interview with Fischler Hockey Service reporter Amy Spencer at the Rangers' practice facility in Rye, New York, Langdon talked about everything from his neighborhood pond rink to his fighting style. The oral history drawn from the interview follows:

My home town was Deer Lake, Newfoundland, a small place that had about four or five-thousand people and where just about everybody knew everyone else. It wasn't like a big city that might have bad neighborhoods. I don't think you can have a bad neighborhood in a place with only four thousand people.

I have one brother and one sister and we were pretty much a normal family. Everybody worked, came home and watched Hockey Night in Canada whenever we could. My brother wasn't into hockey the way I was. He was more of a woodsman; always was out in the forest, doing stuff like that which I don't have a clue about. He is younger than me as is my sister, who I didn't hang out with very much.

People ask if I was a troublemaker as a kid. Actually, I never got into much trouble when I was growing up. I kept quiet and did my own things and I didn't let too much bother me. I was — and am — an easy guy to get along with. Not many things bother me.

It was easy for me to get into hockey. Up where I come from everybody plays when it gets really cold. There's the river that freezes over and also ponds where the kids play outdoors. We didn't need any arena to get our hockey games going. I started on a little pond near my house and went from there.

When I was five years old I started playing minor hockey and it was then that I knew that I loved the sport. Besides, that's all there was back home and almost all my buddies played. It was a lot of fun then and it still is now The difference is that there was no fighting back then. In Deer Lake there was just enough players to get a team which meant that we were scraping for players all the time. This was good because everyone got to play and there was little pressure.

I was always a centerman although I can't say that I was all that tough. Besides, how tough can you be when you are twelve or thirteen-years-old? I was just a hard-nosed player who didn't mind going into the corners. I wasn't all that fast but, then again, I didn't need much speed being a center. It's not the way it is now.

Slowly but surely, I progressed up the hockey ladder but I don't remember any meaningful fights until I was seventeen or eighteen-years-old. At the time I was playing in a senior league and there was one big guy who was supposed to be a real tough player. We got into a fight and I found myself doing pretty well against him. To this day, that fight stands out because of who he was in the league and that I held my own. It was pretty exciting for me.

It wasn't that I only played hockey. I loved soccer and played it throughout my childhood and beyond. When the weather was warm, I'd play fast-pitch softball but I knew all along that hockey was for me and as I got better, I looked ahead to see how I could make a career of the sport. The turning point came when I went to Summerside on Prince Edward Island to play at the Junior level.

I was nervous about the move because it was the first time I would be leaving home and I didn't know whether I would be good enough to make the team in PEI. In a sense I was starting at the bottom again. I said to myself, "Darren, if you don't make it, you'll go back home and do something other than hockey. But I made the club in Summerside and even had time to go to the university on the side when I wasn't playing. It was among the best two years of my life and I wouldn't have traded it in for anything.

How did I get to be a fighter? It pretty much got started in Juniors. As it happened, I was one of the top scorers on our team so it wasn't to our advantage for me to be fighting all the time. Besides, the league had a rule that if you fought more than once a game, you would get thrown out. What I did was wait until the end of the game and then get into a fight. To tell you the truth, it was fun to me. I mean, I didn't have to fight but I liked doing it so I'd fight at the end of every game.

You have to understand that nobody egged me on to fight. And there were no special incidents that made me mad. Not too much gets me upset and I don't really like to hurt anyone or beat up anybody. But sometimes guys on the other team would want to fight me and see what they could do against me. Likewise, I was curious to see how well I would do against them. That's the way it was done back then in Juniors and, to be honest with you, I loved doing it.

Not that I was a skilled scrapper right of the bat; far from it. But I guess that if I had gotten the crap beaten out of me every time back then, I wouldn't have wanted to continue playing that way. Fortunately, I did well in my first big fight and I held my own after that. In life you don't usually do something you love, if you're getting beat up all the time. Still, I soon learned that I was going to take my smacks with the best of them and I also found out soon enough that there were a lot of tough people out there. I decided that, win or lose, I would have the same attitude going into every fight and after the fight as well. Fighting is part of the game and I knew that, whatever happened, I would go on after that.

After Summerside, I moved down to the States and played in Dayton of the East Coast League. Colin Campbell was coaching the Rangers' farm team in Binghamton at the time and needed a checking forward. He called me up for a look-see and liked what he saw. I knew that he wasn't calling me up to score goals; he had enough people around to do that. Being in Binghamton was a pretty big deal since I now was only one step away from the National Hockey League. Actually, getting called up to Binghamton was quite a surprise for me at the time and what happened next was just as big a surprise. Here I am in the next-to-the-top league and in my very first game in the American Hockey League what do I do but score a goal. What's more the game was on local television and later on I learned that the goal I scored was featured on the AHL's Game of the Week telecasts.

I got more major penalties than goals during my first year in the AHL and some of the scraps were good ones. At the time Binghamton was the Rangers farm team and Albany was the farm team of the New Jersey Devils. Albany-Binghamton, Rangers-Devils — those were neat rivalries and you could tell by what went on during the games. During the 1993-94 season the (Albany) River Rats acquired a tough forward named Reid Simpson who would play opposite me in all the games.

The way we got along — or didn't get along, as the case may be — says a lot about the relationship of role players like me and Simmer. I know him off-ice and he's a great guy. But once the game started we knew that we each had a job to do and we just liked fighting each other. Every time we played against each other, we tried to do something. We both understood that this was all part of the game and that once the fight was over we respected each other.

Binghamton was a good place to play and I was quite happy there. I didn't think about the NHL at that point. Sure, when I was a kid, I was like anyone else my age in Canada, saying, "Man, I'm gonna go to the NHL." But that was kid talk and, realistically, I didn't think I was going to get that high. But in 1994-95 — Boom! — I got the call and there I was in The Show.

I played eighteen games in my rookie year and wound up with 62 penalty minutes. I was averaging more than three penalty minutes per game and I felt I was doing the job that they had intended me to do and that was to be a sparkplug. Sometimes when a team is doing badly a fight will give that team a spark. Then again, sometimes it doesn't. But I felt that it was something that I had to do.

Most every one of the role players like myself know when it's time to do it and when it's not time to fight. There's always the right place and the right time for it. You just have to abide by those rules and not be stupid out there. It's not as if there are a lot of guys who got under my skin. That's not the case because most of the guys in the NHL are really great guys. I just had to go out there and do my job just like they do their's.

What I learned pretty quick was that the referees watched us a little more closely than they do a superstar like Eric Lindros. Everybody knows that the fans come to see the stars so, I guess, the refs figure they have to be a little lenient with them compared to a player like myself. I know that I wouldn't want to pay good money for a ticket when Philadelphia plays and find out that he was suspended.

The other thing I learned was that I didn't have to fight all the time to be intimidating — and do my job effectively. I watched other role players such as Randy McKay of the Devils and Bob Probert of the Blackhawks and noticed that they did a lot more playing than just intimidating. I watched them and said to myself, "That's the type of player I'd like to develop into."

Meanwhile, I went about the business of keeping my job with the Rangers. In 1996-97 I stayed the entire year with the big team and played in sixty regular season games as well as ten playoff games. I had 197 penalty minutes altogether and did my share of fighting. My style? I usually let the other guy start off a bit at the beginning. He gets his few punches in and then tires fast while I keep my wind pretty good so that at the end of the fight, I've got a little more left to give. It seemed that I usually had more left at the end than my opponent and that's when I came back with my own punches.

The difference for me would be when I would fight a left-hander. Being a rightie myself, I have a little more trouble with them and, usually, righties take a couple at the start of the fight with the lefty. The lefty gets a little more confidence. When I fight a right-hander, the two of us are swinging with our rights and don't have to give in as often. Given a choice, I'd rather be fighting a righty but I found out that I couldn't take anyone lightly. I would go into a game not thinking about who I had to fight but rather how I would play my game. Smart. Get the puck in deep and don't make any stupid mistakes. That was my game plan. Whatever else happened, happened.

That's hockey. You can never figure how things are going to turn out on the ice. Take my first NHL goal as an example. Jeff Beukeboom, our defenseman, shot it and the puck supposedly hit me and went in behind Patrick Roy, who was in goal for the Montreal Canadiens at the time. The next thing I knew, the referee said he was giving the goal to me but I told him, "It didn't even hit my pads." I didn't even touch the rubber but the goal has stood up right to this day. You can look it up in the record book.

My first NHL fights were with Randy McKay. Twice. They happened in exhibition games and, to tell you the truth, I thought I did well in both of them. Unfortunately, some of my teammates recently read a magazine and said that the magazine commented that McKay beat me twice. (Laughs). That proves that you should never believe what you read in magazines.

Since the McKay fight, I went at it with many of the NHL's big guys, even Bob Probert who I had idolized when I was a kid. Just to fight him was a good experience for me. It was nice to get the chance to do it. Same with a veteran like Craig Berube of the Capitals. I only fought him once but he was tough and big.

If you ask me whether there was any one particular fight that stands out, I would have to say none in particular. Every one of my opponents was tough in his own way otherwise they wouldn't even be in the NHL. But if you ask me who has that one big punch, I would have to say Tony Twist of the St. Louis Blues.

The odd things about tough guys is that the average fan misunderstands them. Fans have the idea that enforcers are bullies and that's not really the case. They are all really tough, true, but they also are all really nice guys. And very well-liked on their teams. Bob Probert is a good example. Same with Stu Grimson. If he wasn't in the lineup you could be sure that the other team would be taking advantage of his teammates.

Most tough guys are honest and that's the way I like to be. I don't like cheap shots or anything like that. I don't see too many tough guys cheap-shotting anybody. But if someone on the other team does something unpleasant to one of our players, I have to do my job no matter how tough the opponent. In my position, I can't afford to say to myself, "Hey, that guy is really tough and I'd better avoid him." No way. I have to do the best I can, win or lose. I have to stick up for my teammates and show them I'm doing my best for them. Naturally, I would rather win every fight but sometimes I don't. That's life.

On the other side there are always opponents who are difficult to figure. Matthew Barnaby of the Buffalo Sabres is a good example. I don't know what he does and I don't like his style; the way he goes about things on the ice. It seems that every time you touch him, he dives and the ref calls it for some reason. He does that thing where he throws his head back when he gets hit. I don't know if players like that. As a matter of fact, I don't know whether his authorities like that. I watch the highlights of Buffalo games and say to myself, "What is this guy doing?" Then again, to each his own.

I know there are people who say that fighting should be eliminated from hockey but usually those are people who don't really know too much about the game. Some believe that more fans will turn out if the NHL presents a cleaner game with more goals — as if when a fight goes on the fans go quiet. The idea of eliminating fisticuffs is like taking away bodychecking because bodychecks might hurt somebody. Everyone knows that some of the loudest moments in an NHL arena come when big bodychecks are thrown.

The bottom line on fighting is this; if it was eliminated, stickwork would go up and players would be doing things that they normally would not be doing. Personally, I don't think fighting will be eliminated from the NHL. It's part of hockey and has been since the earliest days of the NHL. Canadians love it. Everyone I know loves it. Fighting is something that will never go away.

Francois Leroux

It's my job to respond to the abuse that our players take.

There have been few larger stickhandlers to crisscross National Hockey League rinks than Francois Leroux, an articulate French-Canadian defense-man-forward from Ste. Adele, Quebec. At 6-6, 246 pounds, Leroux takes after his father who died in 1995 of cancer. The elder Leroux stood 6-5, 225 pounds.

"My dad," said Francois, "was an authority figure."

So is the son — on the ice.

He established his authority as a Pittsburgh Penguin following a few NHL cups of coffee with Edmonton and Ottawa between 1988 and 1994. Three seasons in the Steel City firmed his reputation for toughness and one episode underlined the point although the incident had terrible repercussions for superstar Pat LaFontaine.

On October 17, 1996 Leroux was skating for Pittsburgh against Buffalo. The Sabres captain Pat LaFontaine crossed the Penguins blue line when he was confronted with the huge defenseman. Leroux's elbow made contact with LaFontaine's head, knocking the wispy center face-first to the ice. Although LaFontaine played in seven more games for Buffalo, he never was able to fully recover from the concussion administered by Leroux's elbow and retired in the summer of 1998.

Does that make Leroux a bad boy?

As the bromide goes, he was merely doing his job. Leroux never meant to disable his foe but he did try to stop him. That's the way he played in Pittsburgh and later — he was dealt to Colorado on September 28, 1997 for a third round draft choice — with the Avalanche.

"I understand the role I have to play," Leroux explained.

With the multi-talented Avalanche, Leroux's ice time often was limited and coach Marc Crawford even moved him up to the front line to provide some added attacking muscle. Francois wasted no time taking on Sandy McCarthy of the Flames on October 3, 1997. The two exchanged punches in an all-out, toe-to-toe encounter worthy of a highlight-reel fight.

"Francois is a good fighter," said McCarthy. "Not a great fighter. But he's big and he's game. I've fought him, oh, four times now. In one fight, he hit me a honey of a shot and my knees almost buckled."

During a 1997-98 encounter with Edmonton, Leroux caught the Oilers

Kelly Buchberger with a right that deposited Buchberger to the ice. That brought a smile to Leroux's then coach Crawford's face.

"I was happy with Frankie," said Crawford. "He did a good job in the realms that he was used. And he was very popular on the team."

Amiable and eloquent, Leroux is a pleasant sort; an easy interview. Fischler Hockey Service correspondent Mike Wray made that discovery in Denver when he did a one-on-one with the big guy during the 1997-98 season. The following oral history is a result of their encounter.

Ste. Adele, where I grew up, is forty-five minutes north of Montreal. The area has four villages together and altogether, the place is very friendly. It's like a farmers' town, where you can just about walk in any house whenever you want and find friends.

I had one brother — no sisters — and he went on to become an earthquake chemist. When I was about seven my parents got divorced, but both my father and mother were around. My dad had been a police officer and after that he did construction work. He did it all. My mom was a cook for the University of Montreal. When my dad couldn't be with us, my mother was there.

My father was a huge hockey fan. He had played a lot of hockey in his youth and even had a tryout with a Montreal Junior team. He probably could have gone on to become a good one but he had to give up hockey on account of the fact that his family, at the time, didn't have the financial means to enable him to keep at hockey.

As for me, I started skating when I was about three-years-old. I would follow in my older brother's footsteps. If he would play baseball, I would tag along. And when he put on the skates, I put on the skates. What made it difficult was my age. I was younger so it meant that whenever I played along with my brother's friends, they were bigger guys than me. They were a good three or four years older and, of course, they were better.

At first, I had trouble with my skating, but by the time I was five, I had that part of the game figured out. Plus, I had begun filling out. I was already a little bigger than everybody else who was playing and I really loved it. I can honestly say that at age five, I was on fire!

The strange thing was that I quit hockey once because my brother had quit hockey to take up skiing. At one point we were both skiing a lot. I liked my brother so I followed him and when he returned to hockey, I returned to hockey. That wasn't easy because I loved skiing.

I can't say the same for school. I was not a big fan of school. When I was a kid it seemed as if I wanted to do everything else but go to school. Still, I had to go and everybody — my mom, my dad — they pushed me. I wound up being no more than an average student but I'm sure that I would have been better had I paid attention. Sorry, but I was too busy playing every kind of sport; that's why I couldn't keep my focus in school.

My hockey had improved enough during my teen-age years that I eventually made it to the Junior team in St. Jean, Quebec, not far south of Montreal. When I was seventeen, I played for them and in 1987, I was drafted by the Edmonton Oilers, First Round, 19th overall.

In my first two years of Junior I played forward but then I got lazy and switched to defense because I couldn't keep up. I was growing so fast and my coordination wasn't that great for my size. I was too big for my motor skills. It took a while for me to grow into my body. But I stayed back on defense during Juniors and in my early NHL years.

In St. Jean I wasn't an enforcer but I was a physical presence. If there was trouble, I responded to it but I don't especially care for violence. I never had a coach come over to me and tell me to go out and fight. But if I had to go out and take care of business, I always knew when to go. Same thing in the NHL.

Nothing much happened for me in Edmonton and then Ottawa claimed me in the 1994 Waiver Draft. Unfortunately, when I got to training camp in the Fall of 1994 the NHL called a lockout. That's when I came this close to quitting. The Senators had sent me back to Prince Edward Island for 25 games and I wasn't really interested in that. By now I had had four years in the minors and I figured I would play out the last year of my contract and then go back to school or do something other than hockey.

Then, I got a break. Pittsburgh claimed me in January 1995 just before the lockout-shortened season began. All of a sudden I'm on the Penguins and everything began to turn around in my career. Even though I only played forty games in 1994-95 — actually all the games were in 1995 because of the lockout — I had a killer season with the Pens. The team was so good at defense that I learned a lot. They needed me for toughness and I responded big-time. I played aggressive and did it all.

It was in that lockout-shortened season that I realized I could do it at the NHL level. I played in forty games, got two assists and 114 penalty minutes. Plus, I played in a dozen playoff games. Remember, Mario Lemieux was still with Pittsburgh when I was there so imagine what it was like for me just being there alongside him. To put it mildly, it was awesome to be out on the ice with Mario. He could do it all and I would watch some of his moves and just shake my head in amazement. He would win games all by himself.

The important thing was that I played well enough to come back to Pittsburgh in 1995-96 and play a regular season — sixty-six games for me — score a couple of goals, nine assists and finish with 161 penalty minutes. I followed that with eighteen playoff games, my first NHL playoff goal and an assist. On top of that, I had gotten to love Pittsburgh. It's a great city and I made a bunch of friends there.

For that reason alone, I didn't want to be traded. I was in Pittsburgh, getting ready to watch the Steelers on television. All of a sudden, the phone rings. It's Craig Patrick (Penguins general manager). He says, "Frankie, we just traded you to the Colorado Avalanche." I couldn't believe it. I said, "Really? Come on. REALLY?" Sure, I had heard a lot of rumors but nothing had ever materialized before so now I'm on a plane to Denver, starting in with a whole new team.

The difference with the Avalanche was that coach Marc Crawford had so many defensemen that he decided to try me out up front as a forward. Actually, he had no choice. He had so many skilled guys on D and I knew what was going on and, besides, he actually put me on a line with Peter Forsberg and Joe Sakic. It doesn't get much better than that! If anyone on the opposition tried anything with them, my job was to jump in and face them. Make things right.

As soon as I got to Denver, the first thing that impressed me was the talent at every position. It was unbelievable and my job was to learn how to make the best of my assignment with them.

It wasn't necessary for me to fight all the time. Or even drop my gloves. I would just go up to an opponent and give him a wake-up call; a "leave him alone" kind of thing.

One night we were playing Toronto and the Leafs had Tie Domi on the ice. He wasn't the pest that night; I was. I had had a really good shift; which meant that I had rocked a few guys and I was feeling great. When that happens, I feel that I have the luxury of shaking anybody off so when Domi wanted to go, I just shoved him away. At a time like that, I can shake anybody off. There was no point in getting into a fight, especially since Domi had not been a factor in the game. He hadn't been doing anything and nobody on our team was getting any abuse from him so there was no point in me getting a penalty for no reason at all. I had been getting the job done with my presence which was quite enough in that particular situation.

What I discovered in Denver is that some of the skill players are tough, tough guys. Peter Forsberg is a good example. But having me alongside him was just a bonus. He knew that if anyone bothered him, Frankie would go in and take care of business, kick ass or whatever.

How tough is this business? It's not as hard as everybody thinks. It just takes guts; you have to have a lot of balls.

Not that I had to do it alone. The Avalanche acquired Jeff Odgers, who is a scrapper. For me, it was good to have a player like that at my side because there are some nights when I just don't feel like throwing them. It's like any job; some nights you feel like working and other nights you don't. Sometimes it was me throwing them and other times it was Jeff.

Since I came to the NHL quite a few new arenas have been built and that element has changed some of the way we play. For example, my favorite rink always was Boston Garden because the ice surface was so small. There was nowhere to hide and that meant you had to show up. Plus the intensity was unbelievable and the fans, too. It had the mezzanine and the side balcony overhanging the ice so you had the feeling that the fans were right on top of you which, in a sense, they were.

One of my passions has been history so when a historic building like Boston Garden, The Aud in Buffalo or Montreal's Forum is taken down, I feel a bit sad. The new buildings lack personality — and the history of the old buildings.

A big difference for me, coming from Pittsburgh to Denver, was recognition. In Pitt, I was known wherever I went. People would come up to me on the street and give me a, "Hey, Frankie, howya' doin'" kind of greeting. I couldn't go anywhere without being known. In Denver it was different and, in a way, that was great because every so often I wanted my privacy; I want to be able to sit down to dinner with a friend and not be disturbed. In Denver, I could go anywhere and nobody knew who I was.

The main thing for a player in my position was first of all to be in the NHL and stay in the NHL. Once I got to Denver, I figured I could last at least three to four years and, if so, that would be great. What I knew was that tough guys still were in demand and once teams got them, they tended to hold on to them as long as the player can get the job done.

In today's NHL there isn't a tough guy in the league who can't play the game. To stay in The Show nowadays, you cannot do it by just playing rough; you have to be able to play the game as well. Even a Bob Probert, who fights so well, can play the game. You'd be surprised how he can turn it on and how skillful he could be.

By the same token, I rate Probert among the top three enforcers in the NHL. Along with Tony Twist and Chris Simon. It's difficult to pinpoint a number one because on any given night anyone of the tough players can win a fight.

Each of these players is committed to his team and his role. In the Avalanche locker room there was a sign that read, "It's all about commitment." What it meant was doing the real thing; doing the things that you don't necessarily want to do every day but the things that, in the long run, are going to pay off.

As for fighting, I can honestly say that I never got my ass kicked. Oh, once in a while, you lose your balance and you take some punches but that goes with the territory. I don't think I've ever had my ass kicked.

When I'm fighting, I'm not really thinking about anything special. With me, it's instinct. All I have to do is make sure of who I'm fighting; whether he's a lefty or a righty.

I worry about that but, otherwise, I grab and throw. I have no fighting secrets. As a matter of fact, there are few fighting "secrets" around the league. Most of the fighters are aware of the other enforcers' skills, strengths and weaknesses. But the bottom line for me when I get going is just to drop and roll.

Bryan Marchment

In pond hockey it was basically a case of survival because most of the guys were always bigger than me.

Based on events that were well-chronicled during the 1997-98 season, one would be hard-pressed to find a more vilified National Hockey League performer than Bryan Marchment.

To say that he was hated in some quarters — Dallas being one of them — would be the understatement of the half-century.

Loathed. Despised. Crucified.

Those were some of the terms used to describe the destructive defenseman. The reasons are obvious.

Joe Nieuwendyk, Mike Modano and Greg Adams, to name three.

Each, a member of the 1997-98 Dallas Stars, was torpedoed by a Marchment hit that was deemed treacherous in its quality and malicious in intent.

The most discussed of the three was delivered against Nieuwendyk in Game One of the Dallas-San Jose playoff in the spring of 1998. Marchment's slamming of the Stars' ace into the boards effectively ended Nieuwendyk's season and seriously eroded the Stars chances of winning the Stanley Cup.

"I thought it was a dirty play by a dirty player," charged Nieuwendyk in the aftermath of the attack. "Marchment sees an opportunity to hurt and takes advantage of it. In my case his defense was that he was just finishing his check. But he basically grabbed my left leg and carried me into the boards.

"We were going pretty fast. He knew I was in a compromising position with my right knee. I just feel it's a total lack of respect for your competition."

That's one way of looking at it. Marchment's coaches, on the other hand, take a more salubrious view.

"We became a better team because of Marchment," said Sharks coach Darryl Sutter. "We wouldn't have been in the playoffs against Dallas without him. Bryan's check on Nieuwendyk was a good, clean hit."

Perhaps, but some other Marchment checks were considered somewhat to the left of clean by the NHL authorities. He once served an eight-game suspension for a hit against Kevin Dineen. After the hit on Modano — it sidelined Mike for ten games — Marchment again was suspended, this time for three games.

"Bryan has a presence," explained Al Iafrate who teamed with Marchment in San Jose. "He changes the way half the guys on the other team think when they see his name on the board. His name is associated with pain and injury."

Marchment's whack against Adams put the forward on the shelf for 20 games. There have been countless other victims and innumerable verbal assaults against the defenseman by both the media and fans.

Bryan is acutely aware of them but shrugs off the critics with a rather simple explanation.

"If the opposition fans are worrying about me and the other players are worried about me," Marchment asserted, "then it means I am doing my job."

Darryl Sutter claimed that the Sharks never had "a physical player with his skill level that can do the things he can do." Marchment brings variety to his position, along with the intimidating part.

Sutter: "He is disciplined. He doesn't take bad penalties and very seldom does he get called for a retaliation penalty."

Stars coach Ken Hitchcock not only disagrees but does so with as much vehemence as a Marchment check.

"The first thing to remember about Marchment," said Hitchcock, "is that every opposing team wants him on the ice because he's a liability. When he's out there, he'll do something stupid to give the other team an advantage."

Hitchcock's dislike for Marchment didn't begin when Bryan met his Stars in the 1998 playoffs. The antipathy grew back when Marchment skated for the Edmonton Oilers and successively put Modano and Adams out of commission. At that time, Hitchcock told Randy Galloway of the *Dallas Morning News*, "Marchment is a sick guy who has no respect for the other players in the league. Beating him up doesn't help. He's been beaten up many times. He's been crushed many times. But the only way he knows how to survive in this game is to do this stuff."

Marchment considered the Hitchcock appraisal as indiscreet as some of his bodychecks. "I know a lot of guys on the Dallas team," said Marchment, "and the guys I know don't respect Hitchcock very much."

Brian allowed that he could handle the name-calling and the bad reputation but he charged that the NHL had a double-standard in terms of its discipline. "I watched Teemu Selanne crosscheck Theo Fleury from behind into the end boards one night and nothing was called. Another time, when I was with Edmonton, Frankie Leroux, who's about six-eight, is against Doug Weight and I come in to straighten things out and get third-man in.

"I'm not a rocket scientist but I don't think Doug Weight is going to drop the gloves with Frankie Leroux."

Teammates such as Bernie Nicholls point out that the Sharks desperately needed a threat such as Marchment to keep the enemy honest. "Skilled forwards hate to play against Bryan," said Nicholls. "He's always in your face, punching your head, whacking your hands. He's a big, nasty defenseman. There are maybe only ten players out there like him."

In an interview with Fischler Hockey Service Edmonton correspondent Dan Carle, Marchment spelled out his thoughts on the game, his style and interests. The transcript was turned into the following oral history.

✦ ✦ ✦

I grew up just outside of Toronto and started playing on a frozen river near our house. At first it was just pond hockey with my older brother and friends. We played pretty much every day and I got into hockey at an early age. Being so close to Toronto, I became a Maple Leafs fan and watched them on TV every Wednesday and Saturday night. I especially liked it when physical teams like Boston and Philadelphia came in to play the Leafs.

In pond hockey for me it was basically a case of just surviving because most of the guys I played against were always bigger than me. Street hockey and pond hockey down below our house is what I look back on as the really fun part of the game and it was a way for me to grow into the game; to get my licks in until I couldn't take it anymore.

As I played more, I found that I concentrated more on the players who were both skilled and physical. I learned that I enjoyed the physical part of hockey and the more I hit guys on the other team, the more room I got. This happened first on the minor hockey level and later in Junior hockey.

Mostly, I played defense although there were brief moments in minor hockey where I played forward. I enjoyed it but I definitely liked playing the blue line a lot more than wing or center. My belief was that defensemen who are physical and also are able to play the game were few and far between. That's probably one of the biggest reasons I made it to the NHL. There are not many guys who can make the big, open-ice hit or scare opponents into dumping the puck in maybe a little more than they would. Early on, I enjoyed that part of the game.

When I reached the Junior level, I really began to enjoy hockey. I would say that my four years of Juniors were probably the best four years of my life. In my first year — when I was sixteen — we had brawl after brawl. My coach loved and respected players who played physical and we had quite a few including Troy Crowder who made it to the NHL. And when I was in minor hockey, I played against Brendan Shanahan and Adam Graves.

The rough part of hockey was great for me in Juniors. I knew that if I went out and got the snot kicked out of me, I still would have someone to back me up or go right back out there and try it myself. That first year of Juniors was a terrific learning experience. What it taught me was what was necessary to get somewhere as a physical player. I had some 300-odd minutes of penalties as a rookie in Juniors. I wanted to make a name for myself and one way to do that was to try out a lot of the tougher guys around the league.

Fighting rules changed once I got to Juniors. In minor hockey, I would get into one fight and get thrown out of the game. Those were the rules. In Junior hockey, you never got kicked out for fighting. The other adjustment for me was in the speed and size of the opposition. Junior hockey was faster and the other players were bigger. I had to learn how to be physical in that type of competition. In fact, I found that I always have been learning. It started in minor hockey, then Juniors and right up to the pros. Even now I'm still learning. Because the game is changing so much, I find that I am always learning.

Like when I came to the NHL for the first time, in 1988-89, with Winnipeg, I was learning all over again. Let me tell you, that was some experience. Unbelievable to reach the top for the first time. It's hard for me to explain what my true feelings are but I knew that I had to go out there and play as physical as I could and that was all I tried to do in that first game.

What do I remember? Shane Churla jammed his fist into my stomach and I think I broke his wrist. Randy Carlyle, who had been a veteran NHL defenseman by that time, kept telling me that if I was going to play that way, that I had to be ready for certain situations. He knew what I needed to expect from playing the way I did and he taught me pretty well.

When you are a player who runs guys and has a lot of scraps, the biggest thing is not to fear anybody and to keep playing as physical as I could because that was what was going to keep me in the NHL. I knew that sooner or later I was going to get to play on a regular basis and that everything would adjust around my physical play. But, basically, I wanted to become a good NHL defenseman and still play physical at the same time.

Not that I learned everything at once. One of the challenges was penalties and not taking stupid penalties. It took me a long time to learn not to retaliate right away; not to go after somebody after being hit. The trick is to give it out and take it. And if you take it, try to give it back whenever you can but as clean as you can. The games are a lot about power plays and penalty-killing so a player like myself does not want to put his team down because of a stupid penalty. That's for sure.

After four years in the Winnipeg organization, I became one of those Type I free agents. Mike Keenan was with the Blackhawks at the time and told me, "If I could trade for you, would you sign this contract with Chicago?"

At the time, I would have died for the opportunity to play for the Blackhawks. I had burned out my welcome in Winnipeg and really wanted to play for Keenan. They made the trade and it was everything that I had hoped it would be.

My 1992-93 season there was unbelievable. I couldn't have asked to be in a better situation. We had quite a few guys in their late twenties and early thirties and a couple of guys in their late thirties. There were only a few of us were real young at the time but what mattered for me was that I learned what it took to win and just play the game right, game in and game out.

What made it even more special for a player like me was the luxury of being in a home rink like the old Chicago Stadium. That arena was a throwback. More than 16,000 seats, two rows of balconies overhanging the rink; the fans being right on top of you and the big organ bellowing. If a player couldn't get up for a game at the old Stadium, he couldn't get up for a game anywhere.

It was a strange building in some ways. For instance, the dressing rooms were a floor below ice level which meant that the players had to climb a flight of stairs just to get up to the rink. Man, it was something to be climbing those steps and then hearing the packed house roar as we took the ice. Talk about fans being into a game, the ones at the old Stadium were priceless. It was the same in Boston at the old Garden and The Forum in Montreal and Spectrum in Philly. I consider myself very fortunate to have played in those classic, old buildings.

For a time I had thought that I was secure in Chicago but you can never tell in hockey. Strange things happen. Well, what happened was that Steve Larmer, who had been a mainstay with the Hawks, had to be moved and there were certain ways that it was going to be done. It turned out that Paul Holmgren in Hartford had his eyes on me and the deal finally was made in November 1993. I went to the Whalers with Larmer for Eric Weinrich and Patrick Poulin.

In a way this was tough. In my first year in Chicago we had gone to the Stanley Cup Finals before losing to the Penguins. Then, we made the playoffs my second year there but I still looked at Hartford as a good opportunity for me. I enjoyed Connecticut but, as it happened, I only lasted 42 games with them and we didn't make the playoffs.

Meanwhile, things began to fall apart with that hockey club and I became involved in a deal where Hartford signed free agent Steve Rice and I was compensation for Edmonton. That was in August 1994 and I became an Oiler for the 1994-95 season, which was the season of the long lockout.

Frankly, I wasn't crazy about leaving Hartford for Edmonton. I had come to like my teammates on the Whalers and I was tired of moving so much. Edmonton was my fourth team and I still was a pretty young guy. Actually, it was harder on my family than me. I had a wife and kid at the time in Hartford so it was tougher on them.

Of course, the lockout changed things. It dragged on through October 1994, then November, then through Christmas and into January 1995 before it was settled. To tell you the truth, I didn't even think we were going to play hockey that year. What did I do to keep busy? I relaxed — did some fishing, hunting and everything I could to enjoy myself but think about hockey. By the time the lockout had ended, I had become huge. I was in awful shape and just didn't enjoy what remained of that lockout year as far as hockey went.

What was good for me, then, was that I was making exceptional money for an Oiler at that time. In fact, I thought I would be moved because of the financial situation but when I realized that they would keep me, I made a strong commitment to play for Edmonton and be what they had expected of me in the first place. The Oilers were a young, up-and-coming hockey club and I was there to be one of the leaders. My goal was to go out and play a physical game every night, be a good defenseman, be a leader and show that I had matured at my position. The point was that if things didn't work out in Edmonton in the long run, at least there would be opportunity elsewhere.

Sure enough, I got traded first to Tampa Bay in 1997-98. Then came the eight-game suspension after the incident with Kevin Dineen. I was lonely during the suspension. The team was out of town. No one was around. That's the thing I missed most — being around the guys. I went crazy. It just so happened that when I returned it was against the Oilers. But it was just another game. I wasn't going to change anything. I had decided that I was going to keep playing the same style.

There are a lot of tough, physical players around. The interesting thing is that we can be mean to each other all night long but after a game, if we run into each other, we say "hello" and carry on a conversation. A lot of those tough players are the guys I respect the most and a lot of them are good friends of mine. They know the way I have to play and they know that if I don't play that way I am not going to play. If they don't respect me for the way I go out and play the game or if they are sore at me for doing something to them, then they are not really close friends of mine.

No matter how you shake it, hockey is a team game. I am playing for my team and whatever happens on the ice, happens on the ice. Whatever happens off the ice, happens off the ice.

I have been asked where my aggression comes from because reporters who interview me are often surprised that I am what they call "a nice guy." The aggression comes from an intense desire to win. In every game I play, I want to win. I want to be the best player Bryan Marchment can be. And I do believe that I have improved by leaps and bounds since I started with Winnipeg. My skating, my discipline, my puck movement — even my physical play — have all gotten better. I may be quiet off the ice but once my skates touch the rink my striving to win makes me aggressive.

It's pretty clear by now that if Bryan Marchment is not playing his A Game then he is no good. My job is to pick things up and I know when I'm not playing well. What makes my game is my physical play and when I'm not playing that way, I can tell. And when I play my physical game, I don't worry about retaliation. I can't worry about stuff like that.

I don't try to wreck anyone's career. But that doesn't mean I don't go out on the ice and try to be as rough as I can be. I would be lying if I said it wasn't. Of course, I know that the opposition will try to get back at me but that's part of the give-and-take of any game. I know that if I'm handing out punishment, I had better be able to take it as well. One thing I wanted everyone to be damn sure about is the fact that I'll give out physical play and I will take it but maybe the opponent is going to get it worse than me. That's the way I grew up playing not only hockey but all sports.

Not that I haven't taken abuse. I have. After the 1994-95 lockout, I took a lot of abuse and basically grew up and matured. I realized that players coming into the NHL were getting bigger, stronger and faster. If I was to keep up, I had to work out but it wasn't just a matter of getting muscles, it was the will to win in my heart. I have a big heart and a lot of drive so the other team knows that it isn't going to push me over. Heart has gotten me a long way in the NHL

Over the course of my career I have been criticized for my hitting style. My response is this: everybody is entitled to his own opinion but I don't worry much about them. My Mom still loves me and so do my wife and kids. That's the most important thing in my life. I'm out there trying to do a job that I'm getting paid for so as long as my teammates are happy and my family is happy, then Bryan Marchment is happy.

In terms of actual fighting, the dropping of gloves is not a very much intimidating factor anymore. There isn't anyone in the league I won't drop my gloves with to go to the aid of a teammate but there isn't much sense in me dropping my gloves if, after punishing a guy with a hit, they send out an enforcer who might get a penalty going after me. I'm a lot happier to let them go after me and get two or four or even five minutes in penalties.

Mind you, I enjoy a good scrap just as much as anybody but it is something I haven't had to do much and it has not been much in the style of play since I got to Edmonton. I'm not scared of anybody. My nose and my face cannot get much worse. I mean I get sheet plastic in my nose. I get my head rapped off the boards. Getting a punch in the noggin is the least of my worries. If it comes about, then I drop my gloves but, if it doesn't, then I'm not going to go looking for it. I can go toe-to-toe with a guy and — win or lose — I don't think the intimidation factor is there anymore because of the instigator penalty. If there were still brawls in the NHL the way there used to be, Bryan Marchment would probably have to fight in every game. But that style is leaving the game. Now the idea is to punish physically with a good bodycheck or a stiff crosscheck or a little shove to the head with your glove. That is the way to intimidate the enemy.

Having played on so many teams already, I find myself in strange situations sometimes in that I'll be going up against guys like Jeremy Roenick or Brendan Shanahan or Adam Graves and I know I have to go out and hit them even though they are friends off the ice. That's the tough part but I know that for me to do my job, that's what Bryan Marchment has to do — hit them.

I can say straight-out that if I was traded from one team and had to play my former teammates two days later, I would be just as physical against them as if they never had been on the same club with me. That is just the way I am. I'm out there to win; that is the most important thing.

Over my years in the NHL, I have taken good experiences from Winnipeg, Hartford, Edmonton and San Jose. There's good and bad everywhere but that's life! I talk to my father, my brother and my buddies who work back home and I find that it is no different whether you dig ditches or whether you are a lawyer or whatever. You face challenges every day. In hockey, the biggest challenges is just to be ready to come to play every night and be honest with yourself. Do that and you'll be around for a long time.

Me, I want to stay in the NHL until they kick me out. I'm one of those guys who to get rid of you have to take out back and shoot like a horse. In plain English, I want to play as long as I can play or until they tell me, "No, Bryan Marchment, you can't play here anymore."

When I was a kid, my goal was to play in the NHL. I have achieved that and plan to stay at it a while.

Darren McCarty

When I left home to play Junior B, a math teacher said, "He'll be back in a week or two. He won't make it." I fed off stuff like that and worked harder to stick it up his ass and prove him wrong.

In Motown, they thought they'd never see a second coming of Bob Probert. And to a certain extent, they were right.

Over the past decade, Probert has been the prototypical fighter-performer. He was reigning heavyweight champion longer than any other NHL player. And also has enjoyed seasons in which he scored as many as 29 goals, 33 assists and 62 points.

There will never be another Bob Probert as such. But as reasonable facsimiles go, Darren McCarty ranks remarkably high on the list.

And if you don't believe it, ask Claude Lemieux.

The demolition job performed on Lemieux by McCarty already has become legend at Joe Louis Arena even though it took place not long ago. But the evolution of McCarty transcends mere battles with Lemieux and other Filthy McNastys of hockey.

Like Probert, McCarty can play. Big time. If you don't believe it, ask Ron Hextall or Olie Kolzig or any number of other goalies who have fallen prey to his shot.

You get the point: this is a hockey player. And this is a fighter.

At 6-1, 210 pounds, McCarty is by no means a heavyweight champion in waiting nor are the Red Wings going to let his scoring talent be damaged by constant battles. But as a middleweight, Darren has accepted the challenges of foes both in and out of his weight class including Mike Peluso, Tie Domi and Matthew Barnaby.

At 25 years old, McCarty has had a few difficult off-ice battles as well. Recently, he had to come to grips with his father's having cancer, the loss of his grandfather and he has suffered through a bout with alcoholism. Further tightening the bond between McCarty and Probert is Darren's crediting Bob for helping him rebound from his drinking problem. But despite the setbacks, McCarty has become a fan favorite. He has won two Stanley Cups and even scored the sweep-clinching goal against Philadelphia in 1997.

Affable almost to a fault, McCarty is a media favorite and proved it for the umpteenth time sitting down with Fischler Hockey Service correspondent

Jim Ramsey for a third-degree session at The Joe. Their question-and-answer interview follows.

Jim Ramsey: Tell me about your family.
Darren McCarty: My dad, Craig, owns an air-conditioning company and my mom, Roberta, manages a travel agency. I have a sister, Melissa. Our family is really close. They are only about an hour away from Joe Louis Arena so they come to every game. My sister is in Grade 10 in Leamington, Ontario. My mom actually got me started in hockey. When she was a teenager she played for Leamington and Essex, Ontario. My dad used to play a little bit but nothing serious.

JR: What kind of kid were you?
DM: I was into all sports. I was seven when I started playing baseball, hockey, soccer and volleyball up through high school. I was Athlete of the Year in Grades Six and Seven. When I got to high school, I had to decide whether I wanted to concentrate on hockey with all the travel or continue playing all the sports. When I was 15, I played hockey every day. It didn't matter if it was organized practice or out on the pond. I was on the ice seven days a week and that's what helped me.

JR: What about your first pair of skates?
DM: I was three or four-years-old. My mother and I lived with my grandparents until I was five. There was a big pond out back. I remember seeing pictures of myself out there being pushed, trying to learn how to skate. My uncle always played hockey and I was always around. That's how I got my start. I remember I almost never got to play hockey because I didn't want to wear the garter belt. It didn't feel right and I wouldn't want to have it hurt my legs. But I was told if I didn't wear it, I didn't play. I could have started playing when I was five years old but I didn't get to because of this. When I was six, I figured I could suffer through wearing it so I started to play.

JR: Who were the biggest influences on your life?
DM: My grandfather. He passed away a couple of summers ago from cancer. He was like my father to me. He was a very quiet man and someone I learned a lot from. It was one of those special relationships you have in life. He never said anything unless he felt it needed be said. You could sit in a room with him for two hours and he might say two words but you knew those two words were special. I miss him, but I know he's around and watching out for me and keeping me out of trouble once in a while. My grandmother has always been the back-

bone of my family. She's a very strong lady. My aunts and uncles abused me a lot growing up but that toughened me up. They used to throw me around like a play toy when I was little. I always told them to watch out when I got bigger. I actually got them to say "uncle" to me a few years ago! Family to me is second to none. Family is so important and I owe them for making me who I am.

JR: Tell me about your father's cancer.
DM: We've set up the Craig McCarty Foundation for people with multiple melanoma. My dad is really busy with it. For me to see him doing those things is a great lift for me.

JR: How about your favorite team when you were growing up?
DM: Until I was about twelve, I liked whoever was winning. When Paul Coffey and Wayne Gretzky were playing in Edmonton, I liked them. Growing up in Leamington, I liked Toronto or Detroit. Detroit was going through some tough times. It's very ironic sitting here in the dressing room with guys I used to watch on Hockey Night in Canada. Another favorite was Rick Tocchet. I remember when he was playing in Philadelphia. I tried to pattern myself after him. He may not be the most talented guy but he works hard every night. He can score. He can fight. He can do it all and that's the type of player I wanted to be. Tocchet, Wendel Clark, Brendan Shanahan, Keith Tkachuk, players like that: unafraid, sticks up for his teammates, contribute offensively and defensively. I idolized Tocchet. When I play against him, I'm a little bit in awe, but I also want to show him that I belong here.

JR: You scored 55 goals your last year in Juniors at Belleville of the OHL. Was it difficult to serve a different role with the Wings?
DM: No. That's always the type of game I played. I had success in Junior because I played that way. In Junior you're playing against kids and the intimidation factor is a lot more. By the time I got to my third year playing. I got a lot more room to skate and play the game. I have confidence I can score 30 or 40 goals in this league as long as everyone has patience. I won't change the way I play. With more experience. I'll contribute more. Like Steve Yzerman says, "When you stop learning, it's time to get out of the game."

JR: When did you realize you had the skills to play in the NHL?
DM: It's funny but when I left home to play Junior B, a math teacher said, "He'll be back in a week or two. He won't make it." I fed on stuff like that and worked harder to stick it up his ass and prove him wrong. After my second year of playing Junior, I played against guys like Eric Lindros. I worked hard in the summer and had a good year.

JR: Tell me about your first game and first goal in the NHL.

DM: My first game was in Dallas and we lost so it wasn't as good as it could have been. It was really exciting being on the bench for the National Anthem, but once the puck dropped, hockey was hockey, and you just go out and play. When it's over you say, "Well, I got that under my belt." My first goal was scored against Bob Essensa in a game against Winnipeg. It was the second period and I went out to the blueline. Keith Primeau intercepted a pass and drove to the net. He threw it across, I snapped it low under Essensa's glove. When I jumped on to the glass, I thought I was going to break it. I buried the puck with my grandfather. He came down to Adirondack when I played there and saw an exhibition game at Joe Louis Arena. He never got to see a real game with Detroit.

JR: Tell me about your first fight.

DM: Against Cam Russell. It was a five-on-five skirmish and I came in to help Keith Primeau in the corner. Russell hit me from behind. I was trying to make the team and stick up for myself. So I turned around and we went at it. I hit him a couple of times and had him on the ice. He said I had taken advantage of him and had jumped him. But it was the other way around. So I said, "Oh well, why don't we do it again?" I went out, took my gear off, went to center ice and we squared off. It was like an old movie in slow motion. We went to hit each other but he had a bigger reach. He hit me first and cut me for about ten stitches. Then I hit him and we went down. We wrestled around and threw a few more punches with the roar of Chicago Stadium behind us and the adrenaline pumping. I have a lot of respect for Cam. He's an honest player, like most of the guys in the league. Tough guys respect other tough guys. Sure, you beat each others brains out on the ice, but after the game you shake hands and go out for a beer. That's the way it is with hockey players but a lot people don't understand that.

JR: What about your most memorable fight?

DM: It was the seventh game of the first round of the playoffs in my first year in the OHL. It was in Kingston, a huge rival of our's. They were in first place and we were the last team to qualify for the playoffs. We were winning 2-1 and lined up for a face-off. Their left wing said, "When they drop the puck, we're gonna go." I said, "All right." We started out in front of the net, took the helmets off and fought. By the time we were done we both had no gear on, I was holding him by the pants and hitting him. We ended up down on the ice in front of his bench. I had gotten the best of him. I gave him a concussion and he was out for the rest of the game. That put the pin in their balloon and we won the game 3-1. That was the biggest fight I've been in as far as changing the momentum and determining the outcome of the game.

JR: When did you realize that you were good with your fists?

DM: I was told when I played Junior B, that one of the things that would get me to the NHL was if I played tough. I didn't necessarily have to fight, just play tough. When you play like that, people get upset with you and you have to defend yourself. In Junior B that year, I had about 10 fights and it got me drafted into the OHL. In Adirondack, we had the toughest team in the league. This team was scary. I felt sorry for most teams who looked at our lineup. We could put six or seven guys on the ice. It was a joke. We had Kirk Tomlinson, who was, pound-for-pound, the toughest guy I've ever seen in my life. I have seen him break guys' jaws and knock them out cold and Tomlinson is only 5-10, 180 pounds. We had Jim Cummins, Bob Boughner, Dennis Vial, Gord Kruppke, myself. I felt like the low man on the pole. I knew I wanted to get up here and, in order for me to do that, I would have to play tough and hard. With these guys around I felt invincible. I went out with the attitude that I would fight anybody and if they beat me up they had six other guys they would have to fight.

JR: Do you take the game home with you?

DM: It depends on how the game goes. If we lose, I won't be as happy as if we had won. I once spoke to Doug Brown about this and he said, "As long as your kids or your dog is there at home when you get there, they don't care if you are a minus-3 or a plus-3, they are just happy to see you." I am a professional and I know what I have to do. I might think about the game by myself, but I don't take it out on anybody else.

JR: How does your wife feel about your fisticuffs?

DM: You might see her jumping through the glass yelling, "Kill him!" We have been together for about six years and she has been with me through Juniors. She's pretty used to it. Sometimes I think my wife wishes the other guy would give me a couple of good knocks. My mom is the one we had to change. She got mad at me the first time I got into a fight. I said, "Mom, what am I supposed to do? Let the other guy kill me?" Now she's the one jumping and yelling, "Kill him!"

JR: What influence did Bob Probert have when you came up to Detroit.

DM: He meant a lot to me. It's hard to explain this to people who don't know him. You'll never meet a more honest guy. He's one of those players who, if you needed 20 bucks and if that's all he had in his wallet, he'd give it to you. He'll always be a good buddy of mine. When I came here, he took me under his wing. I was in awe, he was always a hero of mine. I asked him, "Probie, what do you want me to do?" "Just go out and have fun and don't worry," he said, "I won't let anything happen to you." He told me that if I went out and fought somebody, it didn't matter if I won or lost. If you drop your gloves and show up, you'll always be a winner.

JR: What makes him so tough?

DM: He can take a punch and he hits hard. Watch him in a fight — the other guy will be tagging him and Probie will stop, adjust his helmet, think about what he wants to do and then proceed to whip the guy. He was showing me stuff he and Joey Kocur — the scariest fighter around — had learned. How to hold a guy's sweater, how to get out of certain things.

JR: Do players talk about other fighters in the league?

DM: You talk about them because there is so much respect for them. There is a code of honor. Most guys you fight are honest because tough guys fight tough guys. You don't go around jumping on smaller players. When Probie fought Marty McSorley, that was one of the greatest fights of all time. When they were about done, Probie's hand was caught up in Marty's sweater and Marty could have hit him, but he said they were done and they agreed. They gave each other a little slap on the head to tell each other, "Good job," and the linesman took them to the box.

JR: When you start a fight, you strike a pose like an old time boxer. Where did that come from?

DM: I don't know. You mess around until you find something that works for you. I'm not the biggest guy when it comes to fighting. Actually someone told me it's called the "Bow and Arrow," because it looks like your you're shooting a bow and arrow. If I have my arms in close to me, then the guy can get in close, but if my arms are extended, it's like a defensive wall. There's nothing too technical to the way I fight. My objective is just to survive.

JR: You've publically stated you were an alcoholic. You were in treatment to get help. Tell me about that.

DM: It's made a great change in my life. Everything is positive. What I realize now is that you have to make a list of things that are important in your life. For me it's family and hockey. Those are the top two things in my life. Alcohol kept me wondering about performing and how good can you be when you're boozing all night. It was probably a few years earlier when I realized it was time and I wanted to quit. I got total support from my family, the organization and all my friends.

JR: How did Probert help you through that time?

DM: Anybody who knows Bob Probert knows he's been through a lot. He has been clean for three years. Just because you're a hockey player doesn't mean you're different from anyone else. We all make mistakes. What really matters is that you deal with them. We talked and he saw a lot of me in him. He didn't want me to go down the same path he did. He never judged, never said,

"Do this" or, "Do that." He was just there to listen and give support. We've both been through a lot of shit so we can relate to each other.

JR: Lets talk about the fight you had with Claude Lemieux on March 26, 1997 (Right off the opening face-off and in retaliation to what Lemieux had done to Detroit's Kris Draper during the 1996 playoffs). How did it start? Some say he suckerpunched you.

DM: I'm not one to criticize people for starting fights, so I've got no problem with it. I'd say it was a return cold-cock. It's part of the game and if that happens my feeling is that I've got respect for him for what he did. He has to stand up for himself and his team. But I still don't have respect for him as a person or a human being. I wondered why he lined up on his off wing (Lemieux is a right wing by trade, but lined up on the left side, next to Darren). But honestly, when the puck was dropped, I watched where it went and I got hit with one or two and I said to myself, "Oh, O.K. If that's the way you want to start the game, that's fine with me." He didn't say anything. He bumped me and I said a few words to him. I don't know if you would call it taunting. I just told him what I thought of him and he took it from there. What we said is between me and him. I just told him he was a gutless player and I have no respect for him. Something along those lines. Still, you have to respect him as a hockey player. You know when he's out there, he can put the puck in the net. He's one of the best playoff performers and you have to be aware of him at that time. That's the respect you have for his skills, but not for the way he is as a human being. In my mind, he's still an idiot because he never has apologized to Draper. Things like that happen in the game but I have no respect for someone who doesn't take responsibility for his actions when they severely hurt someone.

JR: Do you ever get tired of fighting?

DM: It's part of my job and I have to be prepared for it. Nobody wants to go out and fight all the time. I want to play the game, but if it's got to be done, then it's got to be done.

Jim McKenzie

If the NHL ever took fighting out of hockey, the game
would become lacrosse on ice.

Those who meet Jim McKenzie off the ice mistake him for a scoutmaster.

He is amiable, intelligent, courteous, kind and just about everything you would not expect from a National Hockey League enforcer.

Playing for the Phoenix Coyotes in 1997-98, he extended his value as a performer. The career forward moved back to defense and played commendably enough to win coach Jim Schoenfeld's kudos.

"What Jim did was make himself even a more valuable component as a hockey player," said Schoenfeld.

A big-leaguer since 1990, McKenzie has been a travelling enforcer, taking his fists to such outposts as Winnipeg, Hartford, Florida, Dallas and Pittsburgh as well as Phoenix.

To those who suggest that McKenzie simply is too nice a guy to be a hockey cop, bear in mind that he didn't mean it to be that way but things happen.

"When I came up with Hartford," he said, "I was a defenseman. But the Whalers already had six or seven solid defensemen and they wanted to make room for an enforcer. So, they moved me up front and I did the job when they played me. I was still able to take care of the physical part of it up there — the fighting and all that."

He never did go back to playing regular defense but he did maintain his policeman's badge.

"If we want someone in the box serving a five-minute major penalty," said McKenzie, "on most nights it's going to be me."

Yet, McKenzie has always viewed his business — not to mention life in general — with a grain of salt. His personality is laced with the good-natured humor of a Western Canadian from Gull Lake, Saskatchewan.

One day someone asked Jim which was more violent, an episode of "The Jerry Springer Show" or an NHL game?

"Oh, Jerry Springer without question," McKenzie shot back. "How many times do you see two women fighting and pulling each other's hair out during a hockey game?"

But when the 6-3, 205-pound McKenzie squares off, there's nothing funny about his attitude.

"Jim is recognized as one of the elite heavyweights in the NHL," Schoenfeld asserted. "He has a lot of respect from the other people who play that role. But it's a hard way to make an easy living. It really is."

McKenzie expanded on his challenging profession during an interview with Fischler Hockey Service Phoenix correspondent Cathy Duncan. The oral history gathered from that interview follows.

The advantage of coming from a small, Canadian town in the West — the way I did — was that everything I needed for hockey was right near me. Take the rink, for example, I could walk to it from my house and there were times when I not only carried my own big hockey bag to the rink but I also carried my brother's bag.

Another plus for me was my parents' help with my hockey. Although my father was a cop with the Royal Canadian Mounted Police and my mother worked as well, they both had time to help me and they spent as much time at the rink as possible. When I was just starting out in hockey, I always wanted one of them there because I loved to have my skate laces tied tight and I couldn't do it myself.

It's funny. My Dad was a big Montreal Canadiens fan but when I was four-years-old someone got me a Bobby Orr Boston Bruins jersey. The first thing my dad said when he saw that was, "We'll have to get you a real jersey." Which he did, and I don't think I ever got a chance to wear my Bobby Orr jersey.

When I just started playing back home, I would be on the ice two or three times a week plus I was playing street hockey all the time as well. A few years later, when I was about twelve, the routine went like this: right after school play until it was dark and then find the clothes I had taken off — the school jacket or whatever — and then get home before dinner was served.

I started playing organized hockey when I was six and was a player — not a fighter — all the way up to my first year in Juniors. My role model was Larry Robinson, who had been with the Canadiens and was one of the NHL's all-time best defensemen.

When I was fourteen-years-old I moved to Moose Jaw, Saskatchewan and played a couple of years of Midget level hockey there. I was one of the youngest kids on the team and was very homesick about leaving my parents and friends. There were eight or ten of us like that who were homesick, and of the group, two or three guys actually went home. If the truth be known, I was just as homesick but I wanted to play hockey so badly that I found that the good of staying in Moose Jaw outweighed my homesickness; so I stayed and made it through my first year. After that, it was a lot easier on me.

At age fourteen, I had hardly filled out yet. Even though I was strong, I looked more like a pipe-cleaner, but I still was half-a-head or a head taller than most of the other players.

Mind you, I was still playing defense in those days and continued playing on the blue line through my Junior hockey career. At the time, I wanted to be another Larry Robinson and I was willing to do anything that would help me advance my career.

I played two years in Moose Jaw and finished with Junior hockey in Victoria, British Columbia. It was a different culture in those days. One of the things my coaches taught me was to never talk to players on the opposition. Not before nor after a game. The word was, "Don't fraternize with anybody wearing an opposite jersey." Their thinking was that if we talked with the other guys, we would play soft against them.

Up until Juniors, I hardly did any fighting. In fact the very first fight I remember was during training camp and it was with Darren Kimble who later made it to the NHL and was quite a hitter.

The fight happened so fast I didn't know what was happening for a few seconds. It started when he bumped me and, all of a sudden, said, "Let's go!" I had no clue what was going on until he dropped his gloves. Then, I dropped mine and wrestled. I still had no clue, no idea what was going on. But I did manage to put the hug on him because I had no idea how to throw a punch or anything like that.

But I learned something right then and there and kept learning through Juniors. While I was learning, I quietly would think about my ultimate goal; which was to play in the NHL. The thing is that I have always been the type of person who would believe inside in something but I wouldn't go around talking about it for fear that I would jinx myself.

When I want something badly, I don't even want to think about it; all I want to do is keep on working toward that target and pretend that I don't see it until I get there.

One of the big steps in that direction came in 1989 when I was picked as the Hartford Whalers' third choice — 73rd overall — in the Entry Draft. I wound up playing for Hartford's American League farm team in Binghamton in 1989-90 and was that ever an experience. A negative, at least from the win-loss standpoint.

We set a record for futility at Binghamton. The team was just horrible and we had something like fourteen guys who were first or second-year pros, all kids between nineteen and twenty-one years old. The thing I remember the most is that we set a record for losing the most games by one goal.

There was a reason for that: we had a lot of guys who were more than willing to drop the gloves but the opposition had maybe one guy or none at all. So, if they got ahead by a goal, the last thing they wanted to do was run up the score. If they had done that, we would have responded by playing every other shift looking to stir something up and making a name for ourselves.

When I finally made it to the Show with Hartford it was something else. I got the call and from that point on I couldn't sleep a wink. I was so anxious I couldn't do a thing so I went straight to the rink and stayed there the whole day waiting for the game to start.

The first guy to come over to me was Kevin Dineen and right away he said to me, "If you need anything, just let me know." He treated me first-class.

Most important, that experience with the Whalers showed me that I could handle myself in the NHL. When they would call me up, I would have a few scuffles and, from that standpoint, I knew that I could make it as a big-leaguer that way.

It was funny because when the Whalers would send me back down to the minors, I couldn't find a fight. It didn't matter what I did; there weren't many guys who wanted to go with me or were willing. Meanwhile, I still wanted to improve as a player and, like other enforcers, I didn't want to become a one-dimensional player.

Whenever they sent me back to the American League, I never let my nose get out of joint. I went with the idea to come back a better hockey player. I know it's a cliché but I had it in my head, "You've got to come to play every night. You've got to do everything."

Life is this way: there are players who are sent down to the minors or are traded and the move just doesn't make any sense. The guy has done everything he can do yet it just doesn't work out. That's why I've always felt that I was lucky to be in the NHL.

Meanwhile, I began getting more and more ice as a Whaler and, in 1990-91, I was voted the favorite Whaler by the fans. That, to me, was just amazing. The people in Hartford were just great to me and I loved being there. It was a super place to play and the unfortunate thing about the Whalers is that eventually they had to move.

Just when everything was looking so rosy, I ran into some trouble and it all had to do with my conditioning during the off-season. I did weight-lifting but I failed to train certain areas of my body as well as I should have with the result that I blew out both of my hip flexors. By the time I came back, I still wasn't right and it was a terrible year. I couldn't get around on the ice, couldn't make my hits, couldn't jump into the play the way I should and couldn't do all the other things that were necessary to be successful on the ice.

On top of that there were a lot of things going wrong with the Whalers so that they finally traded me. I wound up splitting the 1993-94 season between Hartford, Dallas and Pittsburgh. I was with the Stars for a cup of coffee and then picked up by the Penguins. The NHL, in some ways, is a small world. I say that because Eddie Johnston, the general manager who had drafted me originally as a Whaler, was now the g.m. in Pittsburgh, and he brought me back to his club, only now as a Penguin.

No problem. I had been around the NHL a bit by now and knew the ropes.

And I had had my share of fights. Looking back, one of the most interesting of them all was my very first as a big-leaguer.

We had been beaten badly the night before during a Western Canadian swing and now we were to play the Oilers in Edmonton. Before the game at Northlands Coliseum, our coach gave us a pep talk: "You got to show more fire!" That was the message and it got through to me.

The next thing I know, I'm on the ice for the pre-game warmups. The guys were doing a semi-circle, shooting drill. I was kicking the puck in my skates and not paying too much attention. My head was down and I found myself accidentally running into one of the Oilers.

Frankly, I had no idea who it was but the reality is that the guy happened to be Dave Brown, one of the best fighters in the league who already had made quite a reputation as one of the Broad Street Bullies in Philadelphia before he was traded to the Oilers.

As soon as I bumped into Brown, Keith Acton — he was the pepperpot assistant coach with Edmonton — started chirping at Brown. "Look at that rookie, trying to show you up, Dave." He kept getting in Brownie's ear and the next thing I know, he was making evil eyes at me, skating around, staring at me as the warm-up ended.

What do you think happened?

We're both out for the first shift of the game and away we went, swinging at each other. Truthfully, I held my own and it was a good fight as fights go but, inwardly, I was disappointed with myself. I sat in the penalty box after the fight was over, brooding that I should have done better. In the minors I had thrown guys around and did whatever I had wanted and here I was fighting to just a draw.

But the best part was that I had no idea who I had been fighting. No idea. After I had served my penalty, I returned to our bench and sat down next to our spare goalie, Daryl Reaugh. I turned to him and said, "After that fight, they're gonna send me down to the minors. I shoulda done better than that!"

He looked at me funny; like I had said something really stupid and I had no idea why he was reacting that way. Anyway, on my next shift, I went out on the ice and was hacking and slashing Edmonton players, looking to start something, trying to fight somebody, trying to make what I thought would be a better impression on my coach. To regain what I thought I had lost.

After the shift, I returned to the bench and sat down next to my buddy, Reaugh again. This time, he said to me, "Do you know who that was who you fought before?"

"Yeah," I replied. "Some Brown guy."

He shoots back. "Yeah, that was DAVE BROWN. DAVE BROWN, the same one who did all the fighting for the Flyers. Remember!"

"Uh, oh," I said to myself.

After that I was praying that I would never get a shift for the rest of the game. Fortunately for me, I didn't.

My most memorable moment?

Certainly one of them would be my first career NHL hat trick in 1996-97 with Phoenix against the Kings. I was named first star of the game in a 6-1 win. I got the second and third goals in the second period and had no clue what to do so I went out and fought Matt Johnson. I mean, I had no idea what I was supposed to do.

As for personal rivalries, I have had a few. Over a period of about four years, I've had fights with Sandy McCarthy a lot of times. It was not from any personal dislike for him or anything like that it was just the way those particular games were going. We had a couple of really good ones.

Over the years, I learned my role as an enforcer. That is, I have to be there for the skilled players. That's a huge part of my game. I have to give my skilled teammates more room to operate on the ice; to give the less-than-brave players more confidence. My presence should help them feel an inch taller and ten pounds heavier. Sometimes we go into buildings where the opposition has a big, physical team and our little guys might be intimidated by them.

Let's face it, a fight can be decisive in a game. The biggest thing a team can have in any contest is momentum and a fight can turn that momentum around or it can get momentum going for your club. If it happens to be a blah game, with nothing going on, a fight can ignite a team. If the other team is on a roll, your tough guy can go out and do well against his counterpart and it can stop their momentum. Lots of games are turned around with fights in that way.

Fans seem to like fights. There's an old saying, "No fan ever got up to get a cup of coffee or go to the bathroom when a fight broke out." Nobody ever sits in his seat either. The fight starts and the fans leap out of their seats. Fans go crazy over fights and that's all part of the momentum equation. If I win a fight on the road, it could take the home crowd right out of the game.

If the NHL ever takes fighting out of hockey, it will become lacrosse on ice.

If the NHL ever takes fighting out of hockey, I personally will feel bad for the skill players in the league. I say that because, without fighting, there will be more of the clutching, grabbing and anyone who wants to go after a skill player will do so without the fear that he would be confronted by me or another tough guy enforcer. Take away fighting and the league might as well paint a target on the back of the skill players because they would be the victim of cheap shots and whatever. Remember, it's not so much the actual fighting that's the deterrent to all that cheap stuff perpetrated against the skill players, it's the thought that it could happen that keeps a lot of players from trying that cheap stuff.

Enforcers, you will find, have a very strict code of their own. Enforcers are honorable and respect each other. I can assure that of all the fellows who

I have fought in the league, a good ninety-percent I say "Hi" to before or after a game. If I bump into them after a game we'll have a laugh and have a Diet Coke or something.

Here's a good example of how it works out. In September 1995, I was signed as a free agent by the Islanders and showed up at training camp. The first guy I hit it off with on Long Island was their enforcer, Mick Vukota, who I had already fought a couple of times earlier in my career.

The two of us hung out for the first couple of days of camp, testing and all the other stuff they do before the players actually take the ice. When we finally had our first scrimmage, he was on the other side and the next thing you knew, the two of us were having a scrap. An hour later, after the workout, we went out together and had lunch. The fight was just part of the game.

I'm well aware of the enforcers on the other teams. I start thinking about the next game right after the game I'm playing ends. I think about how the other team's enforcers fight, what they do, who would try to draw me into a penalty, who is a right-handed fighter and who is left-handed. It's important to me to know all these things. I even check out their jerseys to determine whether their sleeves are long or short and if any alterations have been done on their jerseys.

Where do I go from here? Well, I know that I'm never going to be a thirty-goal scorer. For that, I would have to get thirty-goal ice time and that just hasn't happened.

Bear in mind that I don't say that grudgingly. I'm a very lucky guy to have played more than 400 NHL games and I do what I can with what I have. I mean that on ice and off the ice. In Phoenix I even had the opportunity to do some broadcasting and, same as in the other cities, I do as much community work as possible.

It's funny, whenever I get out to meet people away from the rink they are surprised at the type of person I am. Knowing the way I am on the ice, they expect me to talk in one-word grunts, drag my knuckles and eat raw meat with my hands. If anything, it teaches the fans not to stereotype other people, especially those in my profession.

One thing I've learned — and this pertains to some of the charity work that I myself do, as well as other enforcers — is that there's a common denominator regardless of how tough we are. That is, we all feel very fortunate that we are playing and making the money we are making and we are respectful of our position. So when it comes to charitable work, we feel that any time we can help other people, we feel fortunate to do so.

Krzysztof Oliwa

When I went to Maple Leaf Gardens, I sat right behind the net. I was think-ing, "Wow! This is so cool. This is unbelievable. Look at all the people."

O f all hockey's Horatio Alger sagas depicting unlikely players making good, none is more curious than that of Krzysztof Oliwa, hereafter known as Kris.

★ The NHL never knew an enforcer who made the connection from a obscure Polish league to the Show.

★ Of all the Devils' prospects on their Albany River Rats farm team, Oliwa was on the bottom of their list during the 1994-95 season.

★ For a time even the River Rats couldn't decide whether Kris would be better off in the East Coast League and whether or not he should be a forward or defenseman.

The Polish Prince not only surmounted every obstacle in his path but also became so valuable a New Jersey Devil in 1997-98 that he was kept on the Protected List by Devils general manager Lou Lamoriello in June 1998.

Lamoriello had every reason to shield Oliwa. Starting at training camp in September 1997, Kris continually opened eyes with a blend of hustle, skills and, of course, fistic talent.

He made the big club in October 1997 and then proceeded to demonstrate that he not only was one of the most eager battlers but his work on New Jersey's fourth line inspired memories of a younger Randy McKay and Mike Peluso.

What's more, he emerged as one of the more engaging players on the team. He mastered English well enough to hold his own in media interviews and was admired for his fresh view of life in general.

"When things get tough in the NHL," Oliwa explained, "I always look back. Nothing is tougher than the way it was for me back in Poland. I can imagine what the guys back there in Europe would think of my 'problems' here. Like I have to take heat from the coach."

Occasionally, Oliwa was reprimanded by then coach Jacques Lemaire for taking needless penalties. But Lemaire never took issue with Kris' choice of opponents.

He has had bouts with the likes of such notorious NHL enforcers as Marty McSorley, Ken Baumgartner and just about any other tough guy you can name. At 6-5, 235 pounds, Oliwa is a formidable foe but admittedly learned fighting relatively late in his hockey development.

"When I first came up," Oliwa reflected, "I had to set things straight right away no matter who was in front of me. It was weird, though, me a European tough guy."

In 73 games of his rookie season, 1997-98, Oliwa led the Devils in penalty minutes with 295 and finished the campaign with two goals and three assists.

During New Jersey's opening playoff round against Ottawa, Kris attracted considerable attention. *Ottawa Citizen* reporter Lisa Burke described him as "a pitchfork in the Senators' side." He displayed his heavyweight tactics by taking a run at Ottawa defenseman Wade Redden in the final minutes of Game Two at Continental Airlines Arena in New Jersey, infuriating the Senators.

"The hit on Redden was clean," argued Oliwa. "I was just taking my man. They can't be mad at me for that."

But they did get mad at him in Game Four when Kris harshly cracked his elbow on Daniel Alfredsson's head. In so doing, Oliwa enraged Lance Pitlick who jumped the Devil from behind and got a five minute penalty.

"I'm just doing my job," said Oliwa. "I won't stand back from anyone."

Soon after Oliwa completed a scrimmage at the Devils practice facility at South Mountain Arena in West Orange, New Jersey, Kris accommodated Fischler Hockey Service correspondent G.P. Aroldi. The following oral history was drawn from that interview:

Unlike most National Hockey League players, I grew up in different circumstances. My home town was Tychy, Poland. When I was born on April 12, 1973, Poland still was under Communist control and when I grew up it was really tough.

First of all there were hard times in Poland; not much to buy in the stores and always a struggle for food, for just getting stuff. It was very hard to get anything because of the (Communist) system that was in place.

Food was rationed. Each family would get ration stamps so you were able to buy a kilo of this or a kilo of that. You couldn't just go ahead and buy two loaves of bread because that, too, was rationed. We survived because, when you have to survive, you figure out ways and means to do so. And since we didn't have a lot of food on the table, I learned to spread it over my mouth.

In terms of sports, the easiest thing to play was soccer because it was cheap. All we needed was a ball which we took on the field — or even a meadow — and we played.

Every kid played soccer but hockey wasn't as well known. But one day a friend of mine came along and said, "Krzysztof, there's a chance to sign up for a Junior hockey team."

I decided to give it a try although I didn't even own a pair of skates. My mother couldn't afford them but one day my grandfather took me to a store and got the cheapest skates that were on the shelf.

Our Winters were cold — with lots of snow — so there were patches of ice all over the place. In our neighborhood, we had a little pond and some-body made a rink out of it for the kids and that's where I played and learned how to ice skate. I was ten-and-a-half when I first played and the equipment was usually used hand-me-downs. Some of it came from the European Hockey Federation and was used by guys who had been on the national team. Then, complications set in because the hockey practices and the soccer prac-tices took place at the same time, so I had to make a big decision. I chose hockey over soccer because I found it more interesting. I figured that I always could play soccer later if the hockey didn't work out.

Since my mother had been divorced — it happened when I was about seven — she had to work to make ends meet and that meant that I had to go to the hockey rink by myself. I remember the first time I went alone; I had the house key around my neck. Right after school, I took the bus to the rink — I never had a chance to go home in between — and went right to practice, and then back home. That was the routine that I developed when I started learn-ing hockey. Sometimes I would get home as late as nine at night but I loved my hockey and was always looking forward to getting to practice.

When it came to higher education, I decided to go to a mining school. In that way, I would graduate with a Mechanic's Degree and know all about min-ing machines. This could have been a big help in getting a job because where I come from, all we have are mines.

I would get up at six in the morning, go to school and, twice a week, I would work in the mines. This was part of the training but it meant that I had to be up at four in the morning and walk to the train. Imagine what it was like in the winter. Everything was so dark, there were no cars in the street, and the people who were walking to the train with me were just sleep-walking. Then, I'd get on the train, go to the mine, and get sent down 600 meters below the ground. There is less oxygen down there so it made me so tired, I just shut down. As a matter of fact, down there everyone tried to shut down.

In Poland in those days, you didn't even think about a National Hockey League career. Personally, I never thought about the NHL and, to be honest, if someone had told me fourteen years ago, "Yeah, Krzysztof, you're going to play in the NHL," I would have laughed. I didn't even know what the NHL was and didn't even see a game on television until I was about fourteen.

Meanwhile, I kept playing but it wasn't easy. My coach was a great guy but he kept telling me that I was too big to play. "You hit people too hard," he would say. "You keep getting penalties!" Once I punched a guy in the head and got suspended for three months. I had my gloves on and he was wearing a cage. That ended that season for me.

After I returned, I got back in the lineup and they kept playing me and I wound up skating in the European Junior Championships, which were played in Russia, and played against Alexei Kovalev, who's now with the Rangers, and Roman Hamrlik. Kovalev was the best player and his (Russian) team beat us, 7-3. That was the best game we played but Kovalev just danced. He was great! Of course, I was bigger than virtually all the others so when someone my size hit a normal size guy, I would get penalties. My break came when some fellow from Switzerland came to watch and liked what he saw. He invited me to come to his country and skate with the team there. "You have a chance, maybe someday, to play in the NHL." So, I asked for my release papers and went away to Switzerland.

In those days I was a lot skinnier than I am now so I got to lifting weights when I was about seventeen or eighteen and strengthened myself. When I was nineteen I decided to come to North America and try out for a team in Welland, Ontario, near Niagara Falls.

Before I wound up playing Junior, I went to my first NHL game. It was at Maple Leaf Gardens in Toronto. San Jose was playing the Leafs and I couldn't believe how good those guys were. I sat right behind the net and was thinking, "Wow, this is so cool; this is unbelievable. Look at all the people!" I had never seen such a big rink in my life.

Now it was time to make my way up the ladder in Welland. This was a Junior B team and when I got to the rink the manager was immediately impressed with my size but was concerned whether I could skate or not. I put on my skates and there was no problem. The guy said, "Okay, sign here. You're gonna play for us." I said to myself, "Krzysztof, why wait?"

The change from Poland to Canada was like culture shock for me. In Welland the streets were nice and clean and the grass was cut. On the first day, I went for a long run and I was so happy to be over here; it was freedom. I felt a new freedom; like I didn't have to worry about going to work at four in the morning. All I had to do was play hockey and, even if I didn't make it in hockey, I could do something else.

This much I knew, I wanted to stay on this side of the Atlantic. I didn't want to go back because there was nothing for me to go back for. The hangup was that I only spoke a little English; just basic stuff like, "How are you?" The language barrier was really tough and there were times that I was thinking, "This is really horrible; maybe I should go back." Unless you're actually in that situation, you can't possibly understand how bad it felt. I went to school and, after six or seven months, it started getting easier. I mastered the language and could communicate. Compared to Canadian kids, my experience was little. I had played maybe 200 games total but in that first year of Junior, my ambition was to become a goal-scorer. Unfortunately, it was a tough adjustment. I couldn't get used to the style of play and found myself all over the ice. It was really frustrating and that was when I started fighting. I thought, "Maybe if I start fighting, I'll get a chance to play more." And that's how it all started.

It's funny because back home in Poland my mom and I would look at tapes of hockey fights and think they were faked. Yet (laughs), we thought wrestling was for real. We were kind of confused over there.

I finished the 1992-93 season in Welland with a fight — my first in Junior — and wound up going down with the officials falling on top of us. My hand and my shoulder got stuck somewhere between the player and the ref and popped my shoulder right out. It wasn't too cool and I remember thinking, "So, this is fighting; I don't like it too much." (Laughs).

But I recovered from it well and after the 1992-93 season in Welland, there was the Entry Draft held in Quebec City and I went to see what would happen. So, I'm sitting there and now it's the Third Round but, to tell you the truth, I never thought I would be drafted. Next thing I knew my name was called. I said to myself, "This is amazing." I even got to put on the Devils jersey and the cap. It was one of the happiest days of my life — sixty-fifth overall — and biggest surprises.

Then the Devils sent me to Albany for the 1993-94 season. In the American League, I had ups and downs, good times and bad times but more often there were bad times. Once again, I had a hard time adjusting to the system, a hard time finding myself; to be the player that I thought I could be.

Robbie Ftorek was coaching Albany at the time and after two months he told me to go down to Raleigh in the East Coast League for the rest of the year. I went and enjoyed being there but I was not really doing the job. I was still struggling with the system but this much I knew; I didn't want to be back in Poland, working in the mines.

Naturally, if I had been born in North America, it would have been easier for me, so I just had to work through it and deal with the problems. When I did wrong, coaches would talk to me and I would say, "Okay, you're right!" Then, I would try to do what they wanted me to do and eventually it worked out. But, don't kid yourself, it was a long and hard adjustment over five years — and plenty of fights.

My first bout was with Frank Bialowas, who was playing for St. John's, a farm team of the Toronto Maple Leafs. This was in an exhibition game and he was opposite me on the face-off. This was my rookie year and this guy had been around a bit more. As soon as the puck was dropped, he said, "Let's go!"

Remember, I was new to all this. I didn't know the guy; didn't know the AHL tough guys, didn't know the rules, didn't know what it was all about. But I said, "Yeah, okay." He threw and I threw. I didn't win the fight and I didn't lose the fight but I had a few bruises on my face. Afterward, my coach, Robbie Ftorek, came over to me and asked, "You're okay?"

I looked at Robbie and said, "I'm okay." With that, he came back, "All right. Good job. Good job." So, I wasn't that bad. Right then and there I knew it was for real. This was the real stuff although my job, at the time, was not to be the enforcer on the River Rats. I was still trying to be a player, a goal-scorer.

The role change came about in my last year at Albany (1996-97) when my coach said, "I still want you to score goals but I also want you to be the guy who is going to fight on this team."

I said, "Okay," and that's how I became the tough guy on the Rats. After a few years of fighting — and trying different styles — I realized that this was going to be my job if I wanted to play in the NHL. They wanted me to hit people and score goals.

So, I had to pay my dues and play through injuries. Once — this was in 1994-95 during the NHL lockout — I was skating one-on-one with David Emma. He poked me from behind and I fell back, hitting my elbow on the ice. It hurt but I didn't at first realize the extent of the injury; I had busted open my whole elbow.

But first I had put a hand between my pads and there was no blood. After David and I got to the dressing room, he looked at my elbow and said, "Man, you've gotta have somebody look at that arm." It was split right open; the whole thing — and there was nobody around to stitch it up.

About eight hours went by before it actually got stitched, but it was too late. It got infected — my whole arm — and I wound up in the hospital for a week. By the time I got out, there was no room for me on the team so they first sent me to Raleigh and then Detroit of the IHL and then St. John's of the AHL on loan. I was frustrated but I had no control; it was just bad luck. I was back in Raleigh again for four or five games in 1995-96 and that was really something.

Talk about bad luck, listen to this: I had just invited my parents over to the United States for the first time. They had their papers, their visas and flew to New York. I was in Providence with the Rats the day before my parents were scheduled to arrive at Kennedy Airport. I was all set to meet them when Robbie came over and said, "You're not playing tonight; you're going down to Raleigh." I said to myself, "Man, this can't be happening." I hadn't seen my parents for two years but Robbie felt that he was making the right decision and I wasn't going to say no although this was causing a lot of problems with my family.

My wife was in school; she had final exams to take, she was pregnant and there was a big storm happening. Plus, she had to drive to Kennedy Airport to pick them up. This wasn't good — but I had no choice. I went down to Raleigh for three games, came back, and met my parents a few days later. Robbie had been my coach for three years and spent hours and hours working with me on all aspects of my game, especially the physical. At first I couldn't comprehend what he was saying because it was the opposite of what I had been told in Poland but gradually I changed, listened more and things started to turn around. Robbie told me what to do and I did it; no matter what it was.

I told him, "Robbie, I'll do whatever you want me to do," and he liked that. He realized that he had finally gotten into my head. And I had gotten the message, "You want to play, you have to listen." After my second year in Albany, I started to want it more. Before that I had been serious but I had figured that the NHL was too far out of my reach.

While all this was going on, I had met my wife-to-be in Albany and eventually we got married. She was a big factor in my success because she was with me always, through the good times and the bad times and the worst of times. When I was demoted to Raleigh, she went with me. When I was down in the dumps, saying, "I don't know if I can handle this anymore," she would say, "Go, work harder; work harder!" She made me go that extra mile and encouraged me to try all sorts of things to make myself better. It was hard, hard work that I'll never forget and, after three years with Albany I came to realize that now the NHL was something I really *wanted*.

By the time I came to my fourth Devils camp, I worked even harder. I remember saying to myself, "Maybe I won't make the big team *this* year but I see my chance with this organization maybe someday later." And I kept driving for it. When my contract elapsed, Lou Lamoriello came up with a different offer for me and he said, "You are working hard and you have a good chance here." I took the chance, signed another contract and tried to make the best of it.

In 1996-97 I played my last season in Albany and broke my hand in the middle of the year. Every year it was something; not one season without some sort of injury. But I recovered from it real well, came back and tried as hard as I could. By this time I had more experience than a lot of the younger fellows on the Rats and we had a great team.

Meanwhile, Randy McKay got injured on the Devils and that created an opening on the big team. We were playing in Fredericton when it happened and that's when I was told to report to the Devils. Their next game was a Saturday afternoon on Long Island and I almost didn't make it.

I left Fredericton during a huge night-time blizzard and was supposed to report to New Jersey for a practice but I never made it there until five in the afternoon. It was wild because I had been re-routed to Montreal, my bags went somewhere else but, luckily, I had my skates with me. That was a lesson Robbie had taught me; "Anywhere you go, always have your skates with you!"

Eventually, I got my gear and went to Long Island with the rest of the Devils. At first I thought I might actually play in my first NHL game against the Islanders. I skated in the morning workout and the pre-game skate but I wasn't dressed for the game.

But the next night we were in Buffalo, I dressed for the warm-up and actually made it into the game. Here I am, in my first NHL game, on my first shift and I have my first NHL fight. It was against Bob Boughner of the Sabres. He's a strong kid and does his job. I hit him but there wasn't much to it after that. Bob threw a few and I threw a few and then he fell on top of me. Someone took a picture of it and (Laughs) my legs are way on top of the guy. Hey, you win some and you lose some but it's all about showing up. He did his job and I did my job. That was what I was called up for and it was great.

The next day I was sent back to Albany but when I look back on that night at Buffalo, I can honestly say that it was one of the best of my life.

I had my first taste of the NHL and it was delicious. I had been waiting for it, and now that I had sampled what it had to offer, I vowed to work even harder to get back to New Jersey.

In terms of my fighting, I did a little boxing here and there to help my balance, especially when punching and swinging. For a while, I had a balance problem but I solved that and kept working hard through 1996-97, hoping that I would get another call.

When training camp opened in September 1997, I was there. I looked over the roster and decided that if I played hard and physical, Jacques Lemaire, the coach, would like me. That's what he said, "Play hard." So, once the exhibition games began, I always was involved in something and when it came time to put up the Protected List, there was my name. I actually had been protected from the Waiver Draft.

That meant that I had an even better chance of making the team but then Lou picked up Scott Daniels from the Flyers and I thought to myself, "Now there are three (enforcers) here; what's going to happen?"

The bottom line is that I stayed and learned — about the speed of the game, about how hard I had to work to stay — and I had some fights. I fought Tie Domi. I fought Marty McSorley — all good fighters. Domi, especially, is tough. I had a hard time with him because he's so smart as a fighter. He knows what he's doing and has fought so many times.

I have been asked whether there are any tough players who I would rather not fight. The answer is that I can't think that way. For example, during the 1997-98 season we had a game coming up against the Carolina Hurricanes and they had Stu Grimson in their lineup. He's a big guy and everyone knows about his reputation; about how tough he is. But I know what my job is and I knew that I would have to be in his face all night long. I knew that if I had to fight him, then I would fight him. That's the way it goes.

It really isn't about how big the other guy is; it's about how hard you try. I can't step back. I have to be there for the team. I have to do what I have to do. That's my job and I have to do it. And if I won't do it, there will be someone else waiting in line to do it. So, I can't think about these things. In fact, I'll bet that if you put the same question to any guy, he would reply in the same way I am. You go out there; play hard, do you job. I might not have to fight Grimson. I might not even play against Stu. But there always is a chance that I will and in that case, I had better be ready!

In my first full NHL year, 1997-98, I learned a lot — about myself and about the rules. There was a fight I had with Ken Baumgartner of the Bruins when I had tape around my fingers and I was reprimanded for that. I knew about the rule; that if you have your knuckles cut, you can't put anything on your knuckles. But this wasn't my knuckles, it was my fingers. And I had taped my fingers for as long as I had been playing hockey. And even if I had cut Baumgartner with my hand or the tape, it was not intentional. The cut could have been from something else. We don't know, but if you look at the tape of the incident, you can't see if I hit him and cut him. I didn't put the tape on my fingers to hurt anybody because I wouldn't want someone to put tape on his fingers to hurt me.

The thing was, I wasn't aware that you couldn't have tape on your fingers. I only had tape on one pinky — on the end of it! I couldn't hurt anyone with that. Anyway, I got spoken to about the rules after that and I'll never do it again. I learned the tough way and got kicked out of the game and even faced suspension. Thankfully, I didn't get suspended but I learned and, as I've said before, it has never been easy for me.

In one way I was fortunate. Jacques Lemaire used me quite a bit in my rookie season and I loved it. It was amazing how fast the season went. All of a sudden we were at the Olympic break and I was thinking, "Man, I can't believe that it's almost over." I felt that I had learned so much since coming up to New Jersey just by watching the veterans in action.

I like the way Bobby Holik plays the puck. Once Robbie Ftorek asked me, "What kind of player would you like to be?" I said Bobby Holik.

He said, "You are never going to be a Bobby Holik." So, I said, "Ooooookkaay...if I can't be him, I will be the best player I can be as a Krzys Oliwa. I won't try to be like him. I will try to be my best and learn from those guys."

Robbie said, "That's better."

And that was it. Every day I learned something new from this man who has been such a great teacher for me. Robbie has made me mentally tougher.

And, in my last years at Albany, Ftorek's successor, John Cunniff also gave me confidence to play the game.

Plus, all my teammates helped. I like to laugh and talk with them although sometimes I talk too much. Sometimes I will say something stupid. I don't want to be the guy who just sits there and listens. I want to have fun and enjoy the whole experience. That's what it's all about, enjoying it. If you don't enjoy the game, you shouldn't be playing it. And, of course, the other aim is to win the Stanley Cup.

Every so often I'll be sitting in bed and the thought might come to mind that I could still be working down in the mines back home in Poland. I'd think, "Wow! My father has to get up in an hour and go to work."

Now, in my bedroom, I have a miniature version of the "Heaven" photo of when the Devils won the 1995 Stanley Cup. I have it hanging over my bed and it's awesome. I wake up in the morning and it's right there, reminding me that I have a chance, that I'm in the big leagues and this is it. I am here to win the Cup.

I am very happy that I made it to where I am now because there were people who never dreamed that I would. And, sometimes, I doubted myself as well — both here and back in Poland. But I have fought through it and I'm proud of myself and I'm proud of my wife; that she helped me. It's just great!

Rich Pilon

(After the eye injury) I thought about coming back right away. They said I might be done and I said, 'No way.' I wasn't about to live a dream and play in the NHL and have it end in my second year.

To call Rich Pilon a "throw-back," is an easy way to describe a defenseman who has sacrificed more for his team over a decade than anyone could expect from a blueliner.

It is virtually forgotten — and extremely relevant — that the robust Islanders defenseman virtually lost the sight in his left eye during the 1989-90 season.

Just about any performer would have called it a career right then and there but the evidence is quite clear that Pilon not only regained his intensity but in some cases played harder than ever.

One need not go any further than Eric Lindros to find behemoths leveled by Pilon bodychecks. A collision between Pilon and Kevin Stevens during the 1993 Islanders/Penguins Patrick Division Final series nearly ended the big forward's career on the spot.

A native of the Canadian West, Pilon plays the game the way it was played in the frontier days at the turn of the century. That he has survived borders on the miraculous. That he has played for the same team his entire career says everything there is to say of his value to the Islanders.

Fischler Hockey Service correspondent Dan Saraceni sat down with Rich at his home on Long Island to discuss the defenseman's intriguing career.

DS: Tell me about the town you grew up in.

RP: I grew up in a town of 300 people. I had a graduating class of 12. And the 12 people I graduated with, we were together all throughout kindergarten to grade 12. It was a farming community. My mom was a housewife, my dad was a welder. We were lower-middle class, I guess. Growing up we were paycheck-to-paycheck; surviving.

When you grow up in such a small community, everybody knows everybody. The funny thing is, I'm really not friends with any of the people I graduated with. I never kept in touch with any of them. I never really had a best friend growing up. You know, the good kids would hang out together and I was never one of the good boys in school.

I got bullied around, I would say, from kindergarten to about grade five. I was the kid everybody picked on. Then in grade seven, I outgrew everybody. It was payback now and I started bullying kids in grades eight and nine. When I got to grade 11, 12 even grade 10, I guess I grew up and thought, "What am I doin'?" and grew out of it. It seemed people were being my friends because they were afraid, if they weren't, I'd beat the shit out of them. (laughs)

DS: Tell me about your family.

RP: I have two sisters. Both are younger: one is a school teacher and one is a nurse. Everybody lives in the hometown in Canada. Both are married and have children.

Back home it was minus 35, minus 40, — it was cold. My uncle used to take the snow off the ice on the lake and our parents would drop us off. But we used to skate on the road. You'd put your skates on at home and the road was so cold you could skate on it. Your skates were always one or two sizes bigger and you wore two pairs of socks and you had to tie your skates at home because if you didn't, you'd freeze your hands. We would get there and skate free and then walk through the drifts home.

Back then all we did was play hockey, hockey, hockey. Now I don't know anybody that skates on that lake. There's Nintendo now. Not as many kids play hockey now as they used to.

I remember my first pair of new skates were given to me by my uncle. When my father used to get equipment, it was second hand from a store in the city. You could buy new stuff too, but I was used to getting my equipment second-hand.

My uncle bought me a new pair of skates when I think I was 13 or 14 with these tucked blades, and I thought, "wow" because all I had before was steel. I wanted to get them a size bigger because I grew that year and I knew my dad couldn't afford new skates and I wanted them to last a few years. I grew out of them in one year and I didn't want to tell my father. So I continued to wear the skates and I think that's why now, I wear my skates almost a size smaller because I like the tightness. I wore those tight skates all year.

My sisters I used to beat up all the time. We used to fight at home a lot. My mom was the one we depended on. She got the meals cooked, she was a mom. She was there when you needed her. She was definitely the person you talked to before my father. He was a little tough to talk to. It was always his way, he was always right. He's still like that. He would worry about everything in the world and my mom was the counter-balance. She evened the scale. My father was the one who was always up or down. My dad was the breadwinner. He didn't have a steady job all the time and was fighting to make ends meet.

DS: Was the support from your family fierce?

RP: My parents were at *every* game. I remember we used to travel to play in a town called Kanista, which is about 45 minutes away when I played Bantam. We still didn't have much money and we used to travel with six kids and my dad always drove. He never got gas money. It was funny because there was one other native guy in my car, with two other Métis people, and in the other car were the other kids who were French and, I guess, pure-breds if you want to call them.

No matter what, my parents were at every single game. My home games, if we traveled — in Pee Wee's we used to travel in school buses — my mom and my sisters would come. The whole family. In the winter it was hockey, hockey, hockey. My sisters never did anything. They did the volleyball and the school stuff but everything revolved around my hockey. And in the summer it was horses.

DS: Tell me about your Native American background

RP: I'm considered Métis, which is like half-breed. My parents are both half-French and both half-native, which is Cree. Where I'm from they don't pay taxes, they don't go to war. They give them treaty cards and they get to cross the 49th parallel. They can go pitch a teepee wherever they want, basically.

Now the Métis people have basically the same rights as the natives do, except the tax. Right now, with a Métis card, someone can travel here, to Europe, wherever they want. They can come to the States and work. It's like a green card. I haven't gotten mine yet, I'm working on it. My family all have their's.

We went to the pow wows. I remember when I was five or six, we went to a fair and they had a greased pig contest; and my father was in this contest. What it was was you and two other guys and this greasy pig and you had to fight the two other guys to get to this pig, grab the end of the pig and pull it into this circle. You know what they were doing it for? A bag of canned food. That was the prize. They still do it every year. It started out as a tradition for the Métis people where other people could come and watch. Then it became almost all native people and not a lot of Métis people and there started to be a lot of trouble, fighting and stuff. Now its back to how it was before, with the tournaments and stuff. It's kind of weird.

DS: When did you start playing hockey?

RP: I would say I was about four years old. I remember falling once and quitting for a while. I said, "I'm not doin' this." But I started playing hockey again and my father coached us.

When he was younger, he said that when they played against the rich kids, they didn't have a puck so they used to use the hard, frozen turd of a horse. The rich kids had all the equipment and my dad had no shin pads or anything. He never played any kind of hockey, but he was respected. I think when he saw me play out there he saw something good. Like "I couldn't have this chance, now you can."

He coached right from Tom-Toms to when I was 15 years old. And I've never seen him in a pair of skates, despite all the coaching he did. My dad always wears cowboy boots. When he coached us on the ice, he would come out in his boots. He would have a whistle and cowboy boots.

DS: Can you remember your first team?
RP: Yeah. They were in St. Louis, in Tom-Tom. I started and then quit for a while so I started later than everybody, but then I caught up. I used to play forward. I was a centerman and I never played defense until my first year of developmental hockey, after age 15. I was always quick. I didn't really grow until I was 15. I was always 5-10, 180 pounds.

I was small. Then I grew over one summer and my feet started getting bigger and I got clumsy. My father couldn't believe how much slower I was skating, and he was all over me. I didn't quit again, though. A lot of the time, I was the reason we won the game. I used to play the whole game. And I went from playing the whole game to having problems with my coordination because I grew three inches over one summer.

But then I started getting invitations to play for the WHL teams that were 20 minutes away and convenient. I made their midget team there. I went in as a forward, but they had three lines and two extra forwards and six "D." I wasn't going to make the team. One of the defenseman got hurt and they asked me and the other extra guy if we could play "D." He said no and I said yeah because I knew a little bit from foolin' around and I've been there ever since. So I made that team on defense, then on to the Raiders and up until now.

It's funny because when I was younger, all I wanted to do was score goals. Now I get one a year. Every year I match my career high.

DS: How about your first fight?
RP: Yeah. It was a guy by the name of Rod Dolnick. He was Métis, and he was playing for the Raiders and I was in midget. He was a tough guy for the Raiders and we were in an intra-squad game. I knew that the Raiders were looking at me. I was 17 years old. We fought three times and beat the living shit out of each other. He broke my nose.

It wasn't that I got beat up, we beat each other up. It wasn't that he won or I won, it was just a pummeling. Not even holding on to each other. Again, he broke my nose, I got two black eyes, his face was just swollen. That's when Terry Simpson, the coach, said about me, "Put him on the list."

DS: Tell me about getting drafted right out of Midget.
RP: When they moved the midget age to 17, I was kind of lucky. If I had made

the Raiders, I would have been a seventh defenseman. Terry said, "You've only played one year of real developmental hockey, would you like to go play Junior A, which is like Tier 2, with a team a couple of hours or stay in Midget?"

I figured I'd stay in Midget and I got drafted out of Midget that year, when I was 17. Usually you get drafted into the NHL from Tier 1, which is Juniors.

When I played Midget, Triple A, one of my coaches was named Bob Ralphson and he taught me a lot. I don't think he was involved with an NHL team. He would keep me extra all the time. He had these little drills for defensemen. So I used to do extra all the time to try and work on quick feet. He was one of the guys I looked up to and helped me a lot.

DS: Who were your favorite NHL players or team while growing up?
RP: My two NHL favorite teams were always the Canadiens and Islanders. My favorite player was always Guy Lafleur. I used to watch him all the time. But he retired before I got to Long Island.

I ended up playing against Guy Lafleur and Steve Shutt. When they were on an All-star team which came to Prince Albert to play against the Raiders. And I played against Guy. I have this picture with me, him and Steve Shutt when I was in Juniors, I have this graduation suit on. And I met Guy and the team. When I made the Islanders, my first year, he came out of retirement and played for Quebec.

I remember taking a draw with him and saying, "Mr. Lafleur, do you remember me?" He said "No." I said, "In Saskatchewan. Prince Albert? I have a picture with you. I was on the Junior team."

In the game, I had a chance to hit him, but I stayed back. I said, "I'm not going to hit this guy." He still didn't have the helmet on. It was awesome, the best feeling.

DS: I heard that in your first camp with the Isles, you ran everybody in camp. Is that true?
RP: Oh yeah. I wasn't hitting them, I was just running everybody. I was here for maybe 10-11 days, that's it. I did my bumping and grinding. Then I came back at 20 years-old and I was was like, "I'm coming to camp ready." And I just ran everything in sight. I was gaining confidence in Juniors and everything was building. And I made the team.

Guys like Terry Simpson and Rick Wilson were here. Guys who were sort of like my ex-coaches and had watched me play from the time I was 14, for like four years, watching me improve every year.

I met guys like Clark Gillies, Kenny Morrow, Denis Potvin. But it's not like the camps now where everybody is there. Back then, the pros had their own little thing and the rookies, we never saw the guys. They were always the last group on the ice. All we saw them do was walk on the ice and we never got to play against them in practice.

That was the year we had the Al Arbour Cup, with four teams competing. But that was just a fight fest. We had so many fights with the tough guys on the teams. Simpson had to come down and tell the guys to stop fighting.

When we played the exhibition games, a couple of the older guys told me how I had a shot to make the team. I was 20-years old. It was my third camp. And I said, "No. There's too many guys." Ken Leiter was still here. But that year, Leiter retired and it left a spot open for either Dean Chenoweth or myself. They ended up keeping both of us because they wanted to move Kenny Morrow. But then Dean got hurt and I ended up playing full time.

I remember playing in the exhibition games then like the way I play now. Hitting and playing solid "D" and actually being more offensive. But then the game had changed from 10 years ago to now. Everything is so much tighter now. My first eight, nine games, I had eight points in eight games, my first year. Nobody knew who I was, even the players were like, "Where did you come from? Is this your first camp?" When I had been there two years before. I had gained so much confidence hitting in Junior, I played well. But then I ended up having only 14 points all year. Al took me off the power play and that was it.

DS: Now you have the longest tenure on the team.
RP: I never really thought about that. I see those press notes every day and I think it might put a jinx on me. I'll be outta here now. (laughs)

I think that I've been here with Scott Lachance for six years and, yeah, we've got a lot of new faces. I look to when Derek King got traded and he was a guy who I looked up to a lot when I first got here, on the ice and off the ice. Now its a little weird seeing all these young guys and there aren't any older guys for me to talk to. I'm only 29 and I'm the "old" guy. You know, 27, 28 to 32 that's your prime of hockey.

DS: How do you feel playing against former Isles?
RP: When I get on the ice, I really don't worry about it. About the only guy I wouldn't fight is Mick Vukota. No matter what. We're best friends.

It's funny because we grew up an hour apart in Canada and never met until we came here. And we were together for ten years. We bought a horse together. I have nothing bad to say about the guy.

DS: In a fighter's sense, did you and Vukota grow up together?
RP: Oh yeah. He'd tell me before a game to,"look out for a certain guy because he does this or whatever, so if you fight him..." He would tell me what guys to watch out for and he'd help me because I never looked at the sheet before the game. I never used to look to see who's playing. I didn't want to know who's playing. If the coach tells me who's on the other team, fine, but I never worry about what other tough guys are in the lineup.

DS: Would you say there's a science to playing physical?

RP: No. I love to hit. I remember playing soccer as a kid and being in grade seven or eight and playing against grades 10 and 11 and I'd take a run at the older guys. I've always been like that: everything was hitting. We wouldn't play touch or flag football. We'd play tackle with no equipment. And it was always like, "Wow. That's a good hit." It would be forty below outside and you're running down a field trying to take some guy's head off and you walk away like nothing happened. I've always loved that. I've always loved to hit.

People hit harder now than they did 10 years ago. These kids who come into the league right now are huge, like Lindros. Ten years ago, 6-0, 212 pounds, I was the biggest guy on the ice. Now I'm an average guy. Now the guys are just bigger and they hit harder.

DS: How have the different coaches you've had affected your game?

RP: My game is simple. All I have to do is move the puck, keep the puck out of my end and finish my body checks. And I like to finish hard. I'm not a great open ice hitter. I get the odd open ice hit. But if a guy gets a shot off, I'm going to hit him. And I don't want to give him a kiss on the cheek, I'm looking to put him through the boards.

Al Arbour didn't try to take me away, but he could control me more. When I first came into the league I would literally take runs to try and take some guy's head off. I would get myself out of position. It was like, "I have to go get Gretzky." I've hit Gretzky once in my career. No, twice. Once this year and once in L.A. behind the net. But he's so smart. Not that you can't catch him, he's just too smart. He'll just chip it by you. Now I have to pick my spots more, so I don't end up out of position.

In Juniors, I always wanted to get the big hit in the game. Because the games were all about hitting. Whereas now, I try to get three hits in a period and it just may not be there. You might get three hits in the game. Now my game is a little more positional, a little more controlled. I try to take better care of my end.

Now, I think about who we're playing, what style they play, and I'll look to see who's coming down my side.

I look to hit somebody and the chance of hitting someone is always good. If there are five guys out there you always have a chance of making at least one hit. But it doesn't matter who it is, I'm going to finish. I'm on the team with 19 other guys in the dressing room. I want to look at someone after the game and say, "I did my job, did you do yours?" Not put my head down and say, "Oh, I played shitty." I want the other guys to say, "He really worked his balls off."

DS: Tell me about your eye injury, from the shot by Brent Fedyk. How did you feel and how did it affect your game?

RP: I knew it was serious right away. I've been hit in the face before, but with this there was so much pain that I knew it was the eyeball and it wasn't just a knick to the side or something.

When I fell on the ice, I tried to open my eye and it wouldn't open. It didn't bleed all that much, a little out the side. When the trainer flipped me over, he gave a look that said, "This is bad." His first impression was, "Holy shit, the eye is already shut."

It was really a freak accident. I wasn't even in front of the net, I was about three feet off to the side. Fedyk took the shot and I think it actually tipped off of one of our guys. It tipped to the side and I was actually holding a Red Wing and I was turning to see where the puck was and I just met it, it was right there. I had no time to react to it, it happened so fast.

Nobody really knew how serious it was. I was a second year pro and basically everybody said he'll bounce back.

Before they took me to the hospital, I was sitting and the eye was still closed. It was bleeding on the inside of the eye and the blood was actually dripping into my throat and my stomach got full of blood and I ended up getting sick and peeing out blood.

I remember the doctors wondering if they should just take the eye, because of the pressure. They said that the pressure in the bad eye was so great that if it burst, it could affect my good eye. There were two doctors and I could hear them talking. One wanted to take the eye because the pressure was building in the eye and the other doctor wanted to wait a few hours.

I was scared, petrified. I remember waking up in the morning and I was in shock for almost a week. They put these clips on my eye, to keep my eyelids open and the doctor was asking me what I saw. I said everything I saw was blurry and foggy. The other eye was fine.

I thought about coming back right away. They said I might be done and I said, "No way." I wasn't about to live a dream and play in the NHL and have it end in my second year. I had only played 97 games in the league.

My mom was saying, "You'll play again." My family knew I loved the game so much. They were telling me I would be okay and that I would be back. I was also very fortunate with the organization here, with Bill Torrey and Al Arbour. They could have said, "You know, Rich..." I think they thought my career was over but they kept me around for the rest of the season. They kept having me see doctors to make the eye better. But no doctor would clear me because of negligence. If I hit someone else, that guy could sue me because I couldn't see him and he could sue the doctor, too.

I finally got cleared through my insurance and that's why I have to wear the visor. It's one of the parts of my insurance, that I have to wear it to protect my eye. I didn't want to wear it at first, but I think it has helped my game in that some guys get so pissed off that I'm wearing the visor that they try to take it off. A lot of players don't realize the situation that I'm in and might think I'm chicken but I need it.

It didn't really affect my game. I'm the same player I've always been. I think it affected the team, they may have played a little more tentatively after it. But I've always been the same player.

It does have an effect on my fighting, though. Fighting is a spontaneous thing. But if I take my helmet off, I can get two minutes for instigating and five minutes for fighting. Other guys juts have to drop their gloves. So now I have to think about the fight before it starts. That's the only thing I hate about the visor.

DS: I'd like to ask about a specific incident. In the '93 playoffs against Pittsburgh, you had a collision with Kevin Stevens in Game Seven that resulted in a fractured sinus bone and fractured nose for him. Tell me about that event and how his being a Ranger now affects you.

RP: Kevin and I, we battled the whole series. There was an icing call and he tried to take my head off. I saw him at the last second and it was really a freak accident on his part. He said I hit him with the visor, saying, "Oh, the visor did it again." But it was really my shoulder, because I jumped at him.

He ended up being knocked out before he hit the ice and that's what shattered his face. It wasn't the hit, it was the fall. He was out and he hit the ice full on his face.

People ask now if he is the same player as he was then. I know he's not the same goal-scorer that he was but these last few times we've played the Rangers, he's battled just as hard now as he did then. When I play against him, I get the sense that he's still playing as hard, maybe not putting the puck in as much, but still battling hard.

I don't sense a grudge, but I know that if Kevin Stevens is coming down my wing, I'm going to be in his face. It doesn't matter who it is.

DS: Is there a lot of respect between you and other NHL tough guys?

RP: They know I come to play hard. I don't think they think I'm dirty but they know I can be a real prick out there. I use my stick a lot in ways maybe I shouldn't at times, but that's just my style. You can't teach an old dog new tricks. I've used my stick in midget, when I was younger. It not that I just use my stick to protect myself.

DS: Does it bother you that you may not get the recognition that more offensive players get?

RP: You may not get the kind of recognition you want all the time, but if the team is winning, it doesn't matter. If you do well, the whole team does well. Whether it's the guys that night or that year. The crowd is gonna love guys like Ziggy Palffy and tough guys like Ken Belanger and Mick Vukota. I know I'm a hitter. I know I'm not a fan favorite. But the p.r guys, those are the guys they promote, Palffy, Bryan Berard.

No, that's never bothered me. That's great for Ziggy, but it's never been there before, why should it be now? All I want is for the guys to know I played hard. I don't have to be on T.V.

If I do my job and the team wins then I benefit. Whether it's with a new contract or whatever. And nobody likes to lose. I know we have a lot of young guys on the team now and guys have to realize that if we don't win, other teams aren't going to watch a team that has lost a bunch of games over the years. Teams don't want that.

DS: Do you try and show a pure goal-scorer how to play more physically?
RP: I try to teach them how to defend themselves. In the last couple of years, I've tried to become more a leader on the team, try to show guys things. You teach them to always have their stick up. I know when I go to hit guys like Tony Amonte, he always has his stick up. Just get it up there. You won't get a penalty and it might make some guy think twice about taking another run at you if you got him in the shoulder.

Cam Russell

You go out and lose a fight and you can lose your confidence just like that.

Clary Mullane remembered Cam Russell well. Mullane was one of those minor hockey coaches who have such a profound influence on youngsters but who, too often, are forgotten once the player reaches stardom.

Mullane coached Russell on an Atom division team in Cole Harbour, Nova Scotia near Halifax in 1979-80 and saw something extraordinary in the lad.

"Cam was a super kid," said Mullane. "He was special from the first day I had him. He would take any advice."

Russell hasn't changed much in twenty years other than the fact that he has grown and matured into a hulking major league defenseman. When the residents of Cole Harbour honored him in August 1995, Russell reacted with the modesty and humility that have characterized him through the years.

"It's touching and a little embarrassing," said Cam. "I'm a guy who likes to sit in the background. I'm not much of a public figure. This is very flattering."

Russell is what gritty hockey is all about, working his way from the amateur ranks in Nova Scotia to a position on the Hull Olympiques of the Quebec Major Junior League. He played four years for Hull — with one Memorial Cup appearance — before being drafted in the third round in 1987 by the Chicago Blackhawks.

He went to the Stanley Cup Finals with Chicago in 1992 and has been with the Windy City sextet since his arrival in the NHL.

During the 1997-98 season, Russell was involved in a fight with Maple Leafs enforcer Tie Domi. As the fight went on, Russell became tangled in his sweater. As he fell backwards, the back of Russell's skull hit the ice. No one knew how serious the injury was and Russell lay flat on the ice for several seconds.

Though he received only a mild concussion, Russell had to be removed from the rink via a stretcher. While he was being attended to, his combatant, Domi, was preoccupied with Russell's condition. He phoned the Blackhawks dressing room between periods to check on his foe and was described by then Leafs coach Mike Murphy as "pretty much out of it for the rest of the game."

"It disturbed me," Domi said. "I kept thinking about him and what his family was feeling."

Following a Blackhawks practice, Russell huddled with Fischler Hockey Service correspondent Rick Sorci for a one-on-one. Their dialogue follows.

RICK SORCI: How did you get started in hockey?

CAM RUSSELL: Although I was born in Halifax, the family moved to Manitoba and, when I was three, my parents put me on the ice. My older brother already was playing so I just tagged along and watched him. I always wanted to play and after I got my skates, the rest was history. Out there we didn't have much else to do in the winter. Personally, I liked the competition, the pace, the speed — it all got to me and made me enjoy the game.

RS: You eventually returned to the Maritimes and wound up playing Junior hockey in Hull, Ontario.

CR: That route — from minor hockey to Juniors — is the one lots of Canadian kids take when they want to become professionals. So, I was sixteen-years-old when I left home to play in Hull and, as luck would have it, Pat Burns was coaching the Olympiques at the time.

RS: When did you decide to play the physical game?

CR: During my second year of Juniors with Burns. He wanted me to play more aggressively and I took his advice. From there, that style just sort of escalated within me. By the time I got to the NHL, I realized that the Blackhawks were lacking in that area — especially on defense — and if I was going to make it, I would have to play a lot more physical and a lot tougher.

RS: When the Blackhawks sent you to the minors — to Indianapolis — how did you react to the move from Juniors to pros?

CR: For starters, everything was quicker than at Hull and everyone was stronger and bigger and better. The game was elevated by one hundred percent. I had to adjust my speed and my strength and my toughness. My role was being a physical defenseman and I played every single game. I never was scratched. What I do remember was taking a lot of beatings down there because the opposition was so much bigger, stronger and older. I said to myself, "Cam, you're either going to sink or swim!" I knew that if I wanted to make the NHL, this was what it was all about. It was make or break for me in Indianapolis and, fortunately, I wound up making it to Chicago. I took my lumps and worked as hard as I could. The result was that I got called up twelve times to Chicago.

RS: Were you comfortable with the physical aspect?

CR: I realized that my ticket to the NHL was going to be physical play. As far as fighting goes, I don't think anybody is ever really comfortable with it. But I know that if I'm in a situation where I back down from someone, I would find it tough to look at myself in the mirror in the next couple of days. I like to confront my fears. I like to challenge myself and, win or lose, I feel better about it the next day. The best fight I had in Juniors was with Dan Vincelette. We went toe-to-toe for about a minute. It was a real slugfest, yet neither of us went down.

RS: When you got to the NHL, which fight — or fights — gave you some notice among your teammates or coaches?
CR: The first year I turned pro, I fought Kelly Buchberger of the Oilers. It was when Mike Keenan was coaching Chicago and he took notice — this was in training camp — that I had a pretty good fight with a darn good fighter. You see when I came up, the Blackhawks had just lost Behn Wilson, who had played tough hockey for them on defense. They were lacking the physical presence on the blue line.

RS: How much confidence do you get from a fight like that?
CR: Sometimes you tend to even get a little over-confident. Then, you go out and lose a fight and you can lose your confidence just like that! You really have to find a happy medium and stay on an even keel. You can't treat it like a roller coaster ride.

RS: Do you know why you get into a fight?
CR: In one case it would be because I feel that I have to come to the aid of one of my teammates. In another case, it might be an attempt on my part to give the team a little momentum. Or, it might be two tough guys who, sooner or later, are going to fight. Like I bump into someone, he bumps into me, there's eye contact. Who knows?

RS: When you prepare for a game, do you think about those things?
CR: Before a game, I look at the lineup and I might be thinking, "There's that guy on the opposition who I've fought a few times..." I know that if we bump and my opponent feels like going, we're probably going to fight.

RS: If you happened to be challenged and know you've just suffered a recent injury, would you tell the other guy something like, "Look, I've got a sore hand?"
CR: Yep. Most of the time, most of the guys are pretty respectful of that because they have been through the same ordeal themselves. Everybody, at one time or another, has a sore hand or a sore shoulder. If I tell someone on the other team who wants to go with me to lay off because I'm hurt, he'll

understand. He won't bother me after that. He'll play me hard and physical but he won't challenge me to a fight to try to make me look bad.

RS: Can a player make the NHL on fighting alone?
CR: Whether you're a tough guy or not, in order to play in the NHL you have to have the skills to get there in the first place. You can't make the majors on fighting alone. You have to have an all-round game. In my case, I know that I'm not there for fighting skills because I know that I'm not a great enough fighter that I can survive just doing that.

RS: Which NHL coaches did the most for you?
CR: Darryl Sutter had the biggest impact on me in terms of developing my NHL career. He knew how to get me going. He was an intense coach and knew when to kick me in the ass. Darryl also knew when to pat me on the back. If I wasn't giving one hundred percent, I always felt as if I was letting him down. He wasn't much of a verbal communicator; he would communicate through little punches on the shoulders and with his facial expressions. When I looked at him, I just knew what I was supposed to do and what he was thinking.

RS: A lot of young players come to training camp, seeming to look to take on the toughest veteran to make an impression. Is that true or not?
CR: Yeah, they go right to the top — to a Bob Probert. If a borderline player wants to make the team as a grinder, a tough guy or a role player, then he fights the toughest guy. He's basically saying, "Proby, you're either going to make my career or break my career." And Proby has ended a few careers.

RS: Do you remember your first NHL fight?
CR: Yep. It was against John Kordic in Toronto. I fought him twice that year — good fights. In the first one he got the better of me at the end of it and jumped me the next time we fought, but I gave it to him that time. Then, I got a little cocky and fought Dave Brown and he put me right on my ass. Dave was a tough cookie back then. He was in his prime.

RS: What did that prove?
CR: Win a fight and sometimes you get a little too big for your britches. I knocked someone down and, all of a sudden, I started thinking that all the fights were going to be like that one.

RS: Are fights predictable?
CR: The funny thing is that luck often plays a part in the outcome. Of a hundred punches thrown, sometimes only two will land. And if you get hit right on the nose or the chin, the guy getting hit is going to go down. But lots of times it's just luck.

RS: How come when a fight starts, hockey players drop their gloves but don't remove their helmets?

CR: I don't know why that is. I probably don't mind hurting my hand but I don't want to take ten in the head. I'd rather pound on a helmet than have someone pound on my head. Hitting a helmet with a fist hurts like hell. By the next day, when I put my gloves on, my hand is torn to pieces. It kills! Lots of times I ask myself why I do this. But I love the game and it's a great way to make a living.

RS: What's the most difficult aspect of being a tough guy?

CR: It's not an easy job. Injuries can happen. If you worry about fighting, then mentally it becomes a tough strain. In my first couple of years I spent a lot of time worrying about fights — the night before, sometimes a few days before. I'd be thinking, "Oh, my God, so-and-so is coming to town and I'm gonna have to fight him and he could really hurt me." Just thinking about it can be the hardest part because when I go in there and fight him, it might be something like, "Why did I even worry about that? I spent a week worrying about the fight and I came out of it looking great."

RS: Is it still that way for you?

CR: Not so much anymore. I got used to it; I grew out of it. Obviously, I still get scared sometimes but I learned to deal with it and it almost becomes fun. I talk myself into it and don't worry about it as much. I wouldn't say that nobody is scared of anybody because every player has a little fear out there, but that fear is good.

RS: Are there opponents from whom you would rather stay away?

CR: Of course there are guys who I would rather stay away from. But, as I have said, it's easier for me to look myself in the mirror the next day and say, "Y'know, hey, I went after that guy and I know he's a lot tougher than me, but I gave it my all." On the other hand, if I just tip-toed around for the next couple of days I would feel like, "Cam, you know you just didn't do it."

RS: What do you think about in the penalty box after a fight?

CR: If I had a good fight, I hope all my friends were up there watching the highlights. If I had a bad fight, I hope that nobody saw it on television. One thing I can't do in the box is pat myself on the back. I can't rest on my laurels if I have a good one. And, if I have a bad one, I get back on the horse because the next one could be a bad one or a good one. You never know.

RS: Tony Twist said that he didn't have too many fights recently because nobody wanted to go near him. Does he have a reputation?

Big Darren McCarty epitomizes what every NHL team looks for: an enforcer who can skate a regular shift, score goals, play well defensively and, on any given night, be the meanest guy on the ice.

Ready, willing and able, Sandy McCarthy will go toe to toe with anyone in the League and invariably leaves a lasting impression (or two).

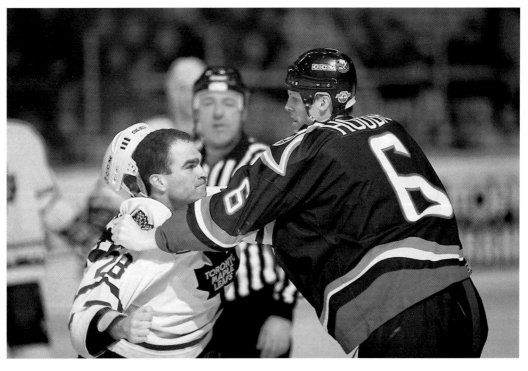

Smaller than the average enforcer, but with superior upper body strength and quickness, Tie Domi always (almost) ends up on top.

At the fore of a new breed of NHL enforcers is Donald Brashear, shown here after a punishing bout.

Many say that Bob Probert, in his prime with the Detroit Red Wings, was the greatest enforcer in hockey history. Perhaps more importantly, Probert could (and still can) play the game with skill.

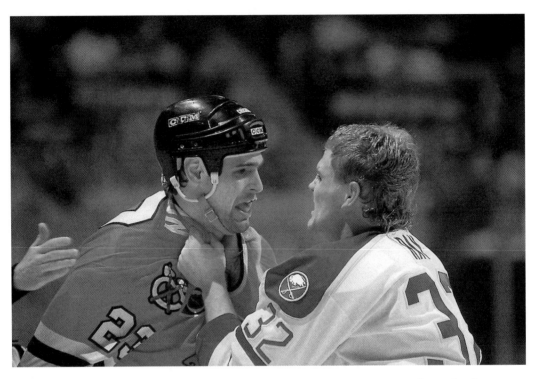

Stu "the Grim Reaper" Grimson prepares to explain reality to a confrontational — and soon to be regretful — Rob Ray of Buffalo.

Occasionally a star player takes a swing or two. Here big Eric Lindros rocks Smehlik of Buffalo.

Two players that define why enforcers exist in the NHL: Claude Lemieux (shown above) before Darren McCarty wiped the ice with his face after Lemieux savaged Detroit's Kris Draper with a potentially career-ending hit from behind; and Bryan Marchment, shown at right getting the worst from Bob Probert. Marchment's string of career-ending body checks is infamous.

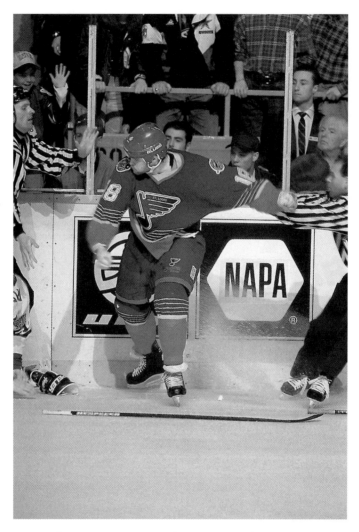

**The current heavyweight champion of the NHL,
Tony Twist, towers over a recent opponent
— note the distance kept by the refs.**

CR: Yeah, because he's a guy who could hurt you. He's put a few guys in the hospital. He's a big, strong player and if you fight him, you have to fight smart. Make sure you tie him up. He's so strong and muscular that it's tough to do that. He's a tough guy.

RS: How long can a tough guy exist in the NHL?

CR: A fellow such as Basil McRae played until he was thirty-five-years-old. The average tough guy plays until he's maybe thirty to thirty-two. But a lot of tough players are really good character guys who coaches like having in the room and around the younger guys. Coaches will keep that type around even if it means only playing them in half the games.

RS: Do fights get personal?

CR: I've never had a fight that's been personal.

RS: You fought Tie Domi, have you not?

CR: We fought in back-to-back games. In the first game it was a good fight, pretty even. In the second, I got a little luckier than he did. That's the bottom line. No matter how tough a guy is, he's going to win some and lose some. I haven't seen any player who has won every single fight.

RS: What kind of fighter are you?

CR: I've taken my share of lumps along the way. I'm happy if I tie a fight. I'm happy if I show up in a fight, win or lose. It all comes down to living with yourself when the day is over.

Ulf Samuelsson

I play a little bit physical, you know, a little bit aggravating at times.

What you have just read above is unquestionably the understatement among any self-descriptions ever made by a big-league hockey player.

For Ulf Samuelsson to describe himself as "a little bit aggravating" is roughly equivalent to suggesting that Godzilla, King of the Monsters, is a bit on the large side.

The Ulf Samuelsson that the civilized hockey world knows has alternately been rated the dirtiest player of modern hockey, a superb defensive defenseman, a backstabber, a Stanley Cup-winner and a realist among realists.

"Sometimes," said Samuelsson in a moment of candor, "I'm dirty. But sometimes this is a dirty game."

True enough.

But is it a dirty game because of The Big, Bad Ulf or is the atypical Swede merely adjusting to the war game on ice?

It is a question that could be answered either way but one thing is certain; Ulfie has been one of the most controversial major leaguers ever since a collision between the Swede and Boston Bruins power forward Cam Neely virtually ended the latter's career as a top performer.

"Ulf always was a rough player," said Christer Rockstrom, the Rangers' Swedish-based scout. "When I saw him as a Junior in Sweden, he played the same style. He was fearless and hitting and running people. You could see the instinct. He wasn't as mean as he became in the NHL. He also wasn't as good. He wasn't as controlled."

By the age of sixteen, Samuelsson had turned pro with the Leksard team in Sweden. By 1984 he was with the Hartford Whalers and instantly proved that a Scandinavian could be as tough as a North American pro.

"There were two reasons why Swedish players were not as rough as those in the NHL," Ulf explained. "First, the ice surface in Europe is bigger, so there's more room for skating. Second, the North American mentality is stronger when it comes to hockey."

While Samuelsson has put himself in league with other pests such as Claude Lemieux, the reactions from other NHL foes has been uniformly harsh. Consider these reviews:

Cam Neely: "I don't have any respect for him."

Bernie Nicholls: "I hate the guy."

Mike Modano: "Really, all he's trying to do is hurt you and knock you out of the game."

Samuelsson has heard it all. When the New York Rangers traded for him, they were making a statement. They wanted a menacing player.

"I knew what they expected of me," Samuelsson agreed.

The bromide states that he who lives by the sword dies by the sword. Ulf is still alive but he has had some dangerous moments, not the least of which was a sucker punch delivered by Toronto Maple Leafs' enforcer Tie Domi that knocked Samuelsson unconscious.

As the hockey world awaited disciplinarian action against Domi, veteran defenseman Mat Schneider was asked his thoughts about a penalty against the Leaf.

"For hitting Ulf? A bonus," was Schneider's reply.

What's fascinating about Samuelsson is that he *is* tough and has been one of the most efficient NHL defensemen for a decade but his failure to actually drop his gloves and fight in the traditional North American style is what grates individuals such as Mike Milbury and longtime savant of hockey violence Don (Grapes) Cherry.

When asked to evaluate Samuelsson, Cherry offered a double-edged sword in return.

"For starters, Ulf is a rough, tough player who is very effective. On the other hand, he is a cheap-shot artist. It's one thing to play that way if, when someone challenges you, you stand up for yourself. The trouble is, Ulf is a guy wearing all that equipment and the only thing that's exposed on him is a little bit of his ear."

On and on the criticism goes while on and on Samuelsson continues to play the game on ice in a manner that, to him, seems to be the role of an ultimate warrior.

"If players on other teams want to say things about me," Ulf concluded, "and if someone wants to write something in the paper, that's fine with me."

By Samuelsson's standard it has been fine for fifteen years of top-grade major league hockey, whether the enemy likes it or not.

During a respite after a scrimmage at the Rangers' practice facility in Rye, New York, Samuelsson participated in a one-on-one interview with Fischler Hockey Service correspondent Amy Spencer. Their conversation follows:

AMY SPENCER: How did Ulf Samuelsson get to be what he is today?

ULF SAMUELSSON: I'm from a town called Fagersta in Sweden. It's a steel mill town and I grew up there into mid-teens. Then, I moved to a place called Leksand

and played there for three years in the Elite League until I came to North America and signed with Hartford when I was twenty-years-old. As a child, I learned to skate on a frozen lake that was situated right behind our house. I joined my first organized team when I was nine. I played other sports besides hockey. I was on my school team for basketball, handball, swimming and track and field.

AS: Were you always a keen competitor?
US: Always. I can remember as a kid playing in a game and when we lost I would be crying. I always had that spirit within me.

AS: At what point did you realize you had a specific knack for agitation?
US: It's always been there. Part of it is that I am very competitive and that's what really helped me to get to where I've gone so far. The bottom line is that I'm basically a defensive defenseman. I get to play against the top lines and I play a little physical, a little bit aggravating at times. That's just the way I am.

AS: As a Swede, when did you realistically think about the NHL as a possibility?
US: When I was seventeen and had broken into the Swedish Elite League. In my estimation it is the second best league in the world. By the time I was twenty, I could have stayed home for a year or two longer, but I took the chance on coming over to Hartford and it worked. Remember, I wasn't the first. My countryman, Borje Salming — he was my hero when I was a kid — had played for the Toronto Maple Leafs in the 1970s and did very well in the NHL. He was my hero and I started watching him on television.

AS: Salming never played the mean, tough game that you brought to North America. What do you feel you've done to toughen the image of European players in the NHL?
US: The only thing I've done is play my style over here. Keep in mind that this is the same style that I have always played. And it is the same style that a lot of other people play in Sweden as well. As a matter of fact, a few years back it was pretty complicated to get players over here. The NHL teams went after the high-skilled Europeans — the offensive defensemen, the goal scorers — yet there always were grinders in Sweden. The thing was there were so many more of the grinders here in North America to pick from so the NHL teams just grabbed them right here.

AS: What was the biggest adjustment you had to make to the North American game?
US: Everything was smaller in the NHL because of the different rink size. I had grown up accustomed to the big European rinks and then, all of a sudden, when I get to Hartford I'm on the eighty-five by two-hundred size rink. I

learned that everything happens quicker in the NHL and there are more opportunities for physical play. That was the only major change for me. But I had to make that adjustment. I played in the minors for thirty games or so. It took me almost half a season to get used to the faster pace but once I got the knack of it everything was all right.

AS: Did you get involved in more fights as a young NHL player than as a veteran?
US: In my first couple of years with Hartford I was involved in a few more fights than I have been lately. Now people know what kind of style I play and to continue that style, I know that I'm going to get beat up a few times. But if I keep coming back, they're not going to bother me.

AS: What was it like being traded for the first time — from Hartford to Pittsburgh?
US: It was hard, really hard. I had built up friendships with the Whalers and the people in Hartford but in the end the move to the Penguins turned out to be all to the good. Pittsburgh needed players like myself and Ronnie Francis at the time and we fit right in with Mario Lemieux and the others. Then, the team started going well and in 1991 I got a special thrill in that we beat Minnesota in the Finals and won the Stanley Cup.

AS: Although you're not known for your offense, you did score the Cup-winning goal for Pittsburgh.
US: Yeah (Laughs). It was a very nervous game for us. We were up 1-0 on the North Stars and I came out at the end of a power play. I took a shot from the blue line and the puck sort of trickled its way into the net behind Jon Casey. It was a strange game. We went up 2-0, then it was three, four, five, six and seven. I still couldn't believe that we were up that much and then time was running out. We ended up winning by a score of 8-0. That *was* unbelievable and the most special experience I ever had as a player. Winning a Stanley Cup is the ultimate for an NHL player. To win it for the first time, why there's nothing like it in my mind. For me it was the ultimate dream come true.

AS: While you were a Penguin, what incident highlighted you as a really tough guy?
US: The biggest one was the Cam Neely incident. It was some kind of leg injury. I don't know exactly what it was. I really don't know exactly what happened but I know that it caused problems for him.

AS: Did you ever get hurt in incidents such as that?
US: Oh, yeah. When two guys are coming together at full speed — which is what happens a lot when I play — sometimes somebody is going to get hurt. Sometimes it is me and sometimes it is the other guy.

AS: While you were in Pittsburgh, who made the biggest impression on you as a player?

US: Bob Johnson, who had coached the Penguins before he got ill. He was an extraordinary man.

AS: How difficult was the trade that sent you from Pittsburgh to the Rangers?

US: It was not as tough as the first trade from the Whalers to the Penguins. By this time I had been in the league for many years and I was well aware that if I was around so long, there's a possibility of being traded. The deal to New York was easier although it took me from twenty to thirty games to really start playing well for the Rangers. I remember struggling for the first half of that season before finding the groove.

AS: When you played against Wayne Gretzky, did you play less rough against him because he was Wayne Gretzky?

US: Probably. I gave him a little more room. In the beginning I did try to hit him a few times but I found that that was impossible. Wayne sees those hits coming so far ahead. What I learned was that I had to limit his ice time with the puck. I learned that I always had to be aware of him because he puts himself in a position so that when he gets the puck, he's always going to have a couple of seconds to make the moves. Same with a player like Jaromir Jagr. Sometimes I think I have him but he'll throw a new move at me. Players like Jagr and Gretzky always have a little extra. Being a defensemen against guys like that is fun and hard at the same time.

AS: Because of your style of play, you have to be aware of the referees. How do you "work" the officials?

US: The "art" of handling the referees is to pretty much leave them alone. They have a very hard job and I'm at the point in my career right now where I try not to make too many outbursts. I respect the work they do and how hard it is for one man to cover everything with one set of eyes. I have respect for the referees.

AS: You have been described as "The Agitator Extraordinaire." What, if anything, agitates you?

US: Losing.

AS: How does your on-ice persona compare with your off-ice personality?

US: It's a job I have on the ice. I don't run around home and beat up my kids. I don't try to trip my kids.

AS: How has the league changed with regards to fighting since your rookie season?

US: It's a lot different. There aren't too many five-on-five brawls anymore. That's good because the NHL is trying to sell the game in the households but I still think there should be some fighting left. It keeps players honest and fans like it, too. Nowadays, the league is trying to get rid of all the holding and trying to get more scoring, more open games. That's one of the reasons why Mario Lemieux retired so early, because he was sick and tired of it.

AS: In retrospect, do you have any regrets about your career?
US: I like to battle as hard as I can but at the same time I don't like to see myself — or anyone else — get injured long-term. Sometimes, stuff like that has happened and I don't feel too good about that.

Reid Simpson

I make sure that if I get beaten, I'm going to go after that guy again.

There is absolutely nothing stereotypical about Reid Simpson, the fighter.

Away from the rink, his demeanor suggests a young sociology professor from your local university.

He is scholarly, articulate, engaging and handsome in a Matthew Broderick kind of way.

The only thing obvious about Simpson, the battler, is his home town — Flin Flon, Manitoba.

Some of the National Hockey League's most tenacious performers — if not the best fighters — have come from the mining community not far from Hudson's Bay. Bobby Clarke, who captained the Philadelphia Flyers to Stanley Cups in 1974 and 1975, is one of Flin Flon's most popular graduates. Another is Gerry Hart, a doughty defenseman who did considerable fighting for the Islanders during the 1970s.

The Flin Flon Bombers Junior team had become a legend in Western Canada long before Simpson had become a teenager and it was axiomatic that if you could handle the bitter Flin Flon winters, you could handle just about anything, including fisticuffs in the NHL.

Simpson not only survived the sub-zero temperatures but thrived on every hockey rink in which he played. He was good enough to move from his home town to New Westminster of the Western Hockey League. A year later he was skating for Prince Albert of the WHL and eventually caught the eye of Philadelphia scouts. In 1989, the Flyers made him their third choice in the Entry Draft (72d overall) and in 1989-90 promoted him to their Hershey farm team in the American Hockey League. He made his NHL debut during the 1991-92 season but it hardly was auspicious. One game as a Flyer was the extent of his career on Broad Street. The Minnesota North Stars next signed him as a free agent and, lo and behold, he played a grand total of one NHL game for his second big-league club. But on March 21, 1994 Simpson's career took an upturn.

Dealt to the New Jersey Devils, he was assigned to their Albany farm club in the AHL and in the spring of 1995 was a prime factor in the River Rats march to the Calder Cup, emblematic of the league's playoff championship. He was promoted to the big club a season later and appeared destined for a lengthy career as one of New Jersey's prime ice cops, but a series of injuries braked his progress and in the middle of the 1997-98 season he was dealt to the Chicago Blackhawks.

Simpson's size is advertised as 6-2, 220 pounds but that appears overly generous to those who have seen him up close. At best, he is a middleweight and sometimes actually appears smaller than that. But there's no question about his toughness nor about his ability to throw punches.

"If he doesn't get hurt," noted one hockey fight critic, "Simpson could be one of the toughest players in the league."

Based on his early history as an NHL pugilist, that remains a big if.

Simpson was interviewed at Continental Airlines Arena in East Rutherford, New Jersey by Fischler Hockey Service reporter Eric Marin. The oral history follows:

Flin Flon, where I grew up, is about nine hours North of Winnipeg. To people in the United States, that's considered pretty far North, but for Canadians, it's just another small town along the way.

What made it famous, in a way, was the fact that Bobby Clarke came from Flin Flon. He was friends with my parents when I was growing up so I can say that I've known him since I was a little kid. When I was just starting to play hockey at home was when Clarke — and the Philadelphia Flyers — won their two Stanley Cups in 1974 and 1975. He was quite a hero in our town and what made it even neater was that he would come back to Flin Flon every Summer after the NHL season was over.

Because of Clarke, people all over the National Hockey League got to know about our town and our Junior team, the Flin Flon Bombers. It was always known that teams from Flin Flon would be tough, rugged and fight for everything they had to in order to win a tournament. That was ingrained in just about every hockey player who grew up in my neighborhood and it was ingrained in me when I was seven-years-old playing on the Squirt hockey level.

Players who had gone from Flin Flon to the NHL helped spread the reputation. Gerry Hart went to the Islanders and he was quite a fighter. Later on it was Ken Baumgartner. He came out of the Western Junior League, made it to the NHL, and fought all over the place.

I can vividly recall that when I started playing for New Westminster in British Columbia, I was singled out as another one of those guys from Flin Flon. People would point to me and say, "There's another one of those fighters." The way I felt was that I didn't want to let down my home town's reputation, so I just wanted to be that type of player so everyone knew what I was capable of doing.

Western Canadian players always have prided themselves on being tough. A lot of graduates of Western teams are kids who came right off the farms.

Their way of life was tough from the beginning because life on the prairies —
just coping with the mean winters — can be quite a challenge. Toughness is
ingrained in the people and it's also a pride thing. The feeling is that we'll do
anything to win no matter how much physical work is involved.

This feeling starts at an early age. In my case, I was five. I was fortunate.
I had a rink right beside our house and lots of times I would go out in the cold
without even putting my skates on and play hockey in my boots. It didn't matter what day it was, I did it all the time.

My move upward in hockey was not smooth. I started playing on the
organized level when I was seven years old but after two years I quit because
I wasn't very good, and also I wasn't playing very much. In retrospect, quitting was one of the best things I ever did because I came back the next year
and enjoyed playing again. From then on, it was non-stop playing. My game
improved and I wound up being the leading scorer in my group. Obviously,
when you are doing well, you want to continue at it and at that point in time
I was loving every minute I was on the ice.

Not once did I dream about making it in the NHL. Never. I played hockey because I liked playing hockey. No more. No less. It was that way through
my early teens and then, when I was seventeen, I got lucky. I went to Prince
Albert, Saskatchewan and got a chance to play there. I say lucky because I
had played two games in New Westminster at the age of sixteen but at that
point I wasn't good enough for the league. I returned to Flin Flon, played
another year at home, and then got the break to skate for Prince Albert.

When I say it was a break, I mean that I just phoned the club from Flin
Flon and asked if I could try out for the team. They knew nothing about me
in Prince Albert but they were good enough to at least give me a chance to try
out even though I was a walk-on and their roster could easily have been filled.
Looking backward, I have to say that that was the turning point of my hockey career in the sense that I got a chance to play for some awfully good coaches, especially Rick Wilson.

I learned a lot in Prince Albert including how to conduct myself as a person both on and off the ice. Wilson also gave me some good advice about
improving my game. This was in my second year at Prince Albert, 1987-88,
and I had come off the ice after having what, for me, was a mediocre practice.
"How do you think you're doing?" he asked.

I can't remember exactly what I said but I do remember what he told me
after I got finished answering him. Rick told me that there are two things that
can happen when you come to the rink. "You're either going to take a step forward," he explained, "and improve yourself. Or, you're going to take a step
backward and go in the other direction. You're never going to stay in the same
spot. Don't put in a half-ass effort or your game will slip and you don't want
that to happen."

Wilson made me realize that I had to give my best every day that I came to the rink and that advice made me a better hockey player. I worked harder and, sure enough, I got a little better. Not that it meant that I was a sure-fire star. Far from it. When I was seventeen, I was not an NHL prospect. But I kept working at my game and working and working. First, I started out as a fourth-liner and eventually progressed to the first line.

I always fought a lot whether I was playing five minutes or thirty minutes a game. By the end of a season in Juniors, I would have totalled up to thirty to thirty-five fights. The question was, how much could I contribute in other parts of the game besides the fighting. But I had no illusions about fighting. It was something that had to be done and it was something that I had done going back to my kid days in Flin Flon.

My first hockey fight? I was ten-years-old at the time. The rules about fighting were different back home than they are now in that we didn't wear face masks when we played. If a player got into a fight, he would be suspended or if you punched someone in the face you would get suspended as well. On the neighborhood rinks it was a little different. Something would be going on and the next thing you knew someone would be punching someone else. On some days on the outdoor rinks, it was like neighborhood fights would break out although it was never anything very personal.

The thinking was, "Well, that's hockey," so you just fought. It wasn't like you were in a schoolyard and you would fight a guy where that was all it was. On the rink it was part of the game and accepted back where I came from. At the same time, even at that kids level, you develop a sense that there are some fellows who don't want to get involved in the fighting. But I must say, where I grew up, nobody would let intimidation get to him. You would just suck it up and play no matter what.

I was smart enough to realize what moved me upwards in Juniors and eventually in the minor pros. For sure it was because of the fighting; there's absolutely no doubt about it. Anyone who plays a tough game and gets into fights and thinks for a minute that the fighting hasn't given him an extra chance to get to the higher level is really fooling himself.

I see that reaction in some players because in those cases, their mentality is such that they actually don't like fighting. They do it because there's pressure and they are trying to live up to an image. As time goes by, that type of individual might get better as a player and fight less, thinking, "Hey, I don't have to fight anymore because I can really play the game." So that player removes fighting from his repertoire. But then it doesn't work anymore. All of a sudden, you'll hear, "Wow! My game isn't quite as good as it used to be." He looks back and realizes that he's not able to make that transition to the next level because he took fighting out of his game.

Me, I recognized early that that was going to be a big part of why I was going to make the NHL. I knew that I had to get as good at that as possible and never change. Granted, that's hard. As you get older, new guys come up and every night there's a new challenge as far as fighting goes. You might lose a couple here and there and start doubting yourself, wondering if you still have it. Before you know it, you're in a rut.

I've made a concerted effort in my heart and in my mind to always believe that I'm as good a fighter as anyone else. I have to tell myself that when I go on the ice that I'm the toughest guy out there. I can never believe anything else because if I starting thinking negatively, that maybe someone else is bigger or stronger than me. That's when I'm going to get beaten and I won't be winning fights anymore.

Naturally, the role of enforcer is not favored by everyone out there in the image business. For example, every once in a while I'll meet someone who will say, "Oh, you're the goon on the team." When I hear that, I say to myself, "Yeah, I am." But, personally, I don't like to think that fighting is all I can do. I have come to grips with the fact that fighting has gotten me to the NHL but there's more to me than being an enforcer. I'm not happy when people think because of what I do, my intellect is low. I often feel like explaining to them, "Hey, don't knock my job; I'm doing the best I can."

Despite the knocks, I've gotten a lot of satisfaction out of what I have accomplished especially since I can remember when I was younger and people would be putting me down. "You're never going to make it. Why are you even bothering?" are words I heard a lot. Now I look back and wonder about the people who said those things and what they are doing with their lives right now. There were always a few people who tried to make me feel ridiculous for thinking I could play in the National Hockey League. My answer to them was learning to be a contributor to every team on which I played; fighting, yes, but also getting fifty or sixty points in a season.

When I was on my way up through the minors, the term "goon" was heard often around hockey rinks. Since then the game has changed and I don't believe that there are goons anymore. Nowadays teams have to be able to put players on the ice who can get the job done in all circumstances. As a limited skills player, I have to know that defensively I have to be as good or better than anyone on the ice at that particular time. And I must remember what my role is; which is to say if I'm going to hit an opponent every time I get a chance, I have to make sure to finish my checks. And if I do get a chance to make an offensive play, I have to take that chance and go for it.

By the same token, every time I go on the ice I'm prepared to be the first guy fighting. I have always had a two games to one fight ratio. I have known that every two or three games I'm going to get into my fight. I've always included that in my thinking and made it a part of my game. I concentrate on that and find that just thinking about it keeps me sharp. If the game is not going well for my team — or if someone on my line gets hit in a way that I don't feel is warranted, or if the opposition has a guy out there doing what I'm doing, then I have to step up to the plate and deliver my challenge. If I challenge someone and he doesn't stand up, then it's going to be noticeable. The whole bench can see that. It's like I'm telling that team that I'm going to win the game. If they don't like it, they can back off.

I wouldn't be naive enough to suggest that I have won all my fights. Far from it. Nobody goes through an NHL career winning every single fight. I've lost some bad ones but I never reconsidered being a tough guy because of those defeats. What the loss made me do was want to fight that guy again. Every so often any fighter will get hit so hard his reaction will be something like, "Wow! That was a hard one." It will set the player back but he can't let that feeling fester in him. He can't afford to think about it too much and he can't afford to wait too long before fighting that guy again. The more you think negative in a situation such as that, the more doubt you create in your mind.

A lot has been said and written about the mentality and the image of enforcers. I respect everyone I fight. It's important to have respect for your opponent so that no one surprises you. I learned that there is a difference between the fighters in the AHL and the NHL and it is a big difference. To fight in the NHL, you have to be one of the best and you have to establish yourself fast once you get to the top. You have to challenge the top guys because word gets around about the new fighters very fast. When I was with the Devils at the start of the 1997-98 season I could see that type of reaction setting in with my teammate Krzysztof Oliwa who had been with me for a while in Albany.

Oliwa knew right off the bat that he had to fight and he knew that he had better do it well. He had to be hungry and prove himself and it was a continual process for him all season. To his credit, he never forgot what got him to the top and he stayed with the big team all season and into the playoffs.

Some players lose that fire after a while. Dave Manson of the Canadiens is an example. When he first came to the NHL, he had fire in his eyes. As time went on it cooled a bit. Then younger guys realized that they wanted to hit Manson a bit more. It's a continual process of proving yourself. Not that I'm knocking Dave Manson. He has taken his game to a point where he contributes in other ways such as working the power play and killing penalties so he doesn't have to fight to get his job done.

I don't have that luxury. If I don't fight for two or three weeks I feel that something is missing from my game. All of a sudden I'll notice that I'm playing against the same team a few times in a short period and that I haven't asserted myself physically. Suddenly, the opposition will be pushing me back a bit, thinking that I'm not going to fight anymore. Then, I have to step back in and beat someone up. All of a sudden, it comes around and I get room again. I know that that's how I'm going to get my space on the ice.

The people in the stands react to fights differently than we fighters our-selves. Usually, the crowd reacts to the peripheral, superficial stuff. They fig-ure that the player who falls on top of the other guy is the one who won the fight but that's often not the case. What the crowd misses are the inside blows. There have been many times when I clocked an opponent and the crowd real-ly didn't understand how hard the blow was — and vice versa. After fights I've won, I know that the other guy is thinking, "Jesus Christ, he really hit me hard." Yet the audience may not have even see the punch.

After winning a fight like that, if I don't hear from the guy I've beaten right away, I'll know that he doesn't want to fight or go through that again. That's when I know that I've made a statement and maybe the other fellow will tell a few teammates about it and the others will know that they don't want to go through the same trouble themselves. On the other hand, I can think of some players who I have beaten badly early in a game who came out in the third peri-od and wanted to fight again. When that happens, I try to figure out what I have to do to get my point across. By the same token, those are the same guys you can always count on to be there. And I, for one, want to be among those guys.

Players like myself, Probert, Domi, who have made it to the NHL level have a mutual respect for one another. If they've gotten this far, they must be doing something right. But because a player is a good fighter does not neces-sarily mean that he's a good guy. I respect a guy for what he is off the ice as much as on the ice. If he's a jerk off the ice, I might respect his fighting abil-ity but not the fact that he's a jerk and it will make me want to beat him even more. Fortunately, there aren't many jerks in hockey and most of the fighters are genuinely nice guys away from the rink. They tend to be more intelligent than most people would think. You almost have to be because we are smart enough to realize what got us to this level.

Fighting styles have changed since I began playing on a competitive level. In the old days, bench-clearing brawls were commonplace but that turned off a lot of people and you don't see it anymore in the NHL. The kind of sponta-neous fighting we now have and the rules that the NHL has in place are per-fect. If a player does not want to fight, he does not have to fight. Nor is a coach going to tell a certain player to fight on a certain night. That kind of hockey doesn't work anymore, although it was common practice in the old days. I can assure you that when I was playing Junior hockey, coaches would send me out there to fight.

Not that I didn't want to; far from it. I've played for coaches who would just give me a look and when I saw their eyes I knew what I was supposed to do. I did-n't have to be a rocket scientist to understand what was expected from me in situ-ations like that. If the club was not playing well and the coach suddenly put me out there, I knew he wasn't putting me on the ice to score a goal; it was to start a fight.

From time to time hockey critics argue that fighting should be taken out of the game, but I disagree. The NHL would be stupid to eliminate it because the fans in the stands get pretty excited when a fight starts. People don't run to the concession stands to get drinks when fights start. Granted, there are some fans who can do without fisticuffs but they can still enjoy hockey whether there's fighting or not. I'm sure most fans understand why fights happen; there are a dozen players in an enclosed area and ten of them on the ice are skating at high speed with sticks in their hands. Furthermore, they are allowed to hit the opposition as hard as they want. In a situation like that, tempers will flare, fights happen spontaneously and in a matter of minutes, it's over with.

I've studied fights on videos going back to the 1970s and the one thing I notice is that there has been a change in strategy. About twenty years ago the fighters would just stand back and throw punches. The player who could land the most and move the best would win. More recently, guys got into the wrestling mode but in the last three or so years, it seems as if we're back to the Irish boxing, where you paint a line on the ground and stand there and just punch each other. That's the way I always fought and I have no problem with that.

I don't know what brought about the change to just throwing punches again but a couple of players seemed to do it a lot better than others and they set an example. I remember when the Devils got big Troy Crowder and he dominated so many fights. Same with Bob Probert in Detroit and, more recently, in Chicago. Probert just sticks his neck out and trades punches. That type of fighter wins more fights.

Some young guys have come along and asked older guys how to fight. They want tips about grabbing arms and whatnot. I was never into that and if any kid ever asked me how to be a better fighter, I would say, "Listen, kid. You see his face — punch it!" That's all you need to know. It's no secret.

I've always been a self-learner but I watched other good fighters just to study styles. When I was with the Devils, I kept my eye on Lyle Odelein, the defenseman. He was one of several who could throw the punches. And let me tell you, it's nice to be on a team when there are five or six other guys who are good fighters; who will support you when the going gets tough. I say that because I have been on teams where I was the only guy who threw 'em and that can be a lonely situation.

If you were to ask me which fighter I most respect the most it would be Probert. He went through some tough times off-ice but got over them and what he brought to the team on the ice — that intangible — is something that not many other players can do. His physical and mental presence have been phenomenal for any club on which he's played. I can say firsthand that when Probert is on the ice, he's the one guy I know is there. What's more, he has proven it over and over, shift by shift, game by game. I know what it's like. When I was a Devil, I went toe-to-toe with Bob.

It was my kind of fight. I hit him with everything I had and he hit me pretty good, too. It was a good fight but I wouldn't say I won and, then again, I wouldn't say I lost it.

Turner Stevenson

The tough guys aren't the problem in hockey. They're not the ones running around two-handing guys. They're not the ones breaking sticks over heads or doing anything stupid like that.

There's something about rural British Columbia that breeds toughness and honesty in hockey players.

Those who watched the Philadelphia Flyers win consecutive Stanley Cups in 1974 and 1975 will remember the exuberance and energy generated by the British Columbians Joe and Jim Watson. No less an example is the New York Islanders Stanley Cup hero from 1980, Bob Nystrom, another native of B.C.

Turner Stevenson is cut from the same lumber.

Born and bred in Canada's westernmost Province, he learned his hockey in a frontier-style and carried those values with him through Junior hockey, the American League and, finally, the National Hockey League.

His indefatigability has shown through even in the most dismal Montreal Canadiens losses. During the 1997 playoffs between the Habs and New Jersey Devils, Stevenson caught the eye of Devils television analyst Chico Resch for his superb teamsmanship.

"Turner has the kind of attitude you want to see on your team if you're the coach," said Resch.

Admittedly not the heavyweight champion of the NHL — nor even a contender — Stevenson nevertheless has been an "I'll take on anyone" kind of competitor and the Canadiens have been all the better for it.

The Habs picked him as their first choice — twelfth overall — in the 1990 Entry Draft. He bounced up and down from the AHL to the NHL until the 1994-95 season, which was severely curtailed by the lockout. Once the labor dispute was settled, Stevenson was called up to the big club to stay.

Following a Canadiens practice, Turner was interviewed by Fischler Hockey Service Montreal correspondent Sean Farrell. The oral history which followed was gleaned from that one-on-one.

When I was a kid I wanted to be like Theo Fleury. He was my idol back in MacKenzie, British Columbia, the first place that I remember playing hockey. Of course, at that age — about four — I wasn't even thinking about the NHL. Hockey was a hobby and my dad played along with me.

I can remember the very first time I put on a pair of skates. It was tough in the beginning but after awhile I got the hang of it. There was an outdoor rink right next to where we lived so I had no problem with ice time and got encouragement from everyone in my family.

There were five kids; myself and four sisters — three older and one younger. My parents had their hands full with us. One minute they were driving me to hockey and the next they were taking my sisters to a swim meet. They sacrificed a lot for us and I'll never forget them for that.

Even, better — sports-wise — they never pushed me. They would come to the games and encourage me whereas other parents would be heavy-handed. Lots of times the heavy-handed father is trying to live his fantasy as a hockey player through his son. Believe me, that kind of attitude ruined a lot of good players and good kids. They just get fed up being pushed by their parents and chuck it all.

The only thing my father would say was, "Turner, always go out and work hard and try to be the hardest-working guy on your team. That's the one thing you can control — working hard."

What's interesting is that that's the same message that NHL coaches say even now. They all stress the value of the work ethic; not to worry about goals and everything else — just work your hardest and everything will fall into place. In retrospect, my father gave me good advice.

The difference between the way my father handled my hockey growth and my mother was in their respective styles. My mom did less talking and more worrying — like all mothers. She was more of the quiet motivator. She was the spiritual one who lifted me up when I was down.

Since I came from a small town, it wasn't easy to get a lot of kids my age playing hockey. For instance, when I was five years old, I had to play with kids who were seven and eight. I remember on Friday nights, I would go to a public skate at the rink, then there would be the game, and then the ice would be free. I would stay at the rink until two to three in the morning, all by myself, shooting, skating. That experience helped a lot in developing my game. That was a fun time to be a kid.

By the time I reached the age of nine, I had grown some. I was the biggest kid in my hockey group. I began to hit during the games and played at a decent speed. Even though I was a Theo Fleury fan, I rooted for the good Montreal Canadiens teams as well as the Edmonton Oilers. Once a year we would travel to Edmonton and catch an Oilers game at Northlands Coliseum.

I wasn't sure what position I wanted to play — except that I didn't want to be a goalie. I was hit in the face by a puck once and that was enough goaltending for me. I played defense for a couple of years and got better by the season. By the time I reached the age of thirteen, my chances of improving as a hockey player were limited in MacKenzie and my father knew it.

He also realized that I was really into the game and that there was a higher quality of hockey in Prince George, British Columbia. "Do you want to move to Prince George and play there?" he asked me.

"Sure," I said.

This would be a great opportunity for me because one of my sisters lived there and I could live with her while improving my hockey. It was a terrific move for me because I had two good years at Prince George and in my second season we won the Provincial hockey championship for British Columbia.

From the Prince George experience on, I stayed up front and forgot about the idea of being a defenseman. By now I was beginning to think about making hockey a career. Watching Wayne Gretzky and the Oilers in Edmonton really got my juices going and I began dreaming about the NHL and scoring an overtime goal in Montreal or Toronto. Wherever!

What made the dream come closer was the way I improved at Prince George. That was the stepping stone for Junior hockey so the next question was who would want me and if anyone did want me, where would I go?

In those days the Western Junior Hockey League didn't have a draft but I got "listed" to play with the Seattle team. It was a good-news-bad-news scenario in that Seattle had not been a good organization until then but the club had just brought in Barry Melrose, the former NHL defenseman, and Russ Farwell, who already had made a name for himself as a top general manager in Medicine Hat. Melrose, who also had been at Medicine Hat, would be the coach and Farwell would be the manager.

Melrose made all the difference in the world for me. He was one of the greatest coaches. I know first-hand because the truth was that when I got to Seattle I wasn't really good enough to play in the WHL. But by Christmas time, I was a regular and getting better by the month.

One of the turning-points was a conversation I had with Melrose. He sat down with me and said, "Look at your assets. You're six-foot-three. Use your size."

The turnaround for me didn't happen overnight. I wasn't really a physical player until after my first year of Juniors. But once I decided which route I would take, I built from there. In my second year at Seattle, I was playing even better and Melrose told me, "You've got a good chance of going in the first round of the Entry Draft."

When I realized that, I knew that I had to finish strong. Up until then, I was basically playing hockey for fun but all of a sudden it became like a business and the draft was one of the things I would focus on to make my hockey better.

Meanwhile, a lot of good things were happening to me. I was named to Canada's World Junior Team and became a teammate of players such as Eric Lindros, Paul Kariya, Darryl Sydor and Scott Neidermayer, plus Trevor Kidd was our goalie. We had a great team but we had a bad year; it was just a matter of the club not coming together at the right time. Nevertheless, it still was a wonderful experience for me, personally. Playing for Canada was quite an honor and the trip to Germany was quite a learning experience as well. But with the talent we had, we should have won. This was one underachieving club, for sure.

One of the things I learned in Europe was that the Olympic-size ice surface is much better for the game. I know the NHL people are always saying that it's too big but the problem with big-league hockey today is that the players are so huge there no longer is room out there on an 85 by 200-foot rink. It would benefit the NHL if we got the bigger ice because then the skilled players like Jaromir Jagr, Eric Lindros and John LeClair would have some room to make the neat plays.

Win or lose, making the World Junior Team was the highlight of my pre-NHL career. That and playing for Melrose. Barry was a very special kind of coach. He had a knack of sitting down with his players and working with them the way very few other coaches do. And he infused a work ethic in all of his skaters. A coach like that makes a player want to play for him and work hard for him.

He was typical of those workhorse NHL players who made his way to the minors and who makes a great coach because he knew what it took to get there. Barry was able to take a kid with some talent and work him harder so that he could go that extra mile and be successful. That's the attitude he put into me and it was one of the elements that helped me get drafted as high as I did.

That Spring of 1990 the Entry Draft was held in Vancouver and that was a break for me. It meant that my family could simply come down from their home in B.C. and not have to travel cross-country to a place like Buffalo or Montreal or whatever. Plus, I had a lot of relatives living in Vancouver so they showed up as well.

Of course, I was nervous. All draft-eligible kids worry about where they are going to get picked — or whether they're going to get selected at all. It's a big day for a lot of kids but the build-up — all the TV, press and radio hype — can lead to awfully big letdowns. Kids my age show up, expecting to be drafted and when they don't hear their name called all afternoon, it's almost the end of the world for them.

Myself, I didn't think I would go as high as I did go and I had no idea the Canadiens were even interested. Nobody from Montreal even interviewed me the way others did before the Draft. I had met plenty of representatives from teams. I did interviews and talked to general managers, but not from the Habs.

What I did know was that some experts had rated me seventeenth or eighteenth and Montreal was picking twelfth. As it happened, the Canadiens were my parents' favorite team at the time and, sure enough, Montreal took me with the club's first pick. Man, that was weird! It was one of the biggest days of my entire life yet, when I look back, I don't remember very much else other than surprise that I went so early. It was a great day but, like my wedding day, I don't remember what else happened.

My first year of pro hockey was in Fredericton. When I went there, the organization didn't want me fighting as much; they wanted me to work on my offensive game. In any event, I had a pretty good year, scored twenty-five goals and almost seventy points.

The Canadiens have a good philosophy when it comes to developing young players. Management takes its time before bringing kids up to the NHL. It makes for a good learning experience and, later on, makes you appreciate more what you get when you reach the NHL. If everything goes nice and easy right from the start — which happens to a lot of guys — they're not as mature.

My experience in the AHL made me a better person. It made me aware of my responsibilities plus I got to play a lot and worked hard to get to the top. Meanwhile, I was watching the Canadiens from afar. They won the Stanley Cup in 1993, beating Los Angeles in the Finals and they decided to keep the same team for the next season. I couldn't blame them for that. But then they started losing and I got my chance.

I would have made the big club at the start of 1994-95 but that was the Fall when the NHL pulled the lockout so there was no hockey with the Canadiens for a while. Management asked me if I would go down to the minors until the lockout was over and I agreed. It was one of the best things I did to further my career.

I played great, made the AHL All-Star Team and when the lockout was over, I was ready to move right in with the Canadiens without missing a beat. The other thing that helped was Jacques Demers' attitude toward me. He was good and patient even though I didn't start off with Montreal as well as I might have. He had me on the fourth line and toward the end of the year we played great. The bad news was that the club missed the playoffs.

By this time I had a pretty good idea what the big club wanted from me. I had to improve my offensive game and be better around the net while still playing a physical game. All the big guys in the NHL who can fight also have to be able to play the game as well. And they do. Instead of just playing one shift a game or going out there and just fighting, they're contributing to the game. Two good examples are Darren McCarty of the Red Wings and Randy McKay of the Devils.

I knew that I wasn't the so-called "heavyweight" but there weren't a lot more guys in the league who were a lot tougher than me. My target was to get fifteen to twenty goals a year and still fight when I had to do it.

What I learned about fighting is that in any given game any fighter can have a big win. Anyone who drops his gloves is tough. Normally, you don't see many guys getting hurt as a result of a hockey fight but there is the odd time when it happens.

Once, I suffered a shoulder injury having a fight in a game against the Kings. It was against Matt Johnson. As a matter of fact, we had two fights in that one game. In the first fight, I fell down and did something to my shoulder. When I got out of the penalty box, we fought and I pulled something — I don't know how I did it — and sprained my shoulder.

Johnson is one of those big, young kids who have come along recently, making the league bigger than ever in terms of the size of the players. Eric Cairns of the Rangers is another like that. But the older big fellows can still handle themselves, starting with Bob Probert.

Of all the fighters, Bob is the most special because he's done it so well for so long. One thing I've learned is that if you fight a lot, you get better at it. Take a defenseman like Paul Laus. One season he had almost thirty major penalties for Florida. Paul isn't the biggest guy in the league but he's still one of the best fighters. Any time you fight him, you're going to have your hands full. Then again, every team has a guy like that who can do the same thing.

From time to time you hear hockey critics say that fighting should be abolished from the game but I don't know about that. Check out the majority of the tough guys and you'll see that they are not the problem. They're not the ones running around two-handing guys. They're not the ones breaking sticks over other player's heads or anything stupid like that. The tough guys have respect for their fellow players and the game. They play hard and they fight. If fighting wasn't there, the game would be worse when you consider the way sticks are being handled. And the slashing. If someone slashes one of my teammates, I should be able to do something about it.

The trouble is that in the past I could do something about it but now they call the "instigator" penalty. All I know is that a lot more players get seriously injured as a result of stickwork that's illegal than get hurt from fighting.

In terms of fighting, it's different for the European players who come over here because they didn't grow up with the same hockey culture we did in Canada. We grew up playing the physical way; play tough, play hard. Overseas, when they're young, they don't fight. They play that way overseas into their twenties. Once they get over here, they're too old to change their pattern.

The other thing I notice about tough guys and the way they are greeted by fans is that they are appreciated for what they do. Fans know that enforcers sometimes try to change the flow of the game if their team is losing. Just go out and grab someone.

If an enforcer wants to fight, he'll confront the other guy and say, "Let's go!" And they will usually fight. That's it although with the instigator rule, it's not as bad as it used to be.

Bad Boys

What amazes outsiders is that a pair of fighters who might have squared off during the game will still be buddies once they get dressed and leave the rink. I might have a fight with Player X and later, I'll run into him after we leave the arena and I'll talk to him. That's the way the sport is. It's all respect. You play hard and tough and whatever happens out there happens and once it's done it's done. After all, this is only a game.

You can't bring the anger that you might momentarily have on the ice and bring it off with you otherwise you get put in jail for that. Every one of us knows that we're playing a tough game at a high speed and emotions often run high.

Who is the toughest player I've fought?

I fought Probert in an exhibition game a few years ago and had my hands full. He's tough. Laus is the guy who hit me the most but I don't know that there was one who was the dominating guy. Some games I'm going to do better in a fight and sometimes not so well. You have to be able to take a few punches; that's the way the game works. You put your twenty or thirty seconds — or whatever — in and that's that.

I personally had one very satisfying fight with Shawn Antoski. The bout was good enough to be shown on one of those "Rock 'Em, Sock 'Em" videos. That was a pretty good fight and Shawn always tells me about it.

P. J. Stock

"I remember driving home from a game and saying (to Rangers goalie Dan Cloutier), 'Wow, Clouts, were in the NHL!' And he says, 'I have three wins," almost in awe. We just sat there, turned the music up and started banging our heads."

P.J. Stock makes a lasting impression wherever he goes.

The moment he first put on a blue, white and red Rangers' jersey, he electrified the Madison Square Garden crowd. New Yorkers love a good fight and P.J. wasted no time throwing the punches.

It was the same in Hartford, with the AHL Wolf Pack. Stock's pugnacious, no-holds-barred assault on the opposition was a sight American League fans won't easily forget.

H he helped rejuvenate a community recently made NHL-hockey-less. Chants of "P.J! P.J!" became commonplace at the Civic Center in 1997-98 and replaced the chants of "Stuuuuuu" directed at former Whaler, Stu Grimson. Stock led the Wolf Pack's charge to the AHL Eastern Conference Championship while racking up 202 penalty minutes in only 41 games with the Pack. He also led the team in fighting majors.

After a bloody game with Worchester, Stock fingered a gash between his eyes."These are my first pro stitches," he said. "My modeling career is over."

When the Rangers called in 1997-98, Stock answered. During his rookie NHL season, the Dollard, Quebec native opened fire on some of the NHL's more established troublemakers including Kris King, Scott Daniels, Rich Pilon and Dale Hunter. With the Rangers, P. J. posted 114 penalty minutes in only 38 games.

He also chipped in with some offense. His first NHL goal was the game-winner in a 3-2 Rangers victory over San Jose. After putting a loose puck behind Sharks goalie Kelly Hrudey, Stock lamented, "I had more of a vision of going end to end, a couple of guys on my back, one hand on the stick and put it top shelf. But I'll take that one.

"I never thought I's have a chance to make a hockey career out of my life," Stock reflected on his first trip to the Show. "So I wanted to get myself an education for something to fall back on."

The Blueshirts offered to pay for Stock's education, a determining factor in his signing. At the time, Stock was playing for St. Francis-Xavier

University, following two years with Victoriaville of the Quebec Major Junior League. In drafting him, the Rangers gained Stock's energy and enthusiasm, which were welcomed by the Garden faithful and the Ranger brass.

"He knows how to get the better of an opponent," said former Ranger assistant coach Dick Todd. "He's got a lot of intensity and gamesmanship."

Of Stock's work ethic, Wolf Pack coach E.J. McGuire added, "Part of that is hustle, part of that is toughness and part of that is the extreme toughness of dropping the gloves and actually fighting."

But behind the grit is a 22-year-old who is still awed by the bright lights of the NHL. Currently pursuing a bachelor's degree in sports marketing, Stock's laid-back attitude on and off the ice are reminders to us all that hockey is, believe it or not, still a game.

In an interview with Fischler Hockey Service reporter Amy Spencer at the Rangers practice facility in Rye, N.Y., Stock candidly revealed his involvement in and philosophy on hockey.

The dialogue follows:

AS: Let's start from the beginning. Where you born? Any brothers or sisters?
P.S: I was born in Dollard. I've got one brother who's a year and a half younger than me and a sister who's a year and a half older than me.

AS: Does your brother play hockey?
P.S: He's right now playing for the Halifax Mooseheads in the Quebec Major Junior League. We played together on the same team, the Victoriaville Tigers. He's always been a year and a half behind me, so we never got the chance to play together until that year.

AS: Did you guys get along as kids or did you rough it up?
P.S.: Oh, we roughed it up a lot! He's younger, so there was a lot of, not jealousy, but competition going on amongst everything. I'm sure if you have any brothers or sisters you know what I mean.

He used to take stuff that was mine all the time because I couldn't fit into his clothes, but he could fit into mine. Just little things like that. Then we'd start pushing and shoving.

When we were younger, my parents would just settle us down and get us a pair of boxing gloves. We would just fool around, but nothing serious.

AS: So you were a troublemaker when you were a kid?
P.S.: No. I was always a good kid. I was walking around with a halo over my head. Never got in trouble, never...

I did get in trouble, of course, here and there. In school I was in trouble a bit. Every now and then I'd sit outside, in the hallway, for being the class clown, more than anything.

I didn't mind school. I just didn't like the studies. School's pretty big in my family. That's why (two years ago), instead of signing a contract, I went to a university. I never thought I'd be playing hockey and I always wanted something to fall back on.

My sister graduated from McGill. It's a pretty prestigious school. We're pretty academic, really. My mon is a nurse and my dad is a good businessman. We emphasis school quite a bit in my family.

AS: Did you play any other sports at school?
P.S.: You name it, I played it at school. I was on the wrestling team and played rugby, basketball, volleyball and soccer. Soccer is my favorite besides hockey. I still play it now in the summer.

AS: What was the neighborhood you grew up in
P.S.: It was a nice area. It was pretty quiet, where you could play hockey in the street everyday after school. There were lots of kids. We were non-stop doing stuff with kids our own age. We were all playing football or hockey or basketball.

AS: Do you remember your first time on skates
P.S.: No, but the flashbacks I have are of my mom taking me to the outdoor rinks, teaching me how to stop. And I remember coming home one day, then my dad coming out with me later on.

I still remember my mom taught me how to stop like a figure skater, dragging the toe, the T-stop. So my dad said, "What are you doing, kid? Stop it! You're embarrassing me out there." And then he taught me of course. He was my coach for all minor hockey.

It worked great, actually. He got to play me a lot and he helped me when I was younger. I wouldn't play the highest level, maybe a level lower, but my father was my coach and I always had good friends on the team, so it was fun.

AS: Does your dad play hockey
P.S.: My dad played, but he's about 5' 5," so back when he played, there were six teams in the NHL. I think he played for the Junior Canadiens. He was a pretty good hockey player back then. He was like a feisty little short guy.

AS: How old were you when you started playing hockey?
P.S.: Five or four, something around there. My dad got me into hockey, be we had an outdoor rink where I lived. We'd freeze up the tennis courts, put some boards around it and that's where I started with my mom teaching me the T-stop.

I probably started playing about that year, six, seven and up. It's pretty common where I live in Montreal. Hockey's pretty big with young kids, so I got into it then. I stayed with the same group of guys until I was about 16, 17-years old, when we all went our own ways. But from six to seventeen, it was the same guys every year. We're all great friends now.

AS: At what level did you start playing organized hockey?
P.S.: Novice. My first was Novice A. We were the Dollard Civic Sentinal or the Dollard Centennials. My father was the coach.

AS: What position did you play?
P.S.: I was a defenseman. I was on defense until about two years ago.

AS: What made you switch to forward?
P.S.: My size pretty much. As a defenseman, I was a little offensive, getting caught up the ice everywhere. The coach got fed up and said, "Well, you're always up there, so we might as well make you a forward." I'm kind of thanking him now for making that move.

As a forward, I know how the defenseman is thinking, so it helps. You know how to get in a guy's way a little better.

AS: Did you have an established style of play at that time?
P.S.: I still played the same way, except for the fighting. You can't fight when you're younger. But I was never a really fast skater, not a goal-scorer. I just like to have fun, play competitive.

AS: What was your favorite team growing up?
P.S.: The Canadiens. Chris Chelios was my favorite player.

AS: Do you remember you first scrap?
P.S.: It was in Hocksbury. I was playing in Tier Two and all my buddies came up to the game. I had left home and it was the first time I was coming to play close to home. We wore full cages (on our helmets) at the time.

So a fight started and we pushed each other. I threw off my helmet and went at him. He dropped his gloves and just came at me with his helmet still on. So I ended up getting two black eyes, cut my lip, cut my nose and he never lost his helmet during the fight.

AS: In regards to fighting, who do you really respect?
P.S.: Darren Langdon. I respect him totally. He's not the biggest guy, and he'll take on anybody. It's hard sometimes from a regular person's point of view to understand the way he fights, but for someone who does the job, he's a bril-

liant fighter. I'm young and small, and I try to watch him and learn things off him because he fights everybody and never walks away from anything.

AS: By the time you got to Major Juniors, had you found your role on the team, your style?

P.S: I was a defenseman at the time, so I tried my best to get into the lineup. I played a bit of a scrappy style as a defenseman and ended up getting quite a bit of ice time. And that was the first time I was really allowed to fight so that's when I really broke out.

I had a big defensive partner and I used to try to hit guys all the time at center ice. If I did, their tough guy would come to fight me, but then my partner would go and fight him, so I was o.k. But traded him away at Christmas of that year and I had to start defending myself.

AS: How would you describe your fighting style?

P.S.: I'm just out there fighting for my life. I just don't like getting hit, how about that. I think everyone's like that. My defensive style? I guess I always try to keep the other guy guessing. You do whatever you can. You throw with one hand and then the other. And pray!

Lefties don't bother me because I fight with both hands. I have to because of my size. I can't hold off anybody, because they're too big, so I've got to find a way around it. I'm always moving because if one of these big guys gets a hold of me, I could be in trouble.

AS: Did you have any stand-out fights in Juniors?

P.S.: My most memorable fight came in my first year of Junior. We were losing 8-1 and it was one of the last games of the season. There were two minutes left to go in the game and the crowd was about to leave. I ended up going at it.

They had a big goon who tried to fight me two or three times during the game. I didn't fight him because, I'd be the kid sent off the ice.

Finally with two minutes left, I went to center ice and we challenged each other. I knocked him down with one punch. We lost 8-1, but the fans didn't care about that.

That really kind of put a punctuation mark on our team for the rest of the year.

AS: Some stats from Juniors. 1995-96 432 penalty minutes, but also 19 goals and 43 assists for 62 points. Do you consider yourself a two way player?

P.S: We have guys here who can score goals. I'm not really expected to put the puck in the net as much as prevent it from going in. Every extra one I can get, I do. But a two way player? What two ways are that? Skating forward and going to the penalty box?

AS: What really gets under your skin and drops your gloves?

P.S.: Believe it or not, I don't really get mad at much on the ice. I have fun. That's all kinds of fun. What really gets under my skin is when a guy knocks me out or doesn't and hits me.

I don't like blatant cheap shots. Agitators are fine, just the little things to get a guy off his game. But I don't like when the play is totally on the other end and the guy takes a dirty slash or spear at you. That's the kind of thing that you just remember in the back of your head and you might not get the guy back at that time, but you'll remember it and get back to him sooner or later.

AS: At what point did you think of the NHL as a possibility?

P.S.: I never did. I never thought of the NHL, never. I always dreamed of it, but when the Rangers offered me a contract two years ago, I never thought I would make it.

I thought I'd struggle in the AHL and I didn't want to lose my school bursary to come play in the East Coast League or something. My dream is to play in the NHL and if I'm in the ECHL, that's two leagues away and quite a struggle.

When I started this year, I was really worried again about playing in the East Coast League. I wanted to make the NHL and when I made the AHL, I began struggling for ice time. And then 20 games into the season, I got a call up and it was unbelievable.

AS: How does more NHL ice time affect your game? Does it give you more confidence.

P.S.: When you get one shift, or a bunch of shifts, it's one thing just to be here. But once you play a little, you want to play a lot.

It's a learning process. I'm still young, these guys are older, all experienced and I'm here to learn as much as I can. Then, hopefully, I'll jump into their spots.

AS: What was your first NHL fight?

P.S.: It was against Rich Pilon, in New York. I think we were down by a goal, two minutes left and I had just been called up. I looked around and said, "Lets get this thing going a little. Let the fans in it." He was saying stuff and hitting guys, so I thought he'd be ok to try. He's tough, though.

It went alright. I came out of there conscious.

AS: Being this young and new to the league, do you feel you've found your role on this team or are you still experimenting.

P.S.: I'm in the learning process, just watching everyone else. I'm just here to be a forechecking type of player. I'm a dump and bump type, nothing fancy. I'm a blue-collar worker. I think you need some blue-collar guys to get things going.

Fans like the body checks and something rough every now and then and I try to provide that as much as I can because I know I'm not going to score many goals. I try to put smiles on guys faces. A lot of them are pressured by a lot of things and I just come here to have fun and try to bring them all into my little game.

AS: Your number with the Rangers, 28, is there any significance to it?
P.S.: They gave it to me. It's Tie Domi's old number. I don't know what's going on there, if they're trying to tell me something.

AS: What would you say to the people who think hockey's getting too rough?
P.S.: I don't know how anyone can say hockey's gotten too rough. It's just different people with different attitudes towards the game.

Nobody says that about boxing when two guys are smacking each other in the head. The only reason we do it is to try and get fans in the game, and get them out there like a sixth player.

One fight every three or four games doesn't really affect that much. I think that it gets blown our of proportion.

Everyone has respect for each other at this level. People who think it's a really rough game, I don't mean to discourage them, but they don't have to come watch the games. They can stay home and watch Oprah.

Bad Boys

Ryan VandenBussche

A lot of people have raw talent, but if you don't have the three D's —
dedication, drive, and desire — to go with it, you're not gonna go far.
You get weeded out somewhere along the line.

Outgoing and down-to-earth, Ryan VandenBussche makes no bones about what propelled him to the NHL with the New York Rangers and more recently, the Chicago Blackhawks: dedication. Whether he is in the locker-room, weight room, or out on the ice, Ryan dedicates himself entirely to improving as a hockey player and, most importantly, as a team player. It could be said that VandenBussche puts the 'T' in Team.

Ryan's wallop was most vividly exhibited during the 1997-98 pre-season. A punch to the head of Toronto Maple Leaf forward Nick Kypreos sent the message that VandenBussche is here to stay. At the end of what had been an even-handed fight, the linesman stepped in to try to break them up. Naturally, he was shoved off by two world-class fighters who wanted to decide the fight themselves. Ryan, a strong second-half fighter, had sufficient energy left at the end to throw a monster left round-house to Kypreos' jaw. Nick fell face first to the ice, not even putting his hands out to break his fall. He was out cold before he hit the ice. The blow effectively ended Kypreos' career.

Ryan has also been known to employ his vicious lefts to defend his vulnerable teammates but he brings much more than a hard left to the rink. The Blackhawks thought enough of him during the summer of 1998 to put veteran Bob Probert on the trading block.

VandenBussche discussed his job with Fischler Hockey Service reporter Amy Spencer when still a Ranger at their practice facility in Rye, New York. He recalled his first days on the rink, his Junior career and minor league experiences as well as the NHL. Their conversation follows.

Amy Spencer: What were you like as a youngster?
Ryan VandenBussche: I was born in Simcoe, Ontario but grew up in Delhi, Ontario, which is 15 minutes from Simcoe. I grew up with a brother who was 16-months older than me. It was a little tough for us to get along when we were

young for some reason. Maybe we were too close in age or too competitive. To say the least I used to get in most of my battles with my brother when I was younger. I'd go to school with bruised ears and black eyes, cuts. I learned how to take a beating early in life. My brother had a short fuse. We'd be playing hockey outside and if I shot the puck and missed the net, he'd get all pissed off at me. Either he'd have to go get it, or I'd have to go get it, and it'd make a delay in the game, and we'd end up fighting out of that. Then my dad would get fed up with us and say, "Next time you guys fight, I'm gonna break it up, make you put the boxing gloves on, duke it out, and the winner of that fight will fight me." [laughter]

AS: How would you describe the neighborhood you grew up in?
RV: I grew up on a farm. I wouldn't say it was a tough neighborhood. We had our neighbors and we used to play road hockey, and go bike riding and all that kind of stuff that kids do. Then I moved off the farm when I was eleven. My parents got divorced and I moved closer to town and lived with my mom. That was a little bit of a change, but then I got to meet my stepbrother that way. He was just like a friend all the time. It turned out to work for the best. I was drafted by the Cornwall Royals of the OHL, Major Junior A. I lived there for two years when I was 17 and 18, and then the team moved to Newmarket and I played there for half a year. Then I was traded to Guelph, the Guelph Storm, and that ended my Junior career.

AS: What hockey signs did you show?
RV: I never really stood out more than anybody else. I was never the biggest guy on a team or the guy with the hardest shot. When I was younger I was always a good skater. I was always in there, mucking it up in the corners and working hard. I had to work hard to reach the next level every year. Nothing was handed to me, that's for sure. A lot of people who play the game could make it, if they had the dedication, the drive and the desire. A lot of people have raw talent, but if you don't have the three D's to go with it, you're not gonna go too far. You get weeded out somewhere along the line. Some make it a little further than others just on their raw talent, like maybe to Junior B hockey, or Junior A, or even to the minors, but eventually if they don't have those three D's, they'll be weeded out. Me, I always was kind of a physical player. I was always lookin' to make a hit, be the first one to the corners. No one would ever beat me to the corner. I just skated hard, as hard as I could.

AS: Do you remember your first fight?
RV: Yeah, actually I do. It happened at the pee-wee level. There was this player on the opposition who was always hitting everybody and doing things dirty. The two of us got into it. We were pushin' and shovin' and then I just stood in

front of him, face to face. We had cages on then, and he was chirpin' at me. I didn't say a word. I just took my right hand and corked him right in the face. I never heard the end of that. But later, when I was playing Junior B, I didn't really know when I'd fight. I'd never go looking for it. Still with the style that I played, it'd always come to me and I never backed down. I never knew I was a left handed puncher, either. I write with my left hand, but I was more dominant with my right hand. And the odd time I'd get in a scuffle in Junior B, the odd time I'd throw a left and catch the guy by surprise.

Then I was drafted in Junior A, a 14th round draft pick. Not a lot of 14th rounders make the team. Marc Crawford was coach and I had to do something to get noticed. I just went out there on my first day and knocked Owen Nolan out with a hit, not a fight. It was a clean hit and he missed the rest of the training camp. On my next day I got my teeth knocked out by another guy, my two front teeth came right out. Then the next day, I ended up fighting the team tough guy and did well. And then the next day I received a concussion from a hit, but I was back the next day. I got in a couple exhibition games, scored a goal. I ended up getting in a fight with some guy in exhibition, and I just strictly threw lefts. I did really well in the fight, and the rest is history. I ended up making the team. And that's the story.

AS: How much does having that strong left help in fights at the NHL level?
RV: It's an advantage, but everyone's so well prepared in the NHL for any type of fighter. They get scouting reports from everybody. It's just that some guys know how to handle lefties better than others. Whether you're a lefty or a rightie, it doesn't really matter as long as you know how to hold your own. And to be able to be ambidextrous, so to speak, when you're in a fight is the key, because if one hand's tied up, you've got the other hand, and vice versa.

AS: Who were your role models?
RV: I liked Wendel Clark, Bob Probert, guys like that. Clark could play the game, and was a good hitter. Plus, he'd drop the gloves if need be, and he was great to watch.

AS: Going into your professional career, at what point did you think of the NHL as a legitimate possibility?
RV: Well, when I was playing Junior A that's when I really thought, "Hey, maybe I could make it to the NHL." Because I saw some of the guys I was playing with, and playing against, were moving on and getting drafted, and that was my next step. When I was drafted to Junior A and I made the Junior A team, my next step was to get drafted to the NHL. And I decided if the guy beside me could do it, I sure as hell could do it too. And it worked out. Marc Crawford coached me my first year of pro too, at St. John's, Toronto's farm

team. I remember one day he asked me in my first year of pro's whether I thought I could make it in the NHL. I was always the type of person who was very modest, and would never really say, "Yeah, of course I can." I didn't really sound too confident at the time, but deep down I was, I just didn't want to come out with that. Marc taught me to be confident, to know in the back of my mind that I will make it.

AS: Do you remember your first professional goal?
RV: I was in Cape Breton. I was playing for St. John's Maple Leafs, and I was racing for the puck. It was kind of a half breakaway. The goalie came out to get the puck, and I was racing to get it, and the goalie was gonna beat me to it. I dove for it, hit it with my stick, and as he dove it went underneath him and into the net.

AS: What about your first professional fights?
RV: There was one in my second year of Junior that must've been at least two minutes long. By the time we were done, I had nothing on barely, and I couldn't even lift my arms at the end of the fight to bring the water bottle to my mouth. That's how tired I was.

AS: How did you come to be a Ranger?
RV: I played two years in the minors, and we played against Binghamton a couple times. I had some battles with Darren Langdon in the minors. Nobody went down. We both threw some, and took some. I was a free agent at the end of my contract, and New York ended up making me an offer. I liked what I saw, so I signed on. Right away I knew my role. I've had the same role since my first year in Junior, working the corners, getting the puck out, skating hard, playing a physical game and maybe dropping the gloves.

AS: What is your thinking about fitness?
RV: I always think the next guy's gonna be working harder than me, so I want to make sure I don't cheat myself. I work just as hard. I don't want them to have an excuse to cut me when I come into camp because I'm not in shape. I can control that. There's not much in this game that you can control, but being fit is something you can.

AS: When the Rangers organization decided to protect you in the waiver draft and let Mike Peluso go, how did you feel?
RV: Actually I didn't know what went on. We had a break and I went back to Binghamton to get some stuff. I ended up having dinner at this place and there was a sports page sitting on the table, so I picked it up and I started reading it. It said the Rangers decided to protect Ryan VandenBussche instead of Mike

Peluso and Shane Churla because they felt he could be fit to do the job for the year or whatever, and I was there with my girlfriend at the time, and I looked at her and I said, "Read this."

AS: Tell me about the Nick Kypreos fight and how much you think that fight had to do with the Rangers' decision to keep you.
RV: I'm sure it had something to do with it. It's just that I have a lot of respect for any guy who drops the gloves in this league. I just got a little bit into it and ended up hitting him in the right spot. It could happen to anybody. It could happen to me, but I'd rather be the hitter than the hittee. There's just really not much more to say about that.

AS: Tell us about your technical fighting style and your strategies?
RV: I just grab onto the shoulder pads and throw my left. If my left gets tied up, I try to throw my right. And if they're both tied up, well, then, there's not much I can do. I don't try to struggle to get free because you're wasting a lot of energy trying to do that. If both my arms are tied up, I'll just wait for the other guy to throw a punch. And then as soon as he's thrown a punch, you know that your one arm is loose and then you try to get one in there too. Basically I have to be able to take 'em before I give a couple. When you're in a fight, it's hard to be able to fight if you're not prepared, or if you don't want to hurt the person. It's pretty sadistic to say, but you have to want to hurt the person in order to do well.

AS: What about your biggest fight that really stands out so far in the NHL?
RV: The one that stands out the most is my first fight in NHL regular season play against Brendan Witt with Washington. It was just a good battle, plus it got on Don Cherry's Grapevine. Another that stands out in my mind that I'd like to redo against Stu Grimson. I took a few there. I just totally went into that fight thinking. Sometimes you think too much. And I was thinking too much. The only thing I proved in that fight was that I could take a punch.

AS: What really provokes you to drop your gloves more than anything?
RV: Seeing a guy on the other team taking liberties on our smaller guys, our skill players, the guys who don't really drop the gloves. But I have to be smart about it too. I can't put my team in jeopardy. I can't step out there and take the guy out and get a two minute instigating and put the team at a disadvantage. Or if we're getting killed 4-0, maybe just to change the flow of the game and the momentum, get it going the other way. I can't stand the thoughts of somebody hitting anybody from behind. If anyone were to do that to me or one of my teammates, I'd be right there and I probably would take the instigator penalty for that because I can't stand that stuff.

AS: Do you consider yourself a "tough guy"?

RV: If I get in a fight with somebody, I usually hit 'em with one. Like I said, I wanna hurt somebody and the other person wants to hurt me and that triggers something in my head, "I don't like that." That's how I get myself mad I guess.

AS: How would you characterize your off ice personality?

RV: I'm pretty calm, relaxed, laid back, very laid back. It takes a lot to get me pissed off.

AS: What would you say to people who say hockey is too tough ?

RV: If you don't like the game, don't watch it. If you think hockey is too rough, watch tennis!

Pat Verbeek

"My game is on the edge. I have to play on the edge."

"Toughness," said Dallas coach Ken Hitchcock, "is only good if the guy can play."

Pat Verbeek can play.

Also, he can score, agitate, dig, chirp and, if the spirit moves, fight.

Now in his 16th season, Verbeek has done tours of duty with the Devils, Whalers and Rangers.

Most recently, he has been a valuable member of the Dallas Stars who won the 1997-98 Presidents' Trophy as the NHL team with the most points.

"This season we didn't have a so-called heavyweight in our lineup," said Verbeek. "But everybody stuck up for each other. We were like a pack of wolves. Sometimes you're worse off facing a whole pack of wolves than just one tough one. That's what we were all about."

Verbeek's gritty style has been evident since his earliest days when he beat up Brian Leetch at the Meadowlands in 1988.

In an interview with Fischler Hockey Service correspondent Bob Matuszak at the Stars practice facility, the Dr. Pepper Stars center, the following question-and-answer segment was recorded.

Bob Matuszak: Where did you grow up?

Pat Verbeek: In a small town about 10 miles east of Sarnia, Ontario, called Wyoming. It's small — about 1,700 people. It's closer to Detroit than Toronto. About an hour and 15 minutes from Detroit, approximately two hours from Toronto. My parents raised pigs and basically were farmers. I have three brothers and one sister.

B.M.: Did you all play hockey?

P.V.: Timmy's playing Major Junior for the Kitchener Rangers, Brian played Junior in Kingston and actually played in the minors for awhile, and my other brother played for St. Lawrence University. We played baseball, soccer, and in the summer time, ball hockey. Other than little spats that we had, for the most part we got along. We like to do things together. As we got a little older we did a lot of training together.

B.M.: What about playing on the ponds?
P.V.: My Dad actually built a rink in the backyard. When the time came, it would be our job to construct it ourselves and he would help us when it came time to fill it up with the water and freeze it over. Everyday, after school we would spend a couple of hours on the rink before supper. And when my Dad knew it was going to be good weather as far as being able to skate, he would let us out of our chores that we had to do after school so we could play hockey. We had floodlights so that we were able to see. If you'd miss the net we'd lose all the pucks so then we'd have to start all over the next day and try and find them again. And then you'd find them in the spring when the thaw came.

B.M.: Who was your favorite team while you were growing up?
P.V.: I loved the Boston Bruins. Probably because I loved Bobby Orr so much. As I got older, I started to watch Bobby Clarke more closely, and I ended up switching my number to his and I've kept it ever since. It was the advice of my mom and dad. They said, "'If you ever want to have a chance at making it — this guy works hard, and he's tenacious, and he's gritty — and if you ever want to make it, this is the way you're going to have to play."

B.M.: When did you first realize that you had a chance of making it?
P.V.: When I was sixteen and drafted to the OHL in the First round. It was a stepping stone. And then becoming Rookie of the Year in the OHL solidified more in my mind that I had a real good chance. But, at the time, my size worked against me. I was fortunate in the route I had taken. Major Junior was still considered a good test as far as how tough you were. I certainly had to prove I was able to play a big man's game and that I wasn't afraid to get my nose dirty. After my first year, I was able to prove to scouts that I wasn't going to shy away from it. Consequently, I was drafted by New Jersey.

B.M.: How tough was hockey in Sudbury.
P.V.: It was tough in that the team didn't do very well. We won maybe 28 games or so in the two years that I was there, so obviously it was tough. I mean, every night it was a battle to win and when you did win, victory was sweet. It prepared me for what was going to happen in New Jersey. Had I been in a different situation, would I be the same kind of player that I am today? Would I be better? Would I be worse? I was lucky in that a situation came along where New Jersey wasn't a very good hockey team and that enabled me to come in and get my foot in the door as far as making an NHL team, or having a great chance at making it, and I was able to do that.

It was actually quite exciting for me because I knew that they were a team that just moved from Colorado. It was a team that was struggling to be good and I knew that this was a legit chance for me to make it. Draft-wise I ranked in the first round as far as in the Ontario Hockey League and then I kind of dropped off a bit. But I wasn't concerned. I had put up decent numbers in my rookie season. I think there was a stretch there where, when I did drop, it was because my wisdom teeth were coming in and I was taking these pain killers and I was playing like shit! Plus, scouts don't travel up to Sudbury. They catch you when you're down south in the more central area, and I just didn't play very well in those three or four games.

B.M.: Where were you when you got drafted?
P.V.: I was in Montreal. We went to the Forum and sat in the stands like every other kid. I was there with my Dad. We made the twelve hour train trip up there. I was there with a teammate of mine who I had played Junior with and he ended up being drafted by Pittsburgh.

B.M.: After you got drafted, you played one more year in Sudbury?
P.V.: Well, I went to Devils camp, signed a contract and then they sent me back. I remember the day they sent me back, I was disappointed because I knew I had a good camp and they thought it would be best if I went back. In hindsight, they were right. The losing that went on that year — well, it was probably a little better to take at Junior than in the pros! I figured I could score. Any kid coming out of Junior whose put up decent numbers thinks he can go to the pros and do that. But I knew I had to play the same style that I had played in Juniors.

B.M.: What about your rookie year in New Jersey.
P.V.: It was fun but a lot of nights were tough. It was a grind. You're not used to playing that many games and you were playing with guys who were a lot stronger than what you had played against in Juniors. So it was definitely a different game. I was one of those guys who was constantly being tested. After a while you had to start initiating stuff just to make room for yourself and try to gain respect of the other players. Yet I can't remember my first fight. You would think that would be something I'd remember. I don't remember a lot of my fights. It's just one of those things. We had a few tough guys on our team. John Wensink was there, Mel Bridgman and Phil Russell. Each one showed me different things. What I should do, how I should do it. When I first played I was with defenseman Joe Cirella so I had somebody my age who I could hang out with. We used to always go over to Don Lever's house. He was one of the veterans.

B.M.: When did the Devils start turning it around?

P.V.: We had Rocky Trottier, Ken Daneyko, Cirella, Kirk Muller, John MacLean. Then Brendan Shanahan and Sean Burke came. My fifth year there, you could see it start to take shape. But we were still kind of raw. We had some veterans such as Mel Bridgman, Don Lever, Ron Low, Chico Resch — players who showed us how to be a team off the ice. That was more important than anything that we did on the ice. The closer we were off the ice, the closer we were in the heat of battle. When games got tough, we all stuck together.

B.M.: When you were traded to Hartford, your penalty minutes started racking up. Did you change your style of play at all?

P.V.: I hadn't changed anything. It was the same amount of penalty minutes that I had put up in New Jersey but in the Adams Division, the checking was tighter. We played teams that you had to try and gain a little extra room on.

B.M.: At that time, you were the only player in the NHL who led his team in scoring and penalty minutes.

P.V.: For my game, they go hand in hand. The more I'm battling it seems, the more in the heat of the battle I am, the better I play.

B.M.: Have you ever got any advice on how to fight or were you self-taught?

P.V.: Well, you watch players that you saw who were good and you try to do the same things that they did. The other part of it is, when you get involved, you just have to fight for your life! Last year I went over the edge with the wrong guy — Sandy McCarthy. Someone grabbed me from behind. McCarthy was the first guy I saw that was around, so I just automatically assumed it was him, and swung at him. Well, it didn't take long for him to start swinging back! It's just heat of the moment stuff. It actually ended up getting me going that night. When I can hit a guy good, it can get me going. Good scoring chances really get me going as well.

B.M.: In your career? Have you ever developed a personal rivalry with anyone?

P.V.: Every time you strap on the skates, you know it's going to be a battle. You always look at who you're going to play against that night. I mean, you can pick anybody on any team that I've had a run in with. I can't back down. That's the way my game is.

B.M.: What about your career, has there ever been anyone who has taken you under their wing and showed you the ropes?

P.V.: Mel Bridgman was a good influence for me. As was Don Lever. Chico Resch was a tremendous influence as far as teaching me how and where to shoot on goalies and how to beat them. Ronny Low and I had similar interests as far as farming. He looked after me when I was eighteen-years-old.

B.M.: Are you doing that now to anyone on this team?

P.V.: We don't really have a young team. I don't have too many people over to my house because I've got five kids and they'll drive everyone nuts!

B.M.: What about your farming accident that you had?
P.V.: Well, I didn't think I'd ever play hockey again after I looked at my thumb and it wasn't there. It was May 15, 1985. I was going into my third season. Well, I went to pull a piece of paper out of an auger on this corn planter and I slipped on its frame. My hand went in the machine and it sliced my thumb off. It felt like just a little paper cut but when I looked, it was gone. I couldn't believe it. It was like, "God, give me those three seconds back that I just had." It was like a *déja-vu*. My brother radioed home and told my parents, who were about to leave the house. If it had happened five minutes later, I would never have played hockey again. They went back and found the thumb, and Brian drove me to the hospital. Then the doctor wasn't going to sew it back on. We made a few phone calls and found a doctor out of London (Ontario) who was able to do it. Six hours of micro-surgery later, it was re-attached. I still keep in touch with the doctor and I see him in the summertime. He was explaining to me later that he was about to give up on me. Out of desperation and frustration, he had to take a vein out of my foot and re-install it back into my thumb. But they couldn't get the blood to flow. As a last ditch, he flicked my thumb with a pen and it went. Then, three days after that, it was like a broken thumb. Before my thumb was reattached, though, I had a different perspective on hockey. I didn't tell anyone from the Devils organization for awhile because I wanted to make sure everything was all right. I told Joe Cirella first. Then I spoke with the general manager Max McNab probably a week after I got out of the hospital.

B.M.: Who was the most influential coach in your career?
P.V.: Tom McVie. In my first NHL year, he really showed me what it took, as far as a strong work ethic. He demanded it. Doug Carpenter pushed other buttons that got me to play better. Then Jim Schoenfeld brought in an enthusiasm that maybe some of the other coaches didn't have. They let me play the way they knew I had to.

B.M.: You're still playing the same game you were thirteen years ago when you were a rookie in Jersey. Has anyone ever tried to change your style?
P.V.: No. My game is on the edge. I have to play on the edge. I can be so agitating to the other team that they don't worry about playing the game. Or I can be so aggressive that I'll take penalties. Coaches realize that if I know where the line is and they give me the freedom to play both sides of it, everything will be fine.

THE ULTIMATE, ALL-TIME

HoCKEy fighERs LIST

Who are the best fighters in the National Hockey League?

The answer should provoke heated debate because there really is no definitive "champion."

What we have are many worthy contenders who, on any given night, can defeat the other.

To obtain a legitimate consensus, we consulted three of the most insightful students of hockey fighting in North America.

Randall S. Chadwick, David Singer and Joe Lozito have analyzed NHL enforcers as assiduously as any hockey scientists could possibly X-ray a stickhandler. They obviously disagree on certain sluggers but their reviews cover the entire gamut of enforcers and their respective techniques.

The following is what we consider the most comprehensive hockey fight rating list ever published.

RANDALL S. CHADWICK

I have forsaken the point system to compare fighters. While I still use a 10-point system to rank a given player's strengths and weaknesses, I have not "ranked" fighters on issues such as knockout punch, smartness etc. I do not believe such a system has much value in determining who would win in any particular fight. With some exceptions, I believe that on any given night any of these fighters could beat any other.

A hockey fight is a microcosm of the game itself. Parity is the rule and it is often the *fight*, not the fighter, that determines who wins. Aspects of the fight itself such as how far into a shift each combatant is, the grip on the other's jersey, styles of the combatants, all determine who will win more than, say, a harder punch or a longer reach. Some of the characteristics I have been asked to rate simply do not apply in some cases. For example, "switching hands" is simply a strategy some fighters choose not to use. What score do you assign for that? It is not that the fighter is *poor* at switching, he simply does not use that strategy. Many fighters do not seem concerned with tying up the opponent, another characteristic that then becomes "not applicable" for some. Because some of these characteristics are not applicable to every fighter (and thus some fighters do not have scores for that characteristic) it is impossible to compare across fighters by "adding up the scores." The numbers I give for each fighter indicate much less how he compares to others and more to ho (relatively) strong or weak he is on that aspect of his fighting game within himself.

I provide a profile of each enforcer and have included for each the scaled measurement on the following characteristics: Willingness (W), Stamina (ST), Knockout (K), Strength (SR), Quickness (Q), Switching Hands (SH), Tying Up (T), Balance (B), Fairness (F), Intimidation (I), Smartness (SM), ability to Take a Punch (TP) and Future Potential (FP). I present them in alphabetical order.

KEN BELANGER (6'4", 225 LBS.)

In Belanger's rookie year with the Islanders (the 1996-97 season) he easily led the team in the Penalties Minutes Per Game Ratio (PMR) of 5.67 minutes, a lot given his undoubtedly limited ice-time. He is a southpaw who used his left effectively vs. Hicks last season. He did suffer a concussion at the hands of a hard Paul Laus right-hand haymaker but later came back and challenged Laus and did well. He had a decent scrap with Luke Richardson where he threw left but also took some Richardson lefts and went down. My knowledge of him is pretty limited; I've seen less than 10 of his fights. He's too new to really be an intimidation factor and I've never seen him try to switch hands or tie people up; he might do well to attempt tying the opponent up as it seems he is vulnerable to the big punch. As he is big and young he should have a nice future.

	W	ST	K	SR	Q	SH	T	B	F	I	SM	TP	FP
Belanger	10	8	8	9	9	n/a	n/a	8.5	10	7	8	7	10

DONALD BRASHEAR (6'3", 223 LBS.)

Despite the fact that Brashear was second only to Odjick last year for Vancouver in PIM's and is one of the top five busiest fighters this year, Donald sometimes seems reluctant to really *fight*. Maybe it is just his style; he is very defensive minded and often likes to get in close to the opponent as he has done against Churla, against Severyn (in Nagano) and against Leroux in Colorado. With Montreal he had some good early scraps and showed an ability to go either right or left, although it seems he prefers left. Against Darren McCarty he used both hands and in a good fight against Probert (Probert a Red Wing at the time) he displayed very much a boxer's stance and an ability to use both hands. He has had inspired fights against other big opponents, such as Matt Johnson where Brashear used both the right and left and against Jim McKenzie where he dropped McKenzie (in Vancouver) with the left. His reluctance did show when, in Chicago, he had to be practically forced into a fight with Probert (in 1996-97) but at the same time he has thrown the odd sucker-punch, notably one during the same season against LaPerriere in L.A. One of Brashear's best fights of the 1996-97 season was against poor Cam Russell on January 12th (Cam's birthday no less) where he stunned or "TKO'ed" Cam with two very quick but powerful lefts.

	W	ST	K	SR	Q	SH	T	B	F	I	SM	TP	FP
Brashear	9	9	9	10	10	9.5	10	9.5	7	7	10	9	9

ERIC CAIRNS (6'5", 217 LBS.)

Cairns is an obviously huge kid who is only in his 2nd year in the NHL and apparently still going back and forth to the minors. Again, I've only seen a few of his fights but from what I have seen he is still in his learning stage. Against Berube he was quickly pulled down. Against Rob Ray in Buffalo, Cairns showed himself to be a right-hand puncher and a good skater, but a much smaller Ray was able to nail Eric a couple of times which really bloodied Cairns badly. But hey, he's young and has great teachers in New York in such as Darren Langdon (one of my favorites, more on him later). Because I've seen so little of him the numbers below may not mean much; I used his statistics on paper and my limited viewing of him to come up with these.

	W	ST	K	SR	Q	SH	T	B	F	I	SM	TP	FP
Cairns	8	8	8	8	9	n/a	7	7	10	6	5	5	10

ENRICO CICCONE (6'4", 210 LBS.)

This kid is big and tall with a good reach. He also has a wicked temper, which has gotten him into trouble before. My wife and I used to see him play for the Kalamazoo K-Wings (IHL, now the Michigan Wings) and he went nuts a few times there. Ciccone uses a big, right hand and doesn't seem too concerned with tying his opponent up. He can use the left also; he fought Wayne Primeau and went exclusively left-handed (dropping Wayne with about four, left upper-cuts) so maybe he is smart enough to choose hands based on his opponents' style. In a big fight versus then-Wing Jamie Pushor (EC a Blackhawk) he knocked Pushor cold with a left haymaker but then hit Jamie after he was down, a bit un-sportsmanlike. He fought Jim McKenzie in Phoenix and there used short rights; that fight ended in a draw. On the playing side he's a defenseman who is not really a liability (overall he's been an even plus-minus between Carolina, Vancouver and Tampa Bay) and this season has a PMR of 3.95. I have not seen him in any long fights nor have I seen him take any big punches, so I really cannot judge him too well on those aspects.

	W	ST	K	SR	Q	SH	T	B	F	I	SM	TP	FP
Ciccone	10	9	9.5	10	10	9.5	n/a	8.5	7	8	9	10	10

JIM CUMMINS (6'2", 203 LBS.)

Jim Cummins is one of the most under-rated fighters today; he is very tough and is all heart. I've not seen too many fighters more willing to go with someone simply to protect their team-mates. He was just edged out of the "top 10 busiest fighters this year (1997-98) but has 19 fights to his credit. His willingness to go is evidenced by the fact that he has *challenged* this season fighters such as Twist, Oliwa and Kris King. Jim likes to use the right hand and early on was a friend and protégé` of Bob Probert, in Detroit. At one point before going to Philadelphia he had even spent the summer working in the Krock gym to hone his boxing skills. Not that it helped him fight Probert the next season in Philly, where Bob pounded him with some huge rights, but it shows he's trying! Cummins gets hit a lot but can take a punch very well. He fought Blouin and threw fast rights. Has had great fights with opponents such as Chris LiPuma and Patrick Cote (a huge player in the Dallas system) where against the latter he showed an ability to go to the left. Fought Oliwa this year to a draw and drew against Tony Twist when Tony threw one of his right haymakers so hard he threw himself off balance (Tony's Achilles heel). Had a memorable scrap this season versus Mark Janssens where he marginally suckered Janssens (although it was really Mark's fault) and then proceeded to trade right-hands. He won't intimidate or knock out opponents, but he won't lose either! Although he only played eight games for the Red Wings, folks in Detroit will remember Cummins for being involved in an infamous melee against St. Louis on January 23, 1993 which initiated with a Cummins versus Chase fight and ended with everyone on the ice, including goalies Cheveldae and Joseph, going at 'er. Jim was suspended 11 games in that melee for leaving the penalty box to re-enter the fracas, an instance where his heart got him into some trouble. But he is Mr. Heart and a team/fan favorite wherever he plays.

	W	ST	K	SR	Q	SH	T	B	F	I	SM	TP	FP
Cummins	10+	10	8	9.5	10	9	n/a	9.5	10	7	9	10	10

LOUIS DEBRUSK (6'2", 215 LBS.)

I see so little of Tampa Bay and never really caught him when he was with the Oilers, so I know very little about this player. The one fight I saw him in was versus Ryan VandenBussche, where DeBrusk did pretty well; he threw left-handed (so I'll assume that is his dominant hand) and threw fast, holding VandenBussche off effectively. He was given the win in that scrap. I don't want to post numbers on him because I would really be rating the fight itself more than the fighter.

ROB DIMAIO (5'10", 180 LBS.)

Pound-for-pound one of the more impressive fighters I have seen. He does not really fight all that much but when he does he is very good at it. He had a huge fight this year versus big Jason Marshall where Rob switched with ease back and forth from right to left punches. He does seem to favor, however, his left. Another memorable fight was versus Steve Leach, where Dimaio again showed mastery of that style of fighting where the fighter throws with one hand, grabs with the same hand then switches to the other and throws (the "throw-grab-switch" style; pretty creative, eh!). Rob felled and bloodied Leach, no slouch himself, with his ability to switch hands.

	W	ST	K	SR	Q	SH	T	B	F	I	SM	TP	FP
Dimaio	7	8	6	9	10	10+	10	10	10	5	10	9	8

TIE DOMI (5'10", 200 LBS.)

Does anyone remember that episode of *The Simpsons* where it was discovered that Homer had an extra quarter-inch of skull and could therefore withstand almost any punch to the head? Well that seems to summarize Tie Domi quite well. You have to love this guy; there is no-one more enthusiastic than he about dropping the gloves! Domi is an almost strictly southpaw fighter; he will switch to the occasional right but he plays a pretty simple fight game. Domi grabs the jersey with his right, arm extended, taking on a bent-over position with his head facing away from the action and keeps his left hand cocked back for huge haymakers. Willing? He has fought everybody. Take a punch? Domi took 46 punches courtesy of Bob Probert in Madison Square Garden (see my write-up in the "The Greatest 10 Fights" section) and got up smiling! He can get dropped by a punch (he was dropped by the last Probert right) but they don't seem to affect him all that much. He can hit very hard when he gets the chance and will, again when he can, get the opponent's jersey over their head and hit them blind. He knocked out Cam Russell very recently (last weekend of the 1997-98 season) doing just that. That fight against Russell also gave Domi 363 PIMs (he added to that in the same game v. Probert) which broke his idol Dave "Tiger" Williams' season PIM record in Toronto. His rivalry with Bob Probert is one of the best in hockey; you are almost guaranteed a fight when they meet. In fact, about the only fight Probert had upon returning from major surgery on his rotator cuff (which knocked him out of 64 games) was with Domi. Many will not fight Domi because in their words "You can't beat this guy." He is not a liability on the ice and is a strong community supporter. I love him despite his enmity with Probert; it makes for great hockey! He gets my vote as, pound-for-pound, the toughest fighter in the game.

	W	ST	K	SR	Q	SH	T	B	F	I	SM	TP	FP
Domi	10+	10	9.5	10	9	7	n/a	9.5	8	10	10	10+	10+

KRIS DRAPER (5'11", 185 LBS.)

I know Kris very well as a player as he has been a Red Wing since the 1993-94 season and I can tell you that he is not by any means an enforcer or fighter. Of course it is well known among hockey fans that the hit from behind put on him by Claude Lemieux in the 1996 Detroit v. Colorado playoff series was the catalyst for what is now considered sports' biggest rivalry, which reached a peak on March 26, 1997 (I have more to say about that game in my "The Greatest 10 Fights" section). Kris has been in two fights since becoming a Red Wing, at least. He fought Darcy Tucker (then a Canadien) and surprised Tucker with some very fast rights, literally skating/pushing Tucker to the endboards. Draper spent the rest of that fight absorbing some short rights but held on fast until the linesmen came in. Draper fought Svboda last season, again showing surprising strength and balance and a quick right hand. No damage was done and after a few punches, Kris maintained a close, defensive position. I do not see him ever becoming a fighter, which is the reason for the low "future potential" (which I read to mean potential as a fighter) score.

	W	ST	K	SR	Q	SH	T	B	F	I	SM	TP	FP
Draper	5	8	5	9	10	n/a	9.5	10	10	n/a	10	8	5

ADAM FOOTE (6'1", 202 LBS.)

I know Adam best from his battles with Brendan Shanahan, a one-on-one rivalry that is fast eclipsing the McCarty/Lemieux rivalry. Foote and Shanahan fought in the infamous March 26, 1997 game between Colorado and Detroit; Shanny got the edge in that fight, bloodying Foote's nose, but Foote showed his great balance and ability to tie the opponent up. Foote is a dominant right-hand thrower, but can go to his left. Shanahan and Foote fought twice in Colorado this season (1997-98); both times Foote was susceptible to Shanahan's right and was bloodied in both scraps. The second of the fights was the better (the first was more of a scrum with linesmen in the middle); Foote used both lefts and rights in that match but Brendan popped Adam with some hard rights, bloodying his nose. Foote had a very good match against Brian Noonan this season, showing a smart mixing of right-hand uppercuts and haymakers. Foote landed two particularly hard right upper-cuts which hurt Noonan and put him in a defensive mode. Foote does not really play the hardcore "enforcer" role (nor do Noonan or Shanahan, for that matter) but is nevertheless a good middle-weight fighter who, on defense, plays a regular shift and is not really a liability (although this season he was a minus player).

	W	ST	K	SR	Q	SH	T	B	F	I	SM	TP	FP
Foote	7	9	7	9	10	9	9.5	10	10	6	10	8	8

STU "GRIM REAPER" GRIMSON (6'5", 227 LBS.)

Stu Grimson is a huge, extremely tough and articulate fighter with a solid knockout right hand. He is a very fair and enthusiastic fighter who led his team in PIM's last year with 218 and has had over 22 fights this year to put him in the "top 10 busiest" category. Last year he destroyed Shane Churla, who was not too smart in taking on Grimson with an already broken orbital bone. Stu was actually reluctant to fight Churla because of Shane's injury but did what he had to, sending Churla off the ice extremely bloodied. Obviously Stu has great size and the reach to go with it, which he uses effectively. He has fought everyone: Ewen, McCarthy, Probert (a great rivalry when Stu was a Blackhawk and Probert a Red Wing), McKenzie, Huard etc. and has started a good rivalry, it seems, with Krzysztof Oliwa taking him on twice this year (or rather, Oliwa has started a rivalry with Grimson). Against Sandy McCarthy a couple of seasons ago Stu showed the ability to take a punch; he can and is knocked down occasionally by a punch but hangs on and gets back up. I am glad to see Carolina is giving him the ice time he never got in Detroit; he has shown himself not to be a liability and is in fact a plus player this season.

Grimson learned some early lessons versus Dave Brown, while Stu was in Calgary. I learned the most about Grimson when he was a Red Wing, where he took on the likes of Domi, McKenzie, Brashear, McCarthy, Marshall, Ewen, Bonvie and Laus (among others). Stu goes almost exclusively right and throws big haymakers that tend to be much more accurate and only a touch less lethal, than a Tony Twist. Stu has much better balance than Twist, perhaps because his punches are more accurate and tamed, but as I have said can let an opponent's punch knock him down briefly. He has had memorable wins over both Domi and McKenzie (his rights really hurt McKenzie on one occasion) and beat down Grant Marshall twice in one game a few seasons back. Stu is usually satisfied with holding off the opponent, not necessarily tying up the opponent's dominant hand, and swinging those big, right haymakers. Off the ice a very eloquent speaker who actually considers his answers and avoids giving the "athlete cliché's."

	W	ST	K	SR	Q	SH	T	B	F	I	SM	TP	FP
Grimson	10+	10	10	10	9	n/a	n/a	9	10	10	10	10	10

MATT JOHNSON (6'5", 223 LBS.)

Matt is a very young (only 23 years old), promising player and enforcer and the Kings would do well to keep him. He led the team last year (his rookie year) in PIMs with 194 in only 52 games for a PMR of 3.73. This year he is one of the "top 10 busiest" fighters with 23 (at last count) fights. He fights the big guys; Stojanov, Brashear, Odjick, you name it. Johnson is a right-hand dominant puncher and really uses his left hand (at least in my viewing of him) only to grab; that is, if his left hand is free he is using it to reach for the opponent. Matt won a big decision against Gino Odjick last season, putting Gino off balance and getting in right upper-cuts. In another fight I viewed this season, Johnson dominated the smaller but game Rob Ray (but who doesn't? — just kidding, Rob, you're OK in my book!). My lower scores for stamina and intimidation only reflect that I have not seen him in a long fight and that he is new and is only beginning to make a reputation for himself, respectively.

	W	ST	K	SR	Q	SH	T	B	F	I	SM	TP	FP
Johnson	10	8	9.5	10	10	n/a	9.5	10	10	9	10	10	10+

DAN KORDIC (6'5", 220 LBS.)

Kordic is a big, tough Flyer, possibly their best fighter. Kordic likes to use the left (he went left versus Vukota and Oliwa this season). He and Ryan VandenBussche had one of, if not *the*, best fights of the year (see a write-up in my "Greatest 10 Fights" section). In that fight Kordic took several pops from Ryan early but came back big with the left (although he showed an ability to use the right also in that fight); it was a real showcase for them both. One of Kordic's strategies is to get the opponent's helmet off before swinging his big, left haymakers; with some fighters you can detect a concerted effort to get the helmet off and Kordic is one of those. Dan was involved last season in a fantastic fight versus Brendan Witt — both went toe-to-toe exchanging big lefts, not even attempting to tie up each other. Against Sandy McCarthy, Dan showed the ability to go quick with the lefts, but was dropped by a McCarthy right. He has also had some good matchups against Francois Leroux where he took some big Leroux rights but got in left haymakers late (after himself going right). Kordic tops his club in PIMs this year.

	W	ST	K	SR	Q	SH	T	B	F	I	SM	TP	FP
Kordic	10	10	8.5	10	10	9.5	n/a	10	10	9	10	10	10

DANIEL LACROIX (6'2", 205 LBS.)

Lacroix is another in the Flyers' great lineup of fighters, though not as busy as Kordic or Myhres. Dan is another southpaw; he demonstrated his ability to throw big lefts versus Sheldon Souray this season, actually chasing Souray down at one point after losing his jersey in the fight. Dan showcased his good balance and left hand versus Jason Weimer last season; both fighters skated from the blue-line to the end-boards and back, all the while grappling and throwing punches. Lacroix had a great bout last season also with Alex

Stojanov; there he showed that he could take a punch, taking several rights by Stojanov and waiting until he unleashed several lefts which dazed Alex. In another fight versus Brent Severyn (who is very strong), Daniel took several Severyn lefts, all the while talking to Brent! Daniel throws almost exclusively left; he can tie up his opponent (he had Weimer pretty tied up) but sometimes is either unable or more interested in simply trading punches.

	W	ST	K	SR	Q	SH	T	B	F	I	SM	TP	FP
Lacroix	10	10	9	9.5	10	n/a	9	10	10	7	10	10	10

DENNY LAMBERT (5'11", 200 LBS.)

I saw much more of Lambert with Anaheim than I have with Ottawa, where he is the team's dominant enforcer followed by the newly-acquired Chris Murray; last season he was the only Senator to even break the 3-digit PIM mark with 217. Denny's biggest problem is his balance, which often gets him into trouble. Against Matthew Barnaby I saw him throw some good rights, but then knock himself off balance with a miss whereupon he resorted to a Vukota-style take-down (you know, grab the leg of the opponent then throw him down). His lack of balance has lost him fights against other middleweight and marginal fighters like Sylvain Lefebvre. Lambert has also lost to Kenny Baumgartner (not a middleweight!) and Bob Boughner, again by letting himself be thrown about. He often gets tied up in such a way that it makes him hard to throw his dominant right-hand.

	W	ST	K	SR	Q	SH	T	B	F	I	SM	TP	FP
Lambert	10	8	7	7	9	n/a	7	5	10	6	7	8	9

DARREN LANGDON (6'1", 200 LBS.)

I will say right now that Darren Langdon may be my favorite fighter to have come up in the last three years, or more! Darren is much like a smaller Bob Probert, a very smart, second-half fighter who can switch hands, take a punch, tie up an opponent and do all those things a second-half fighter needs to be able to do. His fight versus Marty McSorley on February 2 this season (1997-98) was the best fight I've seen in years! Elucidating more on Darren's style, he is always in a fight for the long haul; he can and will take however many punches he needs to in order to get position and start giving punches himself. He keeps his head up, thereby not opening himself up for many of the more lethal punches (putting ones head down is the worst strategy, according to many fighters). Like all second-half fighters, Langdon has great balance and the ability to tie the opponent up, although he is also comfortable (as he showed in another showcase fight vs. Domi this season) with simply trading blows. Langdon's dominant throwing hand is his right, but he can and does switch to left when strategically advantageous, as he demonstrated in the Feb. 2 bout with McSorley (a full write-up is in my "Greatest 10 Fights" section). In that fight, Langdon nailed McSorley with a straight-arm left uppercut (which looked very "Probertesque" in fact) which was probably the best single punch of the fight. I would be surprised if Langdon has not studied Probert's style.

Despite his size, which is below average for many of today's enforcers (just examine this list!), Darren is afraid of no-one. He has fought Probert, Grimson, Simon, Stojanov, Ewen and Leroux, among others, obviously giving away size and reach. Langdon topped the Rangers in PIMs last season with 195 and is one of the "top 10 busiest" fighters this season with 21 scraps under his belt. Darren does a few things especially well: He is very good at getting in both rights or the occasional left while his arms are being held! Also he is very hard to pull down (just ask Randy McKay!). Versus Stojanov last season he took about 15 punches and actually told the linesmen 'Don't come in!' before letting loose with several rights of his own and taking the edge. Darren had a simply incredible fight versus Bob Probert last season at MSG; Langdon was given the win but in all honesty Probert took the edge there. In fact, Langdon was the one to go down, as much from exhaustion as anything else. Maybe a case of the student being slightly bested by the teacher? It really was like something out of Stephen King's The Gunslinger where the student fights the master to graduate. The only weakness, if you could call it that, is that Langdon really doesn't have a knockout punch, at least not that I have seen (and I have seen many of his fights), but it is really hard to knock out many of today's fighters; it simply does not happen that much. Darren did very well also against Chris Simon last season, where Darren used his left as much as his right; he held Simon off very well and actually got in the better punches! His best fights this year were versus McSorley, Lakovic and Randy McKay. One last humorous tidbit; when asked this year who he thought was the hardest hitter (in the fighting sense), Langdon is said to have thought for a moment and then reply, "I've never been hit hard!" You have to love that!

I would be surprised if Langdon has not studied Probert's style, and if he says he hasn't I won't believe him (how is *that* for a confirmation bias!)

	W	ST	K	SR	Q	SH	T	B	F	I	SM	TP	FP
Langdon	10+	10+	8	10	10	10	10	10+	10	8	10+	10	10+

PAUL LAUS (6'1", 216 LBS.)

I wish I knew more about Laus, but Florida just is not an incredible market as far as televising games! Paul really has only made a big splash in the league for the past couple of years, so hopefully he has a big future, despite already being 28 years old. Enthusiasm is his middle name; he led the league in fighting majors last year and, as you would expect, led his team in PIMs with 313. Oddly enough, he was also second on the team dramatic knocking-out of Ken Belanger with a huge, right haymaker. Laus does well against the big boys, too, fighting well against big Stu Grimson (it's the law, you know, you have to call him "big Stu" Grimson!) when big Stu was a Red Wing. In that fight, Paul got in several rights on Stuie but finally went down (due to the balance factor) after a few Grimson rights to the body and head. Laus also bested Darren McCarty this season with a few good right upper-cuts.

	W	ST	K	SR	Q	SH	T	B	F	I	SM	TP	FP
Laus	10+	8	9.5	9.5	10	10	9.5	9.5	10	7	10	9	9.5

FRANCOIS LEROUX (6'5", 236 LBS.)

Leroux is an obviously big guy who seems to have an inordinate amount of trouble with the smaller fighters. I saw him fight Brad May a few seasons back (granted May is a very good fighter, as I note in my write-up on him) where Leroux had to settle with throwing May (and himself) down. What I thought was maybe an anomaly turned out to be a pattern as I saw more of his fights; Leroux was pounded by Domi a year or so ago and this season was tossed about like a rag doll by the same Mr. Domi. It is a bit intuitive that a tall fighter would have trouble with a much shorter fighter, but with Leroux it seems to be more of a problem than with others of similar stature. Langdon, admittedly one of the smartest fighters, bested Leroux; Langdon had Leroux's right (Frankie goes almost if not exclusively right) tied up and was at the same time getting rights and lefts off and finally knocked Leroux down with a left upper-cut. Heck, even Olaf Kolzig (!) took on Leroux back during the Penguins/Capitals playoff series (remember that one, where Shoenfeld got booted?). Leroux does do a bit better with bigger fighters; this season he earned at least a draw versus Brashear, getting in several short rights. Each had the other pretty tied up (as I've said, Brashear likes to get in close) around the elbow and shoulder areas. He is really not a terribly active fighter, with only 81 PIMs in 59 games last year with Pittsburgh and only a 2.82 PMR this year.

	W	ST	K	SR	Q	SH	T	B	F	I	SM	TP	FP
Leroux	7	7	6	9	8	n/a	8	6	10	6	7	7	6

DEAN MALKOC (6'3", 200 LBS.)

Dean is not an incredibly busy fighter, with less than 100 PIMs each of the last two years. But he is very good when he does decide to drop the gloves! Malkoc and Darren McCarty had a couple of memorable fights in the pre-season this year; in the second fight Malkoc got beat by McCarty but landed several good lefts. Dean seems to prefer the left-hand punch but I say 'seems' because he goes to the right with ease (and did so against McCarty). Against Kypreos, Malkoc stayed in close and fired lefts, but against Rychel he used the left/right combinations very effectively. Against Rob Ray, Malkoc again switched very comfortably between left and right. One of the best switchers I have seen.

	W	ST	K	SR	Q	SH	T	B	F	I	SM	TP	FP
Malkoc	8	9	8	10	10	10+	10	10	10	6	10	9	10

BRYAN MARCHMENT (6'1", 205 LBS.)

Byran is, unfortunately, known more for his sometimes, shall we say, 'marginal' hitting tactics than for anything else. This is a bit unfair because he is actually a very good defenseman, having the best plus/minus last season for Edmonton. He is also an impressive fighter, although he has slowed down a lot on that front from his Chicago days when he finished with 313 PIMs one year. Bryan had a great fight against Tie Domi last season, where Marchment showed the ability to use both lefts and rights, landing several of each on Domi. Bryan also showed good balance in that fight as Tie, as he is wont to do, tried to spin Marchment down to the ice to no avail. Bryan has fought Darren McCarty well, putting several rights into Darren until McCarty, sans jersey, felled Bryan with two left upper-cuts. Not such an intimidating fighter but he will have people looking around on the ice when he's out, due to his fierce checking; he raised the wrath of the Anaheim team in a recent game and had a great go with Jason Marshall.

	W	ST	K	SR	Q	SH	T	B	F	I	SM	TP	FP
Marchment	8	8	7	9	9.5	10	7	10	8	9	10	10	8

BRAD MAY (6'1", 210 LBS.)

Brad May is a terribly under-rated fighter; this kid is smart, throws hard and is incredibly good at using both hands to throw punches! In my opinion he was Buffalo's most effective fighter, from a win standpoint, but lacked the flash of a disrobing Ray or the outward passion of a Matthew Barnaby. Injuries the past few years have also hampered his career, but this kid has a big up-side not only due to his tremendous fighting skills (more on those in a bit) but also due to his ability to score. His fighting style is furious; he unleashes a hailstorm of lefts and rights and both are big punches. Against big

Chris Tamer, May took several Tamer punches standing up only to unload with both hands, beating Chris. May has had a few scraps with Terry Carkner and Jay Wells, two Buffalo nemeses. May has beaten Carkner with big lefts and in one game vs. the Rangers KO'ed Jay Wells in one fight and in a second fight the same game beat Wells down with both lefts and rights. May has beaten opponents with his right also; against Rudy Poeschek, May grabbed with the left and threw right, putting Poeschek to the ice. Others who found May's left/right combinations too hard to handle include Rob Pearson, Steve Leach, Doug Zmolek and Mike Peluso. Oddly enough, Rick Tocchet has seemed to have May's number. Hopefully May will have a healthy 1998-99 season with Vancouver, an already very tough team where May's scoring touch may (no pun intended) find its way back.

	W	ST	K	SR	Q	SH	T	B	F	I	SM	TP	FP
May	10	10	9	10	10+	10+	8	10	10	8	10	10	9

SANDY McCARTHY (6'3", 225 LBS.)

Sandy is a very strong fighter who likes to throw big, right punches while using the left hand to grab the opponent. For as strong and fearsome a fighter as he is, he has not put up huge numbers in the PIM column. Last season, injuries limited his playing time and he had a respectable 3.42 PMR in 33 games. This year his PMR rose to 3.78 so maybe being healthy is the key. When he fights, though, he is certainly good at it! He places his punches very strategically; against Todd Ewen he held Ewen to zero punches while at the same time firing right after right into the back of Ewen's head, until Todd dropped his head whereupon Sandy went to the upper-cut. This is the same strategy many of the better fighters use; Lyndon Byers used that, as does Darren McCarty and Bob Probert. Next to Twist and Joey Kocur (or rather, alongside both) I think McCarthy has the hardest punch. McCarthy's hard rights have felled such heavyweights as big Stu Grimson and Dan Kordic.

More to illustrate that it is often the *fight* and not the *fighter*, Sandy has had a lot of problems beating Tie Domi but recently this season beat Tony Twist — who'd figure? One of McCarthy's best fights was against Bob Probert in 1993-94, Sandy's rookie year with Calgary and Bob's last year with the Red Wings. In fact, I believe that was Probert's last fight as a Red Wing. This fight was a showcase for McCarthy; it was a long, drawn out fight where Sandy got the majority of the punches in, hitting Probert several times square in the face, actually with both his left and right hands. To Probert's credit he did not go down, but he was not in the fight and it ended when a tired Probert head-butted McCarthy. Sandy also demonstrated the ability to tie up his opponent in that fight as well as the ability to take a punch, as Probert did deliver some solid punches. Against Grimson, Sandy put Stu on the ice briefly (Stu got up) with some hard rights and got the win. Another guy you would not figure to give McCarthy problems is Rob Ray and yet he has beaten McCarthy on at least two occasions! Oddly, Sandy's strategy seems to be one of mimicking the opponent's style; against a fast puncher Sandy will punch fast; against someone who throws slower, Sandy will do likewise. Calgary traded him maybe because of the emergence of a promising young enforcer by the name of Rocky Thompson, but McCarthy has been busy so far in his short stint with Tampa Bay. As big and tough as he is (more fearsome than Twist, in my opinion, due to his greater accuracy in punching) and as he is only 25 years old, I see a bright future for him.

	W	ST	K	SR	Q	SH	T	B	F	I	SM	TP	FP
McCarthy	10	10	10	10	9.5	9	10	10	10	10	9.5	10	10+

DARREN McCARTY (6'1", 210 LBS.)

Considering that the Red Wings were a club who's success in the 1996-97 season (winning the Stanley Cup) exemplified the word "team" it is fairly safe to say that Darren McCarty was personally responsible for three of the most important events of the season. Consider the following: 1). Darren McCarty personally exacted revenge upon Claude Lemieux for Lemieux's nasty hit on Draper the previous years' playoffs in a game on March 26, 1997, 2). McCarty, in that same game, scored the game winning goal 39 seconds into overtime, providing the Wings with their first victory over Colorado that season and 3). McCarty scored the Stanley Cup clinching goal against Philadelphia on June 7, 1997 in, I might add, spectacular style!

McCarty is not an enforcer in the 'goon' sense of the word. His own claim is that he patterns himself after Rick Tocchet; his plan has always been to fight for the purpose of making room for himself and his team-mates (and protect team-mates when needed) with the goal of increasing his point production. He has been successful in that, registering a career best 19 goals and 30 assists in 68 games during the 1996-97 season. Having said all that, Darren is a superb and fierce fighter who has taken on all comers. He had a simply awesome fight (narrated in my "Greatest 10 Fights" section) against Cam Russell in a pre-season game his rookie year. There he used his patented "Jack Johnson" stance and jack-hammer left to put the hurt on Russell in a major way! His rookie year (1993-94) he also battled McSorley, Baumgartner, Brashear, Kocur and Crowe, among others. He has shown a very hard left punch (his left upper-cuts are deadly!) against opponents such as Mark Tinordi (who he knocked out with one punch!), Scott Walker, Marchment, Rob Pearson and others, all of whom have been bloodied and bruised by Darren. Oh, and let's not forget Claude Lemieux, who suffered Darren's wrath to the tune of over a dozen stitches on March 26, 1997.

This season, McCarty leads the team in PIMs, with a PMR of 2.21, not as active as many enforcers but that may be due to several factors including his concentration on scoring, the effects of his father's battle with cancer as well as a recurring hand injury. Nevertheless, McCarty has had fierce fights this year with Claude Lemieux (a November 11 showcase of McCarty's ability to switch hands, tie up an opponent and use his great balance), Sean Brown (a big rookie with Edmonton), Marty McSorley and others. Darren's best punch is the left uppercut and his biggest weakness is that opponents' punches sometimes have the effect of stunning him, however briefly; he gives up reach on some and therefore leaves himself open to such aforementioned punches.

	W	ST	K	SR	Q	SH	T	B	F	I	SM	TP	FP
McCarty	9.5	10	9.5	10	10	9.5	8	10	10	8	10	9	10

JIM McKENZIE (6'3", 205 LBS.)

Jim is a big and very strong player who can throw with both hands effectively. He is not an incredibly active fighter but he has shown the ability to take on and win against very tough opponents. Earlier in his career, with Hartford, he had great success fighting Tony Twist (Twist then with Quebec). He seemed, at least then, to have Twist's number; in one great fight Jim threw three lefts followed by about 8-9 rights followed by a half-dozen more lefts, the last which dropped Tony to the ice. McKenzie can take a punch too, evidenced by a re-match with Twist whereupon Jim took a half-dozen or so of Twist's huge right-hand bombs, but stood to deliver six lefts of his own again dropping Tony. I say this not to derogate Tony Twist but to show McKenzie's ability to go with the very toughest. I would say Jim is about the biggest fighter (with the exception of Bob Probert) to effectively use both rights and lefts — both are bombs! Last season McKenzie had two great fights in one game versus Troy Crowder where he bested Crowder both times, again using both hands.

	W	ST	K	SR	Q	SH	T	B	F	I	SM	TP	FP
McKenzie	9	10	10	10	9.5	10+	10	10	10	8	10	10	9

MARTY McSORLEY (6'1", 235 LBS.)

At 34 years of age, McSorley is not as active on the fighting front as he once was but he is without a doubt the toughest 34-year old in the NHL. Given that he has been a fighting institution in the NHL since the 1983-84 season where he racked up 224 PIMs in 74 games, it is certainly wondrous that he is still as tough and smart a fighter as he is! Because he is in San Jose, where games start at 10:30 p.m. as far as the Eastern markets are concerned, people have seemed to forget about Marty's presence. Looking at just this year, however, McSorley has been involved in what are possibly two of the best fights of the year, one against Darren Langdon on Feb. 2 (for which I give an account in my "Greatest 10 Fights") and one against the very tough Reid Simpson of Chicago.

McSorley is a fighter much like Bob Probert. In fact, the two have had quite a rivalry over the past 13-odd years and were involved in the best fight I have ever seen in my life, during the 1993-94 season (look for my write-up in "Greatest 10 Fights"). Marty prefers, it seems, fights that go long; he is a "second half" fighter, like Probert and like Darren Langdon. Perhaps that is why the Langdon/McSorley bout was so entertaining. Again, like any successful second-half fighter, McSorley has excellent balance along with the ability to tie an opponent up unless and until he has the advantage. Marty hits almost exclusively with his right hand; he switches very rarely and usually only when the other fighter goes left. This is probably to avoid the "left/right" situation where two fighters end up hitting each others' hands when swinging. Still, McSorley will hit wherever he gets the chance; he will go to the body if the head is unreachable, mixing in both upper-cuts and haymakers; anything to land blows and weaken or tire the opponent. He has a very good reach for his height and keeps his head up. Another thing McSorley will do, similar to fighters such as Domi, is he will spin the opponent around; this is also evidence of the great balance on his part. McSorley's Achilles Heel, if you will, is his lack of a knockout punch. Marty has not, over the years, really dominated many fights; often his fights are draws, albeit very entertaining draws. Looking at that glass as 'half full' it also means that McSorley doesn't lose many fights either. If anyone needs evidence for his value, consider the fact that he has followed Gretzky from Edmonton to Los Angeles to the Rangers. McSorley's NYR tenure was not overly successful, why I do not know; maybe Langdon and McSorley on the same team smacks of redundancy?

	W	ST	K	SR	Q	SH	T	B	F	I	SM	TP	FP
McSorley	10	10+	7	10	9	9	10+	10+	10	8	10	10	8

GINO ODJICK (6'3", 210 LBS.)
Gino is very obviously a busy guy when it comes to the PIMs, but between his career being in Vancouver (another western team that does not get much media coverage in the east) and only recently moving to New York (with the Islanders) I have not seen him play that much. I do note that while he has big PIM numbers, he also seems to gather quite a few misconduct's and suspensions, which inflate PIMs. I know he does his share of fighting, however.

I have seen him on a few occasions; from what I have seen he is a right dominant fighter; he used his right versus Domi twice and versus Barry Potomski. He did go to the left against Odgers this season versus Colorado. That is all I know and for me not enough information to really put numbers to this player's fight game.

KRZYSZTOF OLIWA (6'5", 235 LBS.)

Oliwa may well be the future, enforcer-wise, for New Jersey and if he keeps going like he has maybe the next long-term heavyweight champion! He is huge (obviously), enthusiastic about dropping the gloves and young, just turning 25 years old this past week (April 12th, 1998). That he likes to fight is evidenced on paper by the fact that in this, his rookie year, he is the #1 busiest fighter in the NHL with 33 fighting majors. Last year he played one game for New Jersey and received — yep — a fighting major! When you actually see him fight, you know he is having fun! This year he has taken on all comers with the purpose of challenging the toughest; he has fought Grimson twice, Cummins, Domi (a few times), Kordic, Stock, Kris King, Kenny Baumgartner etc. He had a "fight-trick" against Toronto this year by getting three fighting majors in the same game (as I recall, two versus Domi and one versus Kris King). When New Jersey played Chicago at season's end, with Probert back in the line-up after missing 64 games due to shoulder surgery, I was sure Oliwa would want to challenge him. It did not happen and I speculate that it was because Oliwa knew Probert was not operating at 100% (Chicago had him in, I believe, mostly because they were vying hard for a playoff spot).

Oliwa is still learning all the tricks of the trade; he is a right-hand puncher who likes to tie up the opponent when he can, but is sometimes unsuccessful. When Oliwa fought Grimson he took more punches than he gave; Oliwa seemed content to use his huge reach to hold off Grimson, but that did not quite work against Stuie. Still, Oliwa took the punches standing up; his second fight versus Grimson that game broke the old PIM record for New Jersey previously held by Ken Daneyko. Oliwa took some hard Domi lefts in one of their bouts, again standing up although he did get cut. There it seemed Oliwa's height was working against him, but Domi is smart and knows how to do that with the taller fighters (and with Domi, almost everyone is relatively taller). I cannot wait to see him next year! His lower scores for knockout punch and intimidation are merely the result of my not knowing that he has indeed knocked anyone out and that he has not had the time to build a reputation (but he's working on it!).

	W	ST	K	SR	Q	SH	T	B	F	I	SM	TP	FP
Oliwa	10+	10	8	9	10	n/a	8	10	10	8	10	10	10+

RICH PILON (6'0", 205 LBS.)

Despite the fact that Pilon has been around for awhile, I have not really seen that much of him. He has somewhat of a bad reputation, mainly because he hits very tough (some say dirty) but wears a visor. For the record, I have heard the visor is prescription and on doctor's orders, so I am not sure that should be counted against him. He is infamous for the hit on Kevin Stevens which knocked Stevens out and caused him to hit the ice face first and without any cushioning, resulting in many operations on Steven's face and really altering the tough game he once played. Pilon was also involved in a nasty stick-swinging incident last season with Mario Lemieux, but for the record there Lemieux did start the incident with a swing to Pilon's head, but Pilon's response looked much more dramatic and it was against Mario, so...It should be noted that in a fight this season versus Corbet, Pilon actually took his own helmet off, which seemed a pretty fair-minded thing to do. I'm not putting numbers on this guy, because I have simply seen too little of him.

BOB PROBERT (6'3", 225 LBS.)

Excuse any over-pontificating I do on Bob Probert, as I feel I could write a book on this player! I would like to make two statements, which I will support. First, Bob Probert is the most dominant enforcer of the last decade; while his status as "heavyweight champion" may currently be under dispute, I am making the claim that if you examine the last 10+ years, Probert is the reigning enforcer. My second claim, which I will defend before looking specifically at Probert the fighter, is that Bob is one of, if not the, most talented enforcers as far as a "total package" is concerned.

Because Probert is often talked about strictly within the fighting realm, I would like to direct some attention to Probert's talents as a total player, particularly his scoring. How many "enforcers" do you see who have had a six-point game, as Probert did (2 goals, 4 assists) as a Red Wing versus New Jersey, in 1987? In his best year, 1987-88, Probert not only led the league with 398 PIMs, he also rallied for 29 goals and 33 assists for a point-per-game ratio of 0.84! In the playoffs that season, Probert also had the distinction of breaking Gordie Howe's playoff scoring record set in 1955 (9 goals, 11 assists for 20 points) with 21 points (8 goals, 13 assists) in addition to racking up 51 PIMs. In fact, Probert has maintained over his entire NHL career a points-per-game ratio of 0.51, which is very respectable, especially considering that along the way he has spent 2,653 minutes in the penalty box, 6th highest in the NHL all time. For those who have recently bemoaned that Probert is not interested or "washed up" in the fighting arena, note that he finished last year in Chicago with 326 PIMs, his highest total since leading the NHL in 1987-88 with 398. Probert can score not only because he has surprisingly good hand-eye coordination (I have seen him slap pucks out of mid-air into the net) and not only because of his fierce fighting reputation, but because he has incredible balance and his hard to move from in front of the net. In addition, he is a fearsome checker; ironically many of today's enforcers are not necessarily fierce checkers like Probert was and is.

Bob Probert is the icon, the epitome, of the hockey enforcer. In Detroit he and Joey Kocur, the "Bruise Brothers," were the most feared twosome in the league (and that comes from other NHL players!). By any standard, Probert has been the king; no person has been more challenged over the years. Why? Because he was and in many ways still is the standard bar by which other enforcers measure themselves. It is pointless to even try and list who Probert has fought; he has fought everyone, often many times. Some of the biggest and most publicized fights of the last decade have been Probert fights: Probert v. Domi I and II, Probert v. Troy Crowder, Probert vs. McSorley (in 1993-94, the best fight I have ever seen, written up in my "Greatest 10 Fights" section) and the list goes on. Probert was never invincible, no fighter is; when Probert would lose a fight, it was always big news and he always seemed to come back big; again, evidence Probert v. Domi II, Probert's re-match with Troy Crowder, Probert's re-match after being TKO'ed by Todd Ewen (in the same game, yet!). Bob has always seemed to get the edge back on any player who bested him. As with any reigning champion, Bob has always seemed to be the target of inordinate criticism; one announcer said it well when he stated (and I paraphrase) that 'Probert loses a fight if he doesn't win' which is to say that any player who came out of a Bob Probert fight with even a draw would be declared, at least by his fans, to be the winner. I have gotten many the e-mail to my Drop the Gloves! page declaring how Tony Twist "beat up" Probert; well I have those fights on tape and Twist in no way has gotten the edge. In fact, those fights were disappointing in their brevity, both players going down early. Along that line note that in Probert v. Domi I, it was Domi who was on the ropes and Probert delivering the better punches at the end; in fact, the linesmen intervened when it was clear that Domi was in trouble. However, Domi did cut Probert and thereby "took" the win. Bob's Achilles Heel, if you will, was always his desire to get the jersey over his head and off, to free his devastating right hand. More often than not, that was the reason for his loses; he had the jersey over his head when Domi cut him and Crowder's win in their first match also came when Probert was caught in his own jersey.

Probert's style is very complex. He has been the best over the last decade at just about every aspect of the fighting game. He has great stamina and has been involved in some of the longest fights in NHL history. In order to last in a long fight, you have to have great balance and the ability to tie the opponent up as well as take a punch when it is delivered; Probert excels at all those things. Bob is good at switching hands; his right is definitely his dominant hand and he uses that better than any I have ever seen. He mixes hay-makers, upper-cuts, jabs, you name it, he goes to the head and body, wherever he can get a punch in. I have even seen him use the patented "back-hand cuff" effectively against, for example, Marty McSorley in their 1993-94 war. When he switches hands, it is often with devastating results; I have not seen anyone else who can switch hands to get in one punch with the other hand to turn the fight around. Probert is not necessarily the quickest fighter; he likes to take his time to get positioned and will take the punches necessary to do so. Since he is so often challenged, he sometimes needs to "get mad" in the fight and get motivated. I score him a bit down on "future potential" because he has been, admittedly, less than motivated on certain occasions. But as Bill Clement duly noted during the Probert v. Langdon bout, Probert "must get tired" of being the Gunslinger, challenged by every enforcer who wants to make his mark. Probert only played 14 games this year with Chicago, due to some serious injuries; it will be exciting to see him back next season, playing healthy for Chicago.

One last thing and I will shut up; Probert has been an exemplary role model, since coming to Chicago. He has shown perhaps better than any other athlete that a person can do a complete 180-degree lifestyle change and get 'one's house' in order.

	W	ST	K	SR	Q	SH	T	B	F	I	SM	TP	FP
Probert	9.5	10+	9.5	10	9	10	10+	10+	10	9.5	10+	10	10

CAM RUSSELL (6'4", 174 LBS.)

Cam Russell is the bravest fighter in the NHL! I say this because this kid, bless his heart, gets pounded so many times and comes back for more! Russell is not a bad fighter; he is a left-dominant puncher but is good with his right also, a very good switcher. Cam has turned in very good performances at times against very tough opponents; he did well versus Probert during the 1993-94 season, the same year he took the pre-season beating by Darren McCarty (in my "Greatest 10 Fights" section). There he used both the left and right against Probert to get a draw. Russell has also done well versus Tie Domi this past season (1997-98); in Chicago, Russell used the left almost exclusively to get a win over Domi.

More often than not, though, Russell seems to get hit a lot and very hard! I mentioned the McCarty fight; Cam has also gotten knocked silly by Brashear (as I mentioned on Cam's birthday, yet!) and pretty seriously by Domi in one of the last games this season (Cam was taken off the ice on a stretcher but happily was OK and returned home with the team that night). I would say Cam needs to work on his defensive game, as either people are getting punches in that are very hard and/or he is not the best at taking a punch, or some combination of the two. I give him high marks for heart, though!

	W	ST	K	SR	Q	SH	T	B	F	I	SM	TP	FP
Russell	10+	9	7	10	10	10	5	9.5	10	7	7	6	9

BRENT SEVERYN (6'2", 211 LBS.)

Brent is a very strong, moderately frequent fighter. He led the Avalanche last year in PIMs but had a PMR of only 2.92, on the low side for this list of enforcers. His PMR has jumped to 4.03 with the Ducks, however he has played in only 33 games. The skinny on him is that he is often asked to play the enforcer role more than he wishes. Having said all that, Severyn is very strong and tough; he likes to swing big with the left hand and has done very well against fighters such as Brashear and Daniel Lacroix. Against Lacroix, Severyn was able to tie up his opponent and throw several big lefts; against Brashear he did the same. A couple of seasons back, as an Islander, Brent had a good bout against O'Donnell where he used his lefts and rights equally effectively, actually throwing more rights after losing his jersey. He likes to get the jersey off (unfortunately that strategy is penalized with a game misconduct now, thank you very much Rob Ray), which he did also versus Aaron Ward in the infamous March 26, 1997 game versus Detroit. Severyn also did well versus Leboutillier, tagging him with several lefts and dropping him. Brent is a very fair fighter, it should be noted; he could have really tagged Aaron Ward but held back when the referee told him to quit.

	W	ST	K	SR	Q	SH	T	B	F	I	SM	TP	FP
Severyn	7	10	8	10	10	10	9.5	10	10+	7	10	10	8

CHRIS SIMON (6'3", 219 LBS.)

Simon is a very hard puncher who goes almost exclusively left, but will strategically go right to get the opponent turned back into the position he wants. Simon decimated Todd Ewen with some hard lefts in a fight a few years back when Simon was with Colorado. One of Simon's strategic moves is to get the opponent's helmet off; a few players use this strategy while others don't seem to care — Simon cares and that's probably pretty smart for the hands. Simon has had a bit of trouble tying up smaller opponents; Domi got in several pops in a fight once and Darren Langdon, last season, got the edge on Simon with both the right and left hands. This was in the same Washington v. New York game that had the wild VandenBussche v. Witt fight. I have heard, note only heard, that Simon did very well against Probert a couple of seasons back in the playoffs (?) but I have never seen that fight and so cannot comment on it. Injuries have dogged Simon recently; he had a very respectable 3.93 PMR last season with Washington in 42 games but has been pretty inactive in this 1997-

98 campaign. He is relatively young, however, and could have a big upside if he stays healthy.

	W	ST	K	SR	Q	SH	T	B	F	I	SM	TP	FP
Simon	10	9	10	10	10	9.5	8	10	10	9.5	9	10	10

REID SIMPSON (6'1", 220 LBS.)

Simpson is a very tough forward, currently with the Hawks, who has just started making his marks in the NHL in the last couple of seasons. He is not an incredibly busy fighter, but he is very tough and has been involved this season in some very entertaining fights, one against Marty McSorley in San Jose and another against Kris King (in the same game where Domi hurt Cam Russell) in Toronto. Simpson likes to throw big rights and can take a punch, as he took many versus Domi earlier this year when Reid got his jersey stuck over his head (one of Domi's favorite tricks). Reid could not tie up Domi's left and he paid the price! In the fight against Kris King, both players seemed content to trade punches, rather than tie the other up, and Reid took many standing up, also delivering several big rights that ended up pounding King down, albeit briefly. I chose this fight as one of my "Greatest 10 Fights" as it is in recent memory and was a very good scrap!

Getting the jersey over the opponent's head is a strategy not lost on Simpson, either, as he did that in his great bout against McSorley (he tried it against King, unsuccessfully). In both fights, Simpson showed an ability to last through a long bout (both went on for awhile) and use the left hand to punch. But his best punch is the right; he mixes in haymakers and uppercuts with that. Reid had a very nice victory against Jason Marshall, another tough customer!

	W	ST	K	SR	Q	SH	T	B	F	I	SM	TP	FP
Simpson	10	10	8	10	10	8	7	10	10	8	9	10	9.5

SHELDON SOURAY (6'3", 230 LBS.)

As this is Souray's rookie year and has he is not a high PIM producer, I really do not know much about him. I have only seen him in one fight against Daniel Lacroix. He preferred to punch left in that fight, but did switch to the right. He did not hold onto Lacroix and took some lefts that appeared to stun him, but he stayed on his feet and finished the fight. I don't want to give numbers due to my lack of knowledge.

P.J. STOCK

This kid is so new my The Hockey News 1997-98 Yearbook didn't even list him! Stock is still making his way back and forth between the New York Rangers and their AHL club, but his performances in the NHL demonstrate he wants to stay! Stock is very brave; he took on Oliwa (who simply towered over him), which is evidence of bravery in my book! In that fight Stock showed himself to be very intelligent; given the size discrepancy, Stock stayed inside and delivered several short lefts to Oliwa (Stock appears to be a left-dominant puncher). P.J. even used the glass along the boards, grabbing the partition to pin Oliwa against the boards, keeping him close while P.J. got in those short lefts! Clever guy!

I saw Stock fight Kris King (not on Stan's list, but a very tough, very under-rated fighter!) where Stock went deftly back and forth between the right and lefts, equally effective with both. P.J. fought Dale Hunter, a veteran, twice in as many games and right off the opening whistle! In their second match-up, Stock used his right (maybe he's a righty!) to cut Hunter over the eye. He is very good at tying the opponent up and is quick; he could be a dominant fighter someday!

	W	ST	K	SR	Q	SH	T	B	F	I	SM	TP	FP
Stock	10+	10	8	10	10	10	10	10	10	8	10	10	10+

RYAN VANDENBUSSCHE (5'11", 187 LBS.)

Ryan is an extremely tough kid, especially as he usually gives up size to many of his fighting opponents. Ryan is a left-dominant puncher who swings very fast lefts, much like Darren McCarty. In a great scrap versus Dan Kordic (written up in my "Greatest 10 Fights" section), Ryan was able to get in some lefts that surprised, if not stunned, Kordic while simultaneously holding off Kordic's own huge lefts. Ryan's big lefts proved deadly for Nick Kypreos, who was knocked cold by a VandenBussche left and may not return to the NHL! Ryan was involved in another donnybrook with Washington's Brendan Witt; the two went toe-to-toe, trading punches! Ryan's left proved to be quick and accurate in that fight. Ryan can, when needed, switch to the right as he did versus a much bigger Wade Belak (a huge kid in the Colorado system). Ryan's strategy, many times, is to get in close (smart given his size!). He can also tie up the opponent very well.

	W	ST	K	SR	Q	SH	T	B	F	I	SM	TP	FP
VandenBussche	10+	10	9.5	10	10	9	10	10	10	8	10+	10	10+

So here you have it, my assessments of some of the fighters presented in *Bad Boys IV: Ultimate Bad Boys*. Again, one thing I did not do was rank the fighters as it seemed too much like comparing "apples to oranges" so to speak. But for those who want to know what I think about who is best at what, here are some "awards" if you will, including fighters not in this book:

Hardest Punch - tie between Tony Twist and Joey Kocur (honourable mention Sandy McCarthy).

Smartest Fighter - Darren Langdon and Bob Probert.

Most Willing - tie between Kryzsztof Oliwa and Tie Domi.

Biggest Heart - Jim Cummins (honourable mention to Cam Russell for always coming back for more).

Most Stamina - Bob Probert and Marty McSorley (honourable mention to Darren Langdon).

Strength - Sandy McCarthy.

Quickness - Jeff Odgers, Ryan VandenBussche (honourable mention to Darren McCarty).

Switching - Brad May (honourable mention to Jim McKenzie).

Tying Up - Darren Langdon, Bob Probert and Ryan Vandenbussche.

Balance - Bob Probert and Tie Domi.

Fairness - Dennis Bonvie (he takes his own helmet off!).

Intimidation - Tony Twist (honourable mention to Bob Probert and Sandy McCarthy).

Smartness - Darren Langdon and Bob Probert (honourable mention Marty McSorley).

Taking a Punch - Darren Langdon.

Future - K. Oliwa, R. VandenBussche, P.J. Stock and Matt Johnson (and a host of others!).

DAVID M. SINGER

A floor and roller hockey player and long-time season ticket holder at New York Islanders games, Singer has maintained a website (http://pages.prodigy.com/dmsinger) which is primarily dedicated to hockey fighters. He also has covered the Buffalo Sabres for Fischler Hockey Service and is pursuing a degree at the University of Buffalo. Like Chadwick, Singer is a savant when it comes to pugilists-on-the-pond.

Unlike Chadwick, Singer views the sluggers from a different — but no less intriguing — perspective. His review follows:

WILLINGNESS

1. Krzysztof Oliwa - He had to fight everyone he could as a rookie (1997-98) to earn a spot on the Devils skilled roster.

2. Tie Domi - They wouldn't love him as much in Toronto if he didn't do what he does best.

3. Donald Brashear - He had some superstar teammates to protect even if they didn't play super.
4. Paul Laus - He's had the most fighting majors in the league the past two years.

5. Jeff Odgers - He didn't win them all, but still dropped the gloves as often as possible.

6. Darren Langdon - He showed the Rangers he can fight and is unwilling to let P.J. Stock take his job.

7. Mick Vukota - After the Islanders gave up on him, he went to Tampa and Montreal proving he's still valuable.

8. Stu Grimson - He showed Carolina fans many highlights last season.

9. Kris King - Domi spent so much time in the box, Kris missed him on the bench and decided to be his partner in crime.

10. Matt Johnson - Even though he collected a number of majors last season, he's not nearly as known as some of the other fighters. That can be an advantage.

STAMINA

1. Marty McSorley - He's way ahead of the pack.

2. Matt Barnaby - If a ref steps in Barnaby spends half his time and energy yelling at the zebra to back away.

3. Bryan McCabe - He went five minutes with Barnaby. That was really impressive!

4. Tie Domi - A hard head with a second and third wind.

5. Darren Langdon - He likes to take a few to see what he's getting into and then throw his best. Usually makes it last a little longer than most scuffles.

6. Bob Probert - Probie never seems to mind when someone hits him. If he doesn't KO the other guy, his fights will last a while.

7. Joey Kocur - If his knuckles could last, so could he.

8. Ken Baumgartner - Bomber dislikes losing but usually can't deliver a huge punch so he tries to get in many quick ones.

9. Donald Brashear - Like teammate, Bryan McCabe, Brashear was in a couple of scraps last season that were just too long to ignore.

10. Stu Grimson - He also put together the Hurricanes longest "winning streak."

KNOCKOUT PUNCH
1. Tony Twist - One nasty punch can deposit a foe quicker than anyone else in the league. His opponents won't disagree.

2. Sandy McCarthy - He's a big man and throws a big punch.

3. Chris Simon - Although he didn't get a chance to show many people that nice punch of his last year, it should be back in 1998-99 in full form.

4. Rob Ray - He could win the award for making an opponent's neck look like it broke off several times in a bout.

5. Bob Probert - If his fights don't last a long time, it's because of his Kayo punch.

6. Dave Manson - Half the time he uses his punch like a halfback stiff-arm while playing D. It's probably why he gets so many minors.

7. Brent Severyn - He doesn't get to show it as much as the others on this list, but the power is there when he gets to go.

8. Stu Grimson - Nicknames like the Grim Reaper aren't just concocted because they sound cool.

9. Ed Jovanovski - Out of all his hockey attributes, I wish he'd show this one more.

10. Ken Belanger - There must be nothing more satisfying to a fighter than punching a guy, dropping him, and skating away as if it was no problem.Ken does it well

STRENGTH

1. Tony Twist - It seems as if he started lifting weights when he was an infant.

2. Bob Probert - Although he may not be in his prime, he's remained at the top because of his strength.

3. Chris Simon - He can't always rely on speed. His reputation comes from sheer power.

4. Donald Brashear - When he started he wasn't considered a special fighter. Time in the weight room helped. With Mike Keenan around, he'll probably only be getting stronger.

5. Sandy McCarthy - He works on his legs more than most fighters.

6. Krzysztof Oliwa - His natural size gives him an edge. If he keeps working on his strength, he could become Number One.

7. Brent Severyn - After Tony Twist, no one spends as much time in the weight room.

8. Enrico Ciccone He would be higher on the list if he worked out more.

9. Francois Leroux - He doesn't drop them as much as everyone else, but when he does it's painful because of his power.

10. Reid Simpson -He earned a spot on the Hawks roster with his strength.

QUICKNESS
1. Matt Barnaby - He has the most energy, he doesn't tire and keeps wailing quickly.

2. Kelly Chase - His speed keeps him with the bigger boys.

3. Ken Baumgartner - He prefers quick, short punches.

4. Tie Domi - Getting in two punches to your opponent's one gives him get an edge.

5. Tony Twist - Known for power, not speed. But if he was so slow, that nasty haymaker wouldn't connect as often as it does.

6. Bob Probert - Same as Twist. Pure power needs to be able to connect to be effective.

7. Darren Langdon - He usually never throws less than two or three punches in two seconds. He gets them off swiftly since he doesn't usually get nailed in between throws.

8. Rob Ray - Although he had been faster without his jersey, he's still got his speed.

9. Marty McSorley - Age slows everyone, but Marty was so fast that he still belongs on the list.

10. Enrico Ciccone - He lets them fly as fast as his arms will go.

SWITCHING HANDS
1. Ken Baumgartner - Ken and Marty McSorley use their boxing training to advantage. When was the last time you saw a boxer only use one hand?

2. Marty McSorley - See above

3. Brad May - The best part is that it never looks as if the foe realizes he can throw from either side. What a surprise!

4. Jim McKenzie - Switching hands is his best attribute.

5. Chris Simon - He's not nimble, but he switches hands quickly.

6. Stu Grimson - It's nice to see a big fellow learn to turn in his stance.

7. Mick Vukota - If he didn't learn to throw from both sides, he'd be out of the NHL.

8. Tie Domi - Sometimes it looks as if he's launching both hands simultaneously.

9. Bob Probert - Occasionally it appears as if he'd rather let one hand start bleeding before throwing the other.

10. Matt Barnaby - He studied Brad May when they were teammates.

TYING UP

1. Mick Vukota - This is why some fight fans dislike him

2. Rob Ray - He can still hold the foes.

3. Craig Berube - Chief knows when he's out of gas. He can tie up an enemy to get him to stop swinging.

4. Brent Severyn - If he doesn't want you to swing at him, you won't! He's too strong, and if he grabs his opponent, he won't let go.

5. Ken Belanger - One thing he learned quickly in the NHL — from Vukota — was getting the tie-up.

6. Darren Langdon - If necessary he'll do it but not before getting a few off. Then he grabs and throws his own.

7. Gino Odjick - Sometimes he ties up too much and walks away with a lot of roughing penalties instead of fighting majors.

8. Marty McSorley - His is the boxing trait that I like the least.

9. Bob Probert - He would rather throw punches, but won't swing wildly.

10. Sandy McCarthy - He knows when to throw 'em, and when to hold 'em'.

BALANCE

1. Chris Simon - He likes to spin while he fights. This provides him with an edge on those who don't come close on the "Best Balance" list.

2. Tony Twist - Punch and pull on him all you want, he rarely goes down.

3. Bob Probert - Probie is reminiscent of Twist, but he's been standing for more years.

4. Tie Domi - Because he is smaller, Tie has a low center of gravity and better leverage.

5. Bryan McCabe - Really good punches are required to knock him down. It would be much better, though, if he could throw those punches himself.

6. Matt Barnaby - A lot of pulling and pushing accompanies a Barnaby fight. An opponent must have good balance to match Matt's in order to keep the bout close.

7. Donald Brashear - He assumes a stance and usually maintains it. Considerable power is required for a foe to break free.

8. Rob Ray - Even in losing fights he'll be standing at the end.

9. Ken Baumgartner - His balance must last for Bomber to let him win (or survive) a bout.

10. Sandy McCarthy - His strong legs are a neat match for his strong arms.

FAIRNESS

1. Tony Twist - The Twister will not fight someone he knows he can easily beat. He couldn't be fairer than that.

2. Kelly Chase - He actually gives advice to an opponent after a fight

3. Rob Ray - He's co-author the fighters-code.

4. Sandy McCarthy - He stands and punches. No dancing or tricks are needed.

5. Gino Odjick - I have never seen him hit a man who is down.

6. Bob Probert - His reputation has changed. He's now very respectable (on and off the ice).

7. Ken Belanger - If he wants to fight, he'll tell you to your face. No jumping from behind.

8. Krzysztof Oliwa - He's just interested in the game. Kris hasn't made dirty plays to form enemies.

9. Chris Simon - Don't pull his hair and he won't pull yours!

10. Stu Grimson - The Reaper brings a commendable code of ethics to the rink.

INTIMIDATION

1. Tony Twist - Few are still willing to fight The Twister. Once Tony demonstrated that he could crack a helmet with his hand, he scared off many possible challengers.

2. Bob Probert - If opponents worries about an enemy before he's on the ice, he's in trouble Probert does that to the opposition and has an edge over you already.

3. Rob Ray - Razor brings that truly scary feeling onto the ice every time he's out there.

4. Stu Grimson - He was nicknamed the Grim Reaper for reason

5. Enrico Ciccone - He carries a genuine mean streak on to the ice. Wisely, some foes just don't like to get in his way.

6. Sandy McCarthy - He has that look about him. The size and the grimace are worrisome.

7. Chris Simon - He looks wild and occasionally he acts wild.

8. Tie Domi - Tie likes to fight, and also likes to entertain. Some players dislike being part of his circus.

9. Krzysztof Oliwa - The big Pole went after everyone. Word's getting around.

10. Brent Severyn - He's been on several clubs during his career. Most players would rather have him as a teammate.

SMARTNESS

1. Bob Probert - Experience has taught him well. He won't jeopardize a scoring chance for his team.

2. Chris Simon - He learned when not to drop them after he started tossing a few pucks in the net.

3. Kelly Chase - Sometimes he simply goes out there to push a few guys around or to try and draw a penalty instead of making one.

4. Ken Baumgartner - Experience has taught The Bomber not to pick up an extra two.

5. Tony Twist - He knows his role and he plays it. You won't see total 32 minutes in one shift.

6. Darren Langdon - This Ranger won't value his role over Gretzky's. Smart.

7. Adam Deadmarsh - His smarts cover every aspect of the game. That's a bonus for Joe Sakic & Co.

8. Matt Barnaby - Granted, his big mouth gets him in trouble, but most of the time plays the other team right into his hands.

9. Tie Domi - You only remember him for the problems he causes but think about the grief he gives the opposition.

10. Brent Severyn - He never oversteps his role as an enforcer.

TAKING A PUNCH

1. Bob Probert - His survival quotient proves he can handle anything.

2. Chris Simon - His hair must absorb the punches.

3. Tie Domi - His enemies insist his head is like The Rock of Gibralter.

4. Rob Ray - Razor owns a sturdy chin.

5. Joey Kocur - His head takes punches more easily.

6. Marty McSorley - He likes to duck but if he's late on one or two thrown at him, he's perfectly fine.

7. Sandy McCarthy - If punches do hurt, Sandy certainly doesn't showing it.

8. Darren Langdon - He usually waits before throwing, so he can take one or two if necessary. His absorption of blows is excellent.

9. Matt Barnaby - Go ahead, hit him. For some reason, Matt can laugh off the blows. It usually won't shut him up though.

10. Reid Simpson - You can't have a glass jaw considering the opponents he challenges.

FUTURE POTENTIAL

1. Ken Belanger - He's young, big, and already has won a few from marquee foes.

2. Krzysztof Oliwa - He needs a bit more experience to become a big-time heavyweight.

3. Rocky Thompson - Nothing is more fun than chanting "Rah-kee! Rah-kee! Rah-kee!"

4. Steve McKenna - Hi, I'm big and like to fight. It's a good combo. He could use weight on him. Opponents still are able to tie him in knots. Once he learns to overcome that deficit, he'll be good.

5. Tony Twist - Someone so good will not fade for some time.

6. Cale Hulse - With Hulse and Rocky on the Flames they could be banging a lot of heads this season.

7. Ed Jovanovski - He fights so well, I wish he'd do it more. Should Paul Laus gets less playing time, someone's going to have to stick up for the team.

8. Chris Simon - If he can fight off injuries, he'll fight anybody.

9. Matt Johnson - Steve McKenna could learn a lot from him. Johnson has made a lot of progress.

10. Chris Pronger - Since he is captain of his team too much fighting is no good;. just a little bit.

KEY: W- Willingness; Stm - Stamina; KP - Knockout punch; Str - Strength; Q - Quickness; T - Tying up; B - Balance; F - Fairness; I - Intimidation; Int. - Intelligence; TP - Taking a punch; FP - Future Potential.

Name	W	Stm	KP	Str	Q	Sw	T	B	F	I	INT	TP	FP	TTL
Probert, Bob	10	9	9	10	10	9	10	10	9	10	10	10	10	126
Simon, Chris	9	9	10	10	9	10	9	10	9	10	10	10	10	125
McCarthy, S.	10	9	10	10	8	9	10	9	10	10	9	10	9	123
McSorley, M.	10	10	9	9	9	10	10	10	9	9	9	10	9	123
Twist, Tony	9	9	10	10	10	8	9	10	10	10	9	9	10	123
Domi, Tie	10	10	8	9	10	9	9	10	8	9	9	10	9	120
Ray, Rob	10	9	9	8	9	8	10	9	9	10	9	10	9	119
Baumgartner	10	9	8	8	10	10	9	9	9	9	10	9	9	119
Brashear, D.	10	9	8	10	9	8	9	10	9	9	9	9	9	118
Odjick, Gino	10	10	9	8	9	8	10	8	10	9	9	9	9	118
Belanger, Ken	10	8	9	10	9	8	10	8	9	9	9	9	10	118
Grimson, Stu	10	9	9	9	8	10	8	8	9	10	9	9	9	117
Ciccone, Enrico	10	8	9	10	10	8	9	8	9	10	9	8	9	117
Oliwa, K.	10	9	8	10	8	8	9	9	9	9	8	9	10	116
Langdon, D.	10	10	8	7	9	8	10	9	9	9	9	9	8	115
Vukota, Mick	10	9	8	9	9	9	10	9	8	9	9	8	8	115
Simpson, Reid	10	9	8	9	8	9	9	9	8	9	8	9	9	114
Severyn, Brent	10	8	9	9	8	7	10	9	8	9	9	9	9	114
Chase, Kelly	9	9	8	8	10	9	9	8	10	8	10	8	8	114
Kocer, Joey	8	10	8	10	8	9	8	9	9	8	9	10	7	113
McKenzie, Jim	9	9	8	8	9	10	8	8	8	9	9	9	9	113
Baraby, Matt.	9	10	7	8	10	9	9	10	7	7	9	9	8	112
Jovanovski, Ed	8	7	9	9	8	8	10	8	7	9	9	9	10	111
Johnson, Matt	10	9	8	8	8	8	9	8	7	9	8	8	10	110
Berube, Craig	9	9	8	7	9	8	10	7	8	9	8	9	9	110
Mason, Dave	7	9	9	10	8	8	9	9	8	9	7	9	7	109
Shanahan, B.	8	9	8	8	8	9	9	8	8	8	9	8	9	109
Deadmarsh, A.	8	8	8	8	9	8	9	9	8	8	9	8	9	109
McCabe, B.	8	10	7	7	8	8	9	10	8	7	8	8	10	108
Kordic, Dan	9	9	9	8	8	8	8	8	7	9	8	9	8	108
Laus, Paul	10	8	8	9	8	8	9	8	8	7	8	8	8	107
Rychel, Warren	9	8	7	8	8	9	8	8	8	8	8	9	9	107
Cummins, Jim	10	9	7	8	7	7	9	8	8	8	8	9	8	106
Odgers, Jeff	10	9	8	7	8	8	9	7	8	8	8	8	8	106
Tkachuk, Keith	6	9	8	9	8	7	9	8	7	8	9	9	9	106
Myhres, Brent	9	8	8	8	7	9	8	9	7	8	8	8	8	106
McKenna, S.	9	7	8	8	8	7	8	8	7	9	8	8	10	105
Pilon, Rich	7	8	8	7	9	7	9	8	7	8	9	8	9	104
Karpa, David	8	8	7	7	9	8	9	8	8	8	8	8	8	104
Pronger, Chris	8	9	7	8	7	8	9	8	7	9	7	8	9	104

Leroux, F.	9	8	8	9	8	7	8	8	7	9	7	8	8	104
Kruse, Paul	9	8	8	7	8	7	9	8	7	8	8	8	8	103
May, Brad	9	7	7	7	8	10	8	9	7	7	8	8	8	103
Tocchet, Rick	8	7	8	8	7	8	9	8	7	8	9	8	8	103
Lambert, D.	9	8	8	7	8	8	9	7	8	7	7	8	8	102
Beukeboom, J.	7	8	9	8	8	8	8	7	7	8	8	7	8	101
Tamer, Chris	7	7	8	7	8	8	9	7	8	8	7	9	8	101
Chelios, Chris	7	7	7	8	8	8	9	8	7	8	8	8	8	101
Nolan, Owen	8	7	7	8	8	8	8	7	8	8	8	8	8	101
Hulse, Cale	8	8	7	7	8	8	7	8	7	8	8	7	10	101
Odelein, Lyle	8	8	8	7	8	9	7	7	7	7	8	8	8	100
Wiemer, Jason	8	8	7	7	8	8	7	7	7	8	8	8	9	100
King, Kris	9	9	7	7	8	7	9	6	7	8	8	7	7	99
Berehowsky, D.	8	7	7	7	8	7	7	7	8	8	8	8	9	99
McCarty, D.	8	8	7	7	9	7	8	7	7	7	7	8	8	98
Huscroft, J.	8	8	8	7	8	7	8	7	8	7	7	7	8	98
Debrusk, L.	8	7	8	7	8	8	7	7	7	8	7	7	8	97
Boughner, B.	8	7	8	8	7	8	7	7	6	7	7	8	9	97
O'Donnell, S.	8	8	7	7	8	7	8	6	6	8	7	8	8	96
Thornton, S.	7	8	7	7	8	8	7	7	6	7	8	8	8	96
Samuelsson, U.	6	7	7	8	7	7	8	6	6	8	8	7	7	92

JOE LOZITO

Joe Lozito has been analyzing hockey fights, "for as long as I remember." He began making fight tapes in the late 1980's (1988-89 or 1989-90) and within a few years it became a big-time hobby.

Lozito says, "I detest the word "goon." A goon is somebody like Claude Lemieux or Ulf Samuelsson, who has gone knee to knee with players such as Cam Neely. Tomas Sandstrom is another one."

Lozito's fight expertise has been sought oversees by Pro Hockey Magazine (based in Norway)Ware pleased to have his evaluations.

FUTURE POTENTIAL

1 - Matt Johnson- During his days at Peterborough, he was billed as "the toughest player without a pro contract" and was far and away the toughest player in his Draft class. He dominated the OHL and after a stint in the IHL, he is starting to have his way with NHL-level heavyweights. The scary thing is he's still just a kid. Just as Tony Twist has replaced Bob Probert as heavyweight king, I feel that Matt will someday do the same and replace The Twister.

2 - Ken Belanger- It looks as if Ken still catches enemies by surprise with his left and it's a BIG left. If he can put concussion problems behind him and fight more defensively, he will become the "Beast of the East"!

3 - Krzystof Oliwa- The strides that he has made in his power, intelligence and especially balance since his AHL days are amazing. He fought just about everybody in his rookie season (1997-98) with New Jersey (including Stu Grimson three times) and he can still get better.

4 - Wade Belak- His favorite movie character is "Rocky 4's" Ivan Drago because he's "big and mean". On the ice, Wade is big and mean. He is the "replacement" for Chris Simon for whom the media seems to looking. He defeated Simon in a preseason brawl last season. His brother, Graham, is in the Avalanche organization as well. He's big and mean too!

5 - Ryan VandenBussche- He had two telling fights in the 1997-98 season. He stood in with Stu Grimson after absorbing about eight unanswered huge punches from Stu (Ryan can take it). In the '97-98, This preseason he defeated Nick Kypreos and, unfortunately, Nick hasn't played since (Ryan can dish it out too). He also had a beauty with Dan Kordic.

6 - Peter Worrell - This is a case similar to Matt Johnson. Peter dominated his junior league (QMJHL) and was the toughest in his Draft class. The knock on Peter is his skating and balance, something Panther people say he's improved on since his first training camp. He does have power. Once Peter gets his pins planted firmly and starts throwing, it's "lights out" for most of his opponents.

7 - Rocky Thompson - Rocky made a huge first impression fighting the likes of Brent Severyn, Matt Johnson, David Karpa, and Krzystof Oliwa. He's not as big as most of "future potential" candidates (although that doesn't make him small) but he's got spunk and a tremendous willingness to prove himself against anyone. He seems to accept his role and that could take him far. He does face a challenge in that he inherited his role from one of the best, Sandy McCarthy.

8 - Eric Cairns: There's no reason for his prolonged absences from the New York Rangers. Eric is a huge kid with an even bigger heart. He must play to improve. But he betrays one major flaw — he allows smaller opponents to get inside so either he can't unload his huge punch or they can work in tight where he is susceptible. If he keeps his legs planted and his left extended, very few opponents will be standing after just one of his huge rights.

9 - Brendan Witt: Potentially the most talented player on the list, who will fight the least. He has already had some dandy slugfests with the likes of Ryan VandenBussche and had arguably the best fight of 1996-97 with Dan Kordic in Philadelphia. He appears to be the heir apparent to Mark Tinordi in that Tinordi's number of bouts decrease almost every year and even now, late in his career, he still improves as a player. Brendan will likely follow that path with Tinordi as his teacher.

10 - Shawn Heins- Shawn has the potential to be the total package if he is not rushed by the Sharks. He was playing in the ECHL when Kansas City imparted him to be a physical force on the blueline. He was that and much more, so much that he was voted San Jose's #1 prospect by The Hockey News. He is a big, strong, physical defenseman who — if he plays regularly is capable of scoring 15 goals a season at the NHL level. He won the "hardest shot" at the IHL Skills Competition. As far as the physical side, he is as game as they come. He can take punishment and dish it out with both hands. He also is a maniacal force in front of his net. He has an advantage being a teammate of the toughest in the IHL, Dean Ewen.

11 - Sean Gagnon- His map reads from Dayton to Fort Wayne to Springfield to the Phoenix Coyotes. He may need a bit more seasoning but he could be a force in Phoenix in the near future. He's big and can go righty or lefty.

12 - Terry Ryan- Terry should be a regular with Montreal Canadiens. In a year or two the comparisons to other power forwards should start. He took on Tie Domi in a pre-season bout and his first "official" in 1997-98. was against veteran tough Doug Houda. Another recall brought two more fights, this time against the Sabres, Bob Boughner and a huge performance versus Matt Barnaby. If he reaches his potential, Ryan could be a 25 goal with 200 PIM player in the NHL. He has nothing to prove at the AHL level.

13 - PJ Stock- Every team needs Stock. Buffalo has Barnaby, Vancouver has Scott Walker, Washington has Kevin Kaminski and the New York Rangers have Stock. He is an agitating ball of energy with underrated skills. P.J. is an instant fan favorite wherever he plays for his hard-nosed style. In one of his AHL fights, Stock went toe-to-toe with Sean Gagnon (Springfield), a man with inches and many pounds on PJ, yet Stock held his own.

14 - Kevin Sawyer: Kevin is a hard worker who should have been given a real shot with Boston. He signed with Dallas in the off-season, but the Stars' lineup was solid. He fought everybody he could in training camp, including Tony Twist and did the job on his own in 1997-98 in Michigan (IHL) because fellow roughneck Patrick Cote was injured for the season after he fought Twist. With Grant Marshall improving his play every year, maybe Kevin will be able to show what he's got at the NHL level.

15 - Rumun Ndur: Rumz is loved in Rochester and soon he will be loved in Buffalo. He once teamed with Ken Belanger in Guelph at the OHL where they terrified the league. It had been difficult for him to crack the Buffalo lineup because the Sabres have been it is a tough team with hard-hitting physical defenseman Bob Boughner. If Matt Barnaby is traded, that should make room for Rumun.

16 - Jean Luc Grand-Pierre: A huge kid who should only get better. In 1997-98, Rochester has a very tough team and Rumun and Jean Luc were the toughest. Jean Luc has skills and is banger. He may need one more AHL season before he's ready for the NHL.

17 - Steve McLaren: With acquisitions of Reid Simpson and Ryan VandenBussche, it might be a long shot for Steve to make the Blackhawks. He's very physical with a mean streak to match. Some of his hits are borderline dirty but they stem from a natural, aggressive style of play. His head might be the hardest this side of Chris Murray and Tie Domi.

18 - Fredrik Oduya: With the signing of Shawn Heins there may not be any room for Fredrik on the Sharks. He may have to do his damage with another team. Oduya has a style similar to Tony Twist in that he loves to throw huge bombs. He doesn't have Tony's power, but Odie is a strong guy and the toughest Swede since Bob Nystrom.

19 - Scott Parker: He took a chance going back into the draft, and it paid off. He went from a Third Round pick in 1996 to a First-Rounder in 1998. The toughest player in Junior hockey by far. He has a chance to make the Colorado lineup and would make a very teammate with Wade Belak. Aside from being super tough he also scored 30 goals in 1997-98 with Kelowna.

20 -Brantt Myhres: Off-ice questions drop Brantt to the bottom of this list. On fighting merit alone, Myhres is top five, but after his release from Philly, his future is in doubt. Mhyres owns a lethal left hand and loves to stand back and throw.

UNDERRATED

1 - Brent Severyn- The unquestionably the most underappreciated player in hockey. He has labored honestly, clearing his crease, fighting everybody while leading on and off the ice. His reward was tickets out of Florida and Long Island. While taking on all comers in Colorado and floating between forward and defense, all he heard about was Chris Simon. With Anaheim, he heard how the Ducks are not tough enough and lack a heavyweight. Severyn IS a heavyweight who gets very little respect. Those who see him on a nightly basis appreciate his hard work. In these times of "non-caring, high-priced athletes", it's nice to see players like Severyn who leave everything he has on the ice every night.

2 - Grant Marshall: He's the reason Dallas refuses to employ a full-time enforcer. Not many realize that Grant is as tough as nails. He has overcome injuries, not the least of which was a broken neck in the OHL. His combination of high threshold for punishment and quick, hard punches catch many opponents by surprise.

3 - Scott Thornton- He is the best fighter on Les Canadiens technically speaking. People know Mick Vukota, Dave Manson and Turner Stevenson grasp Thornton's toughness. His fights with the Toronto and Edmonton organizations were acceptable but he has really come into his own with Montreal.

4 - Brad May: He can play and is very tough. In fact, the toughest player of Buffalo's Big Four, he's staggered many opponents including Basil McRae and Ken Baumgartner.

5 - Bill Huard: He made his mark with stints in Ottawa and Dallas. In fact, he performed so well in Dallas, he made Shane Churla expendable. Bill is one of the NHL's strongest players but his problem has been injuries. He has the right attitude and should be a force in 1998-99.

6 - Bob Boughner: With the likes of Brad May, Rob Ray, and Matt Barnaby, Buffalo had a tough team but lacked a physical presence on the blueline. Bob is smaller than many of his opponents but what he lacks in size, he makes up for in guts. Aside from fighting, Bob provides the only true physical presence that clears the Sabres' crease.

7 - Jeff Odgers: With San Jose, he went from second fiddle (behind Link Gaetz) to top gun to team captain, fighting everyone along the way. He was one of the few players who gave their all in EVERY game for the Bruins in 1997-98 and all that earned him was a one-way ticket to Providence. Yet he became a regular with Colorado and someone who could be a huge asset in the development of Wade Belak.

8 - Paul Kruse: Kruse plugs away and can produce if given ice time. Unfortunately he had obtained little respect. In Calgary, he was the perfect compliment for Sandy McCarthy yet the Flames felt the need to play Sasha Lakovic over Kruse. On Long Island, Steve Webb saw playing time over Kruse. He should be appreciated in Buffalo, a team that without a high powered offense, the Kruse Missile might get to fire some pucks in the net.

9 - Chris Tamer: With teammates such as Jaromir Jagr and Tom Barrasso, it's easy for a player like Tamer to get lost in the shuffle. He backs down from nobody but remains a valued member of Pittsburgh's defensive corps.

10 - Mark Janssens: Janssens is the third-line center every team covets. He's big and can shadow the opposition. Few are better on face-offs, and he can throw the dukes. Mark was the center on the Daniels-Janssens and Chase line in Hartford and always made things happen.

GUYS YOU MAY HAVE MISSED

1 - Cale Hulse: His value to the Calgary defense limits his fighting. Cale destroyed foes on a regular basis with Portland (WHL) and Albany (AHL), but now does his job without fanfare. Enemies should think twice before fighting him.

2 - Rhett Warrener: Scott Mellanby might have been regarded as the second toughest player on Florida but in fact Rhett was. He doesn't fight often but his bouts are fun to watch when he does. He'll fight less with the promotion of Peter Worrell.

3 - Rob DiMaio: In some of his early fights with the New York Islanders, he held his own with Al Secord and Darin Kimble and cut Steve Leach. His small size but huge heart and work ethic endear to all fans of "old-time hockey".

4 - Todd Harvey: With the departure of Bill Huard, the fighting assignments on Dallas fell to Grant Marshall and Harvey. Harvey is delights in defeating bigger opponents such as Jeff Beukeboom. He will bring intensity to lackluster New York Rangers squad.

5 - Ethan Moreau: He developed in the OHL and then Indianapolis of the IHL. An intense kid with a long memory, Ethan was suckered and bloodied by Martin Lapointe in 1996-97. He waited patiently and exacted revenge in a later game. He has solid skills as well.

6 - Bill Guerin: Part of Billy's attraction is that he can score 25 goals and doesn't shy from the rough going. He had a classic slugfest with Mike Keane in Montreal a few years back.

7 - Adam Deadmarsh: On a team with as much fire power as Colorado, there's little room for enforcers. Deadmarsh often has to fight for his teammates., just as he did with Portland of the WHL.

8 - Stephane Matteau: He will always be remembered for his playoff goal against New Jersey during the 1994 Rangers Cup run. What people forget is that Stephane is a strong man who, in spite of his long fuse, can fight and is good at it.

9 - Kyle McLaren: Opponents know he is tough, just not how tough. Like Chris Tamer, he is a valuable defenseman so he can't afford to fight all the time. When he gets mad and decides to go, he is effective.

10 - Stephen Leach: Leach hasn't won many fights but always shows up. Almost always the smaller guy in a fight, his grit and determination make him an asset in the long run.

WILLINGNESS

1 - Tony Twist: There is no man in the league more willing to show what he's got. The Twister's problem is finding takers.

2 - Krzystof Oliwa: In 1997-98 he was a strong rookie who fought everybody to build a reputation. He earned respect.

3 - Paul Laus: He led the NHL in fighting majors in 1996-97 before the Peter Worrell era, did it almost all by himself.

4 - Tie Domi: Always ready to go, Domi has great fun doing it.

5 - Sandy McCarthy: He looks forward to fighting formidable foes such as Tony Twist, Jim McKenzie, et. al. to show how tough he is.

6 - Stu Grimson: Fighting is his NHL meal ticket. The Reaper gets better every year.

7 - Bob Probert: He was The Man for so long, young gunslingers still try to earn a reputation against someone who is arguable the best ever.

8 - Darren Langdon: He seems to take on Stu Grimson every time they meet and has fought Reid Simpson almost a dozen times.

9 - Chris Murray: At times, he is the most exciting fighter to watch. He could be the next Randy McKay.

10 - Jeff Odgers: He deserves a Purple Heart for the job he did in Boston in 1996-97. Jeff gives his all every night. He doesn't win them all but you'll never keep him down.

STAMINA

1 - Darren Langdon: Don't throw a ton of punches too soon against Langdon. When the foe is out of gas, he'll put you down.

2 - Marty McSorley: He had more marathon bouts than anyone in his weight class.

3 - Brent Severyn: He is one of the best conditioned — if not the best conditioned — player in the NHL.

4 - Tie Domi: He just keeps going on and on and on . . .

5 - Sandy McCarthy: He'll fight any style you will and win with one shot or after two minutes.

6 - Bob Probert: He gets stronger as his fights get longer.

7 - Matt Barnaby: This ultimate instigator often begs officials not to break up his fights as they prepare to intervene.

8 - Shane Churla: He'll take what you've got. The trick is to get him early or it might be a long night.

9 - Paul Laus: He's unaffected by punches that bother lesser fighters. Being the sole enforcer on his team keeps him in fighting shape.

10 - Stu Grimson: Even after a tough, physical game, if you need Stu, you'll have to wait. He'll be riding the exercise bike.

KNOCK-OUT PUNCH

1 - Tony Twist: Whether he is shattering faces or helmets, his kay—potential is a reason he is rarely challenged.

2 - Stu Grimson: Check with Shane Churla. He'll reveal how hard Stu punches.

3 - Chris Simon: The long-haired sluggert has given many would be opponents jelly-legs.

4 - Jim McKenzie: If Big Jim gets his big left hand loose, he can be as devastating as anyone.

5 - Matt Johnson: Matt will be making foes pick themselves off the ice for years to come.

6 - Sandy McCarthy: His snarl alone is scary; then comes his fists.

7 - Bob Probert: Many have felt the wrath of Probert. This includes Dave Semenko to Troy Crowder to Tie Domi. He hits hard!

8 - Todd Ewen: He KO'd Bob Probert in his second NHL fight. This is a large man who puts every ounce of his weight into his punches.

9 - Paul Laus: He TKO'd Ken Belanger with a concussion punch early in the 1997-98 season.

10 - Joe Kocur: Joe gets an Honorable Mention because he rarely fights anymore. But that lethal has the right hand is always a threat.

STRENGTH

1 - Tony Twist: No question! He is the strongest man in the NHL.

2 - Brent Severyn: Take it easy in the off-season? Never! Sevy works out up to five hours a day!

3 - Matt Johnson: Few can match power with Matt — and he's still growing.

4 - Todd Ewen: Superior strength allows him to rag-doll many of his opponents.

5 - Marty McSorley: The veteran boasts a dangerous combination of power and endurance. He can pummel a foe at the start or the end of a fight.

6 - Chris Simon: Simon says you'll get hit hard, more than likely, you'll go down.

7 - Stu Grimson: He'll render you helpless with his left and destroy you with his right.

8 - Donald Brashear: Bad news for opposing enforcers, Brashear's fighting ability has caught up with his strength and he's really strong.

9 - Krzystof Oliwa: If he's out of position in a fight, he'll move his opponent to proceed with the beating.

10 - Louie DeBrusk: Although his willingness to fight has been questioned by many, nobody can question his power.

QUICKNESS

1 - Chris Murray: While his opponents are wondering why he won't drop, Chris has hit them four or five times.

2 - Jim Cummins: He doesn't win them all but Jim's arms move like pistons when he gets them loose.

3 - Craig Berube- Very few can throw hands as quickly as Craig. That's a big reason why he's been so successful over the years.

4 - Tie Domi: With that head, there's no need for any defense. Tie can let his arms go fast and furious.

5 - Scott Daniels: Scott employs the same style he's had since his days in the WHL: grab on and unload as fast as possible.

6 - Shane Churla: Double-trouble! He throws the punches hard and fast with his left and right.

7 - Matt Barnaby: Since he lacks size, he must be quick. Plus, he has about twenty enemies on each team.

8 - Bob Probert: Once he gets the advantage, he'll look for a quick finish.

9 - Kelly Chase: The man owns quick hands with a quick head and shoulders. That explains why this little big man is still going strong against NHL giants.

10 - Grant Marshall: Speed is one of the reasons he can go with the biggest of opponents.

SWITCHING HANDS

1 - Bob Probert: He's always been dangerous because you could never get away with tying up one of his arms.

2 - Tie Domi: He would have only a fraction of the victories he's earned if he could only throw with one hand.

3 - Ken Baumgartner: He possesses one of the most lethal lefts in the league. Another problem for others — his right is pretty good too!

4 - Marty McSorley: He can throw, hold off or wrestle with both hands as good as any enforcer.

5 - Shane Churla: He's similar to Domi. His ability to throw rights and lefts at great speed has been a reason for success.

6 - Kelly Chase: Beware! Kelly won't knock you out but he will pepper you with both hands.

7 - Brent Severyn: The large man's recipe for success-feed his opponent a steady diet of rights and lefts.

8 - Chris Simon: Chris has knocked out many players with his right hand. Surprise, he's a lefty!

9 - Sandy McCarthy: S.O.S. He's dangerous with either hand.

10 - Darren Langdon: When Darren has his enemy tied up, he'll wait for an opening on either side and go for it.

TYING UP

1 - Marty McSorley: Marty likes this technique tie up because he's stronger than most. When he's tied up, he can throw through his oversized sleeves.

2 - Donald Brashear- The knock on Donald has been that he's too much of a wrestler. Lately, he has tied up more and wrestled less.

3 - Craig Berube: Craig has always liked to try to tie up his opponent with his left and unload with his right.

4 - Gino Odjick: The veteran is good at tying up, sometimes to a fault. He's big enough and strong enough to let them fly.

5 - Darren Langdon: The Ranger does something almost no one else he ties up with both hands rather high on his opponents jersey. He seems to throw punches and tries to get his hand back on the jersey before his opposite can react.

6 - Todd Ewen: The Animal enjoys tying up and rag-dolling his victims before he unleashes blows.

7 - Sandy McCarthy: His vice-like grip with both hands disables opponents. Then Sandy goes to work!

8 - Paul Laus: At first Paul took plenty of punishment. He ties up a lot better now and has become downright dangerous.

9 - Kelly Chase: He's not big nor strong enough to stand back and throw bombs, so he defuses his opponents bombs.

10 - Mick Vukota: Mick is still strong. He'll tie his enemy up until Vukota can toss a few punches. Then he'll try to slam the other through the ice.

BALANCE

1 - Darren Langdon: Even when he doesn't win the fight, he's rarely off his feet.

2 - Tie Domi: His low center of gravity makes it almost impossible to put him on his back.

3 - Bob Probert: Whether his feet are firmly planted or moving about, it's not often he finishes on the bottom.

4 - Marty McSorley: Superior balance is pivotal in Marty's marathon bouts.

5 - Brent Severyn: He can handle bigger men because few are better in terms of staying vertical.

6 - Sandy McCarthy: Strong legs enable him to stand until the end.

7 - Stu Grimson: Punches that ordinarily knock down others early are mere glancing blows.

8 - Chris Murray: What a neat combo — excellent balance and a hard cranium. It's almost impossible to knock him down.

9 - Ken Baumgartner: The Bomber does everything well. His ability to reamin upright is one component.

10 - Craig Berube: If he didn't have good balance, he would fall from the speed of his hands alone.

FAIRNESS

1 - Stu Grimson:The Grim Reaper has come full circle. In a game in 1996-97 against the Rangers, Stu did not want to fight Shane Churla who was playing in spite of a serious injury around his eye. Churla kept pushing and pushing and finally Stu HAD to fight and proceeded to fill Churla in royally. Stu did not want to take advantage but he didn't have a choice.

2 - Tony Twist: He can whip anybody, so why cheat?

3 - Sandy McCarthy: He would rather punch you in the face than hit you in the back.

4 - Jim McKenzie: He enjoyed clearly squaring off in the WHL, and did likewise in the AHL. Ditto in the NHL.

5 - Bob Probert: He is the most respected enforcer in the league.

6 - Brent Severyn: Win or lose, when the fights over, he races to the penalty box to serve his time.

7 - Darren Langdon: This is one honest enforcer with a ton of respect for his role. He's battled from an ECHL enforcer to one of the best in the NHL and all fair and square.

8 - Chris Simon: He has been a dominant enforcer at every level. Jumping foes or sucker-punching would only tarnish his reputation. He stays away from the sneaky game.

9 - Rudy Poeschek: He stands back and exchanges lefts and rights with anyone and everyone.

10 - Craig Berube: Here is the consummate professional. He's an animal during a fight but when it's over, it's over. And there is no finer gentleman-hockey player.

INTIMIDATION

1 - Tony Twist- His legend grows although he fights less and less every year. P.S. There isn't exactly a line to fight him either.

2 - Stu Grimson: Words you don't want to hear from the Grim Reaper, "Let's go!"

3 - Bob Probert: Some of the younger enforcers grew up watching tv and seeing Probert dismantle opponents. They don't want to be his next victim.

4 - Chris Simon: Even though he fights less than ever he still has the look and the big left.

5 - Sandy McCarthy: A lot of players in the Western Conference breathed a sigh of relief when he was traded to Tampa Bay.

6 - Matt Johnson: One of the most physically-imposing men in hockey and still a kid!

7 - Todd Ewen: Has been beating up guys. Warning: don't get him, mad. He'll take pleasure in feeding you lefts and rights.

8 - Marty McSorley: This big, strong man, who will go all night, has taken on all comers in his long career.

9 - Paul Laus: He ENJOYS fighting and has a short, intimidating fuse.

10 - Chris Murray: He's not intimidating, physically, but it's got to be scary to know that Chris isn't going down unless you happen to be aboard a heavy tank rolling into him

INTELLIGENCE

1 - Ken Baumgartner: He can fight in any way, shape or form, Bomber is good at tying up, throws well with both hands, throws hard and excellent defensively.

2 - Darren Langdon: He will wait. You'll get tired trying to put him down early and when you're sucking wind — BOOM! — he attacks.

3 - Kelly Chase: Almost always smaller than his opponent, he is very adept at ducking punches and getting inside on bigger opponents.

4 - Sandy McCarthy: He dictates most his fights go.

5 - Brent Severyn: Intelligence is often overlooked in a fight. Brent is smart and happens the league's most underrated and under appreciated enforcer.

6 - Stu Grimson: The Reaper has made several changes in technique, so much so that he often not only wins, he destroys!

7 - Tony Twist: In Clark Gillies-like fashion-he rations his fights because he does maximum damage in minimum.

8 - Bob Probert: Opposing gunslingers have been gunning for Probert. He's beaten them all.

9 - Marty McSorley: good ole boy Marty will smother you with big arms and jersey. When you're not expecting it, he unloads and you're doomed.

10 - Paul Laus: He's superb at taking punches. As a result, he has become one of the most dangerous enforcers in the business.

TAKING A PUNCH

1 - Chris Murray: He loves to stand back and throw, Chris will get hit — and maybe even cut — but he will not go down!

2 - Tie Domi: The little rascal has absorbed punches that would have decapitated others.

3 - Grant Marshall: Not many people comprehend his toughness. Remember, Marshall recovered from a broken neck in the OHL.

4 - Bob Probert: Part of the Probert mystique is this: after enemies have thrown their best shots at him, he's still standing, usually over them.

5 - Darren Langdon: His strategy is simple: take a few punches, set himself, tie up his opponent, then pick him apart.

6 - Marty McSorley: When he fails to knot his opponent, he's susceptible but he still comes back fighting.

7 - Sandy McCarthy: He has been victorious or held his own with noted heavyweights such as McSorley, Leroux, Simon, and Twist.

8 - Chris Simon: He doesn't get hit often but when he does, the punches have little effect.

9 - Paul Laus: This is an offensive fighter. Sometimes he leaves himself open to retaliation. Considering the shots he absorbs, he seems impervious to pain.

10 - Tony Twist: This is a case of requiring dozens of chops to knock down an oak tree.

KEY: W - Willingness, ST - Stamina, KP - Knockout Punch, I - Intimidation, INT - Intelligence, F - Fairness, B- Balance, T -Tying Up, SH - Switching Hands, Q - Quickness, STR - Strength, TP - Taking a Punch, FP - Future Potential.

Player	W	ST	KP	STR	Q	SH	T	B	F	I	INT	TP	FP	TTL
Twist, T	10	9	10	10	8	9	10	10	10	10	10	10	9	125
McCarthy, S	10	10	10	9	8	10	10	10	10	10	10	10	8	124
Probert, B	10	10	10	9	10	10	9	10	10	10	10	10	7	124
Grimson, S	10	10	10	10	8	9	8	10	10	10	10	8	7	120
Langdon, D	10	10	8	8	8	10	10	10	10	8	10	10	8	120
C. Simon	8	9	10	10	8	10	8	9	10	10	9	10	9	120
McSorley, M	8	10	9	10	7	10	10	10	8	10	10	10	7	119
Baumgartner	10	10	9	9	9	10	9	10	9	8	10	8	7	118
Laus, P	10	10	10	8	8	8	10	7	8	10	10	10	8	117
Murray, C.	10	9	9	8	10	8	8	10	8	10	8	10	9	117
Severyn, B	10	10	8	10	8	10	8	10	10	8	10	8	7	117
Domi, T	10	10	8	7	10	10	9	10	8	8	8	10	8	116
Johnson, M	10	8	10	10	7	8	8	8	9	10	9	9	10	116
Ewen, T	9	8	10	10	7	9	10	8	8	10	9	9	7	114
Berube, C	9	9	8	8	10	9	10	10	10	8	8	8	7	114
McKenzie, J	9	9	10	9	8	8	8	10	10	9	9	7	7	112
Ray, R	10	8	8	8	9	9	9	8	8	7	9	9	7	110
Belanger, K	10	9	9	9	8	8	7	8	8	8	8	7	10	109
Odjick, G	10	9	8	8	9	9	10	7	7	8	7	8	8	109
Chase, K	9	9	7	7	10	10	10	8	8	7	10	7	7	109
Oliwa, K	10	8	9	10	7	8	7	8	8	9	7	8	10	108
Simpson, R	9	9	8	8	9	9	8	8	8	8	8	8	7	108
Churla, S	9	10	7	7	10	10	8	8	8	7	7	9	7	108
Brashear, D	9	8	9	10	7	7	10	8	8	8	8	7	8	107
Barnaby, M	9	10	7	7	10	8	8	8	7	7	8	9	9	107

Poeschek, R	9	8	9	9	7	7	8	8	10	8	7	9	7	106
Kordic, D	9	8	9	9	7	8	8	7	8	9	7	7	8	104
Kocur, J	7	8	10	8	7	7	8	9	9	9	8	8	6	104
Cummins, J	9	9	7	7	10	8	8	8	7	7	7	8	8	103
Odgers, J	10	9	7	7	8	8	7	7	9	7	8	9	7	103
McCarty, D	8	9	8	8	8	7	8	8	8	7	8	8	8	103
Daniels, S	9	8	7	7	10	9	8	8	7	7	7	8	8	103
Boughner, B	9	9	7	8	8	7	8	7	8	7	8	8	8	102
DeBrusk, L	7	7	8	10	7	8	9	7	8	8	7	8	8	102
May, B	7	8	8	8	8	7	7	8	9	8	8	8	7	101
Huard, B	9	7	9	9	7	8	7	7	8	7	7	8	8	101
Kruse, P	9	8	7	8	8	7	8	8	8	7	8	8	7	101
Vukota, M	8	7	8	9	7	7	10	8	8	7	7	8	7	101
Tamer, C	8	8	8	8	7	7	8	8	8	7	8	8	8	101
McKay, R	7	9	7	7	8	8	8	8	8	7	8	8	7	100
McKenna, S	8	8	7	8	7	7	7	6	8	8	8	8	9	99
Ciccone, E	8	8	7	8	8	7	7	7	7	7	7	8	8	97
Janssens, M	7	7	7	8	7	7	8	7	8	7	8	8	7	96
Odelein, L	8	8	7	8	7	7	7	7	7	7	7	8	7	95
Huscroft, J	7	8	7	7	8	7	7	8	7	7	7	8	7	95
Lacroix, D	8	8	7	7	7	7	7	7	7	6	7	7	7	92
King, K	7	7	7	7	7	6	8	7	8	6	7	8	7	92
Manson, D	7	8	7	7	8	7	7	7	7	7	7	7	6	92
Leroux, F	7	7	8	8	6	7	6	6	7	7	7	7	7	90
Lambert, D	8	7	7	6	7	7	7	7	7	6	7	7	7	90
Rychel, W	8	8	6	7	7	7	7	7	7	6	7	7	6	90
Russell, C	7	7	6	7	7	7	6	7	7	6	7	7	6	87
Buchberger	7	7	6	7	7	7	7	6	7	6	7	6	6	86

THE CURRENT CHAMPION

Tony Twist

Tony Twist

— THE HEAVYWEIGHT CHAMPION OF THE NHL

There simply are no ifs, ands or buts about Tony Twist.

He is *the* heavyweight champion of the National Hockey League.

No, not Bob Probert, not Joey Kocur, not Tie Domi, nor Marty McSorley, all worthies in their own right.

The distinction between Twist and the others is that Tony is General-of-the-Army at Fort Neverlose.

Never, ever. At least not in the NHL.

According to one authoritative study of hockey fighting, the last time Twist lost a bout was some time in his dim, distant past as a Junior performer in Saskatoon. Link Gaetz, then the Godzilla of the goal crease, whomped Twist in an early-season fight.

Gaetz would learn that it was a Pyrrhic victory. Twist called for a return bout later in the season, tarring and feathering Gaetz in decisive fashion.

How do I know how menacing Twist can be?

Covering the New Jersey Devils six years ago, I watched large Mike Peluso emerge as a heavyweight challenger. The Minnesota mauler had put together a handsome portfolio of victories at the Meadowlands Arena. But on this night, Twist was visiting with the Quebec Nordiques.

If I have seen a harder punch thrown in a half-century of watching hockey, I cannot remember such a lethal wallop being thrown. Peluso, dreadnought of the Devils, staggered to the ice as if pounded by a pile driver, artfully disguised as Twist's fist.

Suffering a concussion, Peluso was removed to a local hospital for observation. Twist was concerned enough about the damage that he made a bee-line for the infirmary after the game to check out his victim. Fortunately, Peluso escaped with his life.

Twist hasn't killed anyone yet but the word is out, loud and clear. Don't mess with Tony if you can help it!

"There are guys in the league who want no part of him," confirmed Geoff Courtnall, a teammate of Tony's at St. Louis. "There's no one in the league better than he is."

Brett Hull, who played alongside Twist for several years on the Blues, is rather explicit in explaining The Twister's style: "He throws hammers. He throws to kill."

At 6-1, 240 pounds, Twist is not as menacing physically as larger, younger gunslingers like Kris Oliwa and Matt Johnson but even the Young Turks understand that it isn't healthy to annoy Tony.

"You don't want him looking at you the wrong way," said Johnson. "No one in the league matches his pure punching power."

Since signing on with the Blues in 1994, Twist has been challenged with less frequency although his notoriety as heavyweight champion remains as widespread as ever.

In a rare departure from editorial policy in 1998, *Sports Illustrated* zeroed in on Twist, unequivocally listing him as hockey's ultimate puncher. Authored by Austin Murphy, the profile — labelled "Fighting For A Living" — minced no words about puck's bad boy.

"It takes a special talent to stand on skates and beat someone senseless," noted Murphy, "and no one does it better than the St. Louis Blues' left wing."

Courtnall: "When Twister fights, he hurts people."

Some Blues players contend that because of Tony's presence, opponents curb their natural desire to chirp harsh nothings to players on the St. Louis bench. Teammate Kelly Chase credited Twist for this pleasant state of affairs.

One member of the St. Louis hockey writing corps suggested that some enemy enforcers develop "Blues flu" when Twist comes to town.

Fighting comes natural to the Blues enforcer. Tony's grandfather (on his father's side) was a welterweight. Harry Twist — his fight name was Harry Runcorn — once was Western Canadian Welterweight Champion. Harry's wife, Ethel shone at lacrosse and is in the British Columbia lacrosse Hall-of-Fame. Twist's father, Stan, was a member of the Royal Canadian Mounted Police.

"I went out there and there and wanted to earn a job by fighting. I fought everybody at that camp." Twist says of his climb to the podium

"I've hyperextended my elbow a few times. That was from throwing a big punch and missing. You usually throw your elbow out from that. I've also broken couple of knuckles and a couple of fingers. If you look at my hands, you'll see they're all cut up, but they're still working. What I did was start working with a man who was a kick boxer and he showed me how to condition my hands. So I started to condition my hands.

"I would bang them on the floor when I was watching TV When I would tell this to people, they would say to me I must be a stupid person. But I'm not a stupid person — I was conditioning my knuckles. When I played Junior, I was fighting a lot. My knuckles would swell up and my punching hand would swell up for a couple of days. Then I'd end up fighting again and my hand would get bigger. During the off-season, the guy who was teaching me kick boxing said he would condition the damn thing. He said that when I was watching TV to just sit there and bang my hands on the floor for five or six minutes, take a rest and let them swell up the next day. The swelling didn't hurt me, because it made my hands get stronger. Your tendons get stronger and your knuckles get stronger, so the swelling goes away quicker. All it does is condition your hand and make it stronger."

Twist will remain heavyweight champion until a new Tony Twist comes along. For the moment, at least, he appears lefts and rights ahead of his challengers.

And how will the Twister know when he is defeated?

"Blood and guts don't win a fight," he explained. "It's not by what the crowd thinks, or when the crowd cheers, or what the other team thinks — it's what you know. When you are finished with that fight, you know whether you won or lost that fight. And the guy you fought knows whether he won or lost that fight."

Odds are that Tony Twist will be the winner.

PROBERT, KOCUR, DOMI AND McSORLEY
KaYo KiNgs
OF THE DECADE

There is absolutely no question that four of the most penetrating punchers who have terrorized the NHL in the past 10 years have been Bob Probert, Tie Domi, Joe Kocur, and Marty McSorley.

Although each of the TKO quartet is regarded as a senior citizen stick-handler, they command the respect of every other big-league gunslinger because they have done it all.

And will continue to throw punches at the drop of a glove. It is why they are what they are and it also explains why Probert, Domi, Kocur, and McSorley are millionaires.

Their punching prowess not only is appreciated by the audiences but also coveted by management in its endless search for an enforcer.

"The interesting aspect about each of them," says retired NHL general manager Max McNab, "is that Bob, Joey, Tie and Marty also can play the game. Just look at how Joey helped Detroit win two Stanley Cups in succession."

While his physical presence always has been taken for granted, Kocur's offensive ability has been obscured by his lethal punches. Both in the 1997 and 1998 playoffs, Kocur delivered key goals that enabled the Motor City sextet to sweep.

It's worth noting that Kocur also was a member of the 1994 New York Rangers Stanley Cup-winning team. But that never should be misconstrued. Kocur, like his kayo comrades, has always been a big-leaguer because at any given moment he could disassemble a foe in one fell swoop of the arm.

One episode emerges from dozens in The Kocur File. This was during the 1988-89 season at Nassau Coliseum. Tall Islanders forward Brad Dalgarno had solidly checked a Red Wing, whereupon play moved from the visitors' to the home zone.

Dalgarno pursued the puck to the left circle near his net. He was unaware that a stalker was behind him. It was Kocur, who believed that Dalgarno had delivered an illegal check and wasn't about to wait for the video replay.

Kocur dropped his gloves and Dalgarno knew he was in trouble. The Islander tried to defend himself, but the flurry of punches was deadly and, suddenly, one side of Brad's face drooped. Joey literally had rearranged it with one punch, thereby ending the right wing's season and — in the view of some — permanently altering his playing career.

This was not an isolated case. The Kocur punch became so notorious from Vancouver to Boston that only the ignorant or courageous would dare engage Joey in fisticuffs. As a result, the more he played, the more "room" he received. And the more room, the more his scoring opportunities. Which helps explain his 1997 and 1998 playoff heroics.

Imagine, then, what it must have been like for opponents when Kocur and Probert were in their prime as Red Wings. While Kocur's right cross was the most fearsome punch of its genre, the player's total arsenal did not quite match up with Probert's.

Part of it had to do with image. When an enemy saw Bob Probert, it was like watching a dreadnought bearing down on a rowboat. No contest. Don't even think about it.

If looks could kill — and thereby end the fight — Probert had the ultimate glare. It not only menaced but foretold the destruction ahead. His punches were as rapid as they were devastating.

"There always seemed to be players who knew my reputation and felt that they had to give it a shot with me," Probert once explained. "Actually, I never wanted to talk much about my fights."

This would be roughly equivalent to Supreme Allied Commander Dwight D. Eisenhower not wanting to talk about D-Day, the invasion of Normandy on June 6, 1944.

Some fights in which Probert participated demand discussion even now as then, because landmark moments tend to be analyzed and re-analyzed by historians.

In Probert's case it was a bout — or should we say bouts — with the Albanian Aggressor, Tie Domi.

There have been very few in the NHL like Domi. As amusing as he is terrifying, Domi literally leads with his head; and for good reason. Tie is said to be the only player in the NHL who is in no need of helmeted protection. He has taken more blows to the noggin with less damage than any player in this or any other era.

Fortified with this natural first line of personal defense, Domi was able to use his prodigious boxing skills to consummate advantage. Add a visceral love for fisticuffs and you have all the ingredients for the NHL's light-heavyweight champion.

Domi's size always has been his major debit, yet it was not a problem on February 9, 1992, when he not only engaged Probert in combat, but fought the bigger man to a draw. Bob could neither conceal the bruises nor his bloody nose, and although he did as much damage to his opponent, Probert never was given to histrionics.

By contrast, "histrionics" has been Domi's middle name for much of his big-league career. In this case, every word of the small slugger's body language bespoke that he had beaten Probert.

Furthermore, there were clear suggestions from Tie that when the pair met again there would be no ifs, ands, or buts about the winner — and his initials would not be B.P.

As it happened, the Red Wings visited New York on December 2, 1992, a date which Domi had much earlier fixed in his mind. So had the media.

The hype preceding the Madison Square Garden contest was so intense one might have imagined that a boxing match was taking place that night, not a hockey game. One newspaper even went so far as to feature a Tale of the Tape.

Apart from correctly noting that the media "had blown it out of proportion," Probert kept a low profile, although it was apparent that he, too, was a man on a mission.

When the irresistible force and the immovable object finally collided, it was Probert who led the attack. Once, twice, he whacked Domi with his stick and then dropped the gloves and launched a fusillade of fists.

By the time linesmen had separated the pair, Probert had proven his point. In fact, he won the bout on points — 47 punches to 23 hurled by Domi. Naturally, the NHL would not get directly involved, but the unofficial fight referee, Don (Grapes) Cherry, awarded the decision to Probert, who had missed his chance to mummify Domi with a roundhouse right.

Despite the loss, Domi emerged with a fighter's dignity, one that he has retained ever since. No matter how big or intimidating the foe, Tie will take him on if the spirit moves him or if the challenge is laid down by the other.

The same can be said for Marty McSorley, who is built along the generous dimensions of Probert, but who is in stark contrast because of Double M's natural ebullience. If there is any similarity between the two, it is in playing ability.

McSorley has successfully alternated between forward and defense, proving himself valuable at both positions. But because of his raw power, intensity, and long arms, he always is ready to deliver the right blow at the right time.

Unlike Kocur or Probert — but very much like Domi — McSorley savors center stage. During the summer of 1997, he even threatened to enter a traditional ring for an exhibition bout with the then high-profile boxer Butterbean. For unspecified reasons, the fight never came off, but it generated considerable headlines, none of which bothered McSorley.

Because of his advanced age, McSorley has tempered his temper in the manner of Kocur, Probert, and Domi. But Marty has not lost any of his zest for combat. Rather, he has learned when to drop the gloves and when not to get nasty. "It's selfish if I go looking to start a fight," he once explained. "There's no room for that. The main thing is, I want to play."

The best way to gauge the stature of the quartet is by the manner in which they are regarded by Young Turks who enter the NHL. The wannabe Heavyweight champs hopeful of making a name for themselves as legitimate enforcers, view the veteran quartet with a mixture of awe and admiration, constantly alluding to them when discussing their aspirations.

From this reporter's view, Kocur emerges as the most menacing of the four. Although he lacked Probert's massive presence, Joey always seemed the most calculating, the most cold-blooded and the most devastating when it came to delivering a single knockout punch. The destruction of Dalgarno helped shape that image but it was only one of several Kocur TKOs.

Domi falls right behind Kocur, in my view, because of his indestructibility. Tie could be clobbered by a piledriver and still come back swinging. His stature and his indomitable nature make it scary for a foe who mistakenly believes that because he is small, he is vulnerable.

Tie's other asset is his attitude. He makes it apparent that he likes fighting as much as breathing. Fisticuffs not only come natural to him, but they seem to make his day. When someone likes to fight as much as Domi, the foe automatically is at a great disadvantage.

Ironically, that also is a reason why Tie can never be as menacing as Kocur. When you smile as much as Domi does, the sinister nature is diffused by the grin and the Albanian Assassin takes on the trappings of Curly from the Three Stooges. That's not what genuine enforcing is all about. The only time Kocur smiles is when he scores.

McSorley is more like a big Domi. Marty's jovial nature often is betrayed on the ice and slightly — ever so slightly — diminishes his ominous assets. That he remains one of the NHL's most glamorous performers also tends to minimize his fearsome demeanor by about three percent.

Which is not to suggest that either Domi or McSorley have lost their zeal. During the 1997-98 season, Domi finished with 365 penalty minutes in 80 games, while McSorley totaled 140 in only 56 games. If their modus operandi has changed at all it is in the use of their head over emotion. They no longer fight for the sake of fighting. They fight if there's a reason to fight.

Probert is a distinctly different story. After arriving in Chicago with considerable fuss, fanfare, and fists full of dollars, he succumbed to the injury bug and played only 14 games during the 1997-98 season. This followed a year in which he was in 82 games, scoring 9 goals and 14 assists for 23 points as a Blackhawk. Characteristically, he had 326 penalty minutes.

But that was then and this is now. Whether or not Probert still has the fire in his belly is a moot question.

In the eyes of some, Probert is close to the end of the line. He is an aging lion who may no longer lead the pride as once he did in his heyday. Then again, that also may be true of Kocur, McSorley, and Domi.

Nonetheless, this much is certain: as a quartet, they remain the blasters with the mostest and if anyone has any doubts, just check it out with the new breed. Chances are, they'll confirm that Kocur, Domi, Probert, and McSorley are still The Champions in spirit if not power.

PROFESSOR PUNCH'S
ReVEnge

For more than two decades, 42-year-old Mark Topaz has been one of the foremost hockey fight analysts.

By profession, he is a television graphics coordinator and has worked for such networks as SportsChannel, ESPN and other companies.

Topaz translated his passion for ice brawls into a publication called the *Aggressive Hockey Report* which, for many years, dissected the lives of enforcers.

"For years fighters have been disparaged and called names," said Topaz. "But, their value to their teams is immeasurable. Players such as Bob Probert and Ken Baumgartner give their teammates room to play the game. Enforcers in hockey are comparable to offensive linemen in football. They do all the dirty work but only get noticed when they do something wrong."

Topaz has provided us with the following great fights from the pages of *Aggressive Hockey Report*.

1970 QUARTERFINAL BOSTON VS. NEW YORK RANGERS

Long ago, in another world and another time, a playoff series took place between the Boston Bruins and the New York Rangers in the Stanley Cup Quarterfinal. The year was 1970, but in terms of how different the game was played it might as well have been 1870. There were no helmets worn back then, and sticks were carried at ice level. This was due in no small part to the fact that, back then, Americans and Europeans were using their sticks on each other in their own leagues. There were also no rules back then for the third man in, or first man off the bench, although they were put in due no small part to this series.

The Bruins were the first team to use fighting as a game strategy. The coach of this team was the evil twin of current Bruins g.m. Harry Sinden. Even though he was also named Harry Sinden, he bore nothing in common with the current Bruins boss. This Harry Sinden employed a team of hit-men and backstabbers and preached ganging up as a team philosophy. Unlike the current Bruins, this team won. The 1970 Bruins consisted of one legitimate tough guy in wildman Wayne Cashman, and many others who benefited from the Bruins ganging up style of fighting. Derek Sanderson, Ken Hodge, Grant (Ace) Bailey, John McKenzie, Don Awrey, Rick Smith, Dallas Smith, and Gary Doak were all great when it came to three on one fighting, but when the NHL adopted rules to prevent those things they were exposed. When fighting one on one, Sinden's big, bad, Bruins proved to be neither big nor bad. Missing from the squad that year was hatchet-man Ted Green, who had raised his stick one time too many and had gotten pole-axed by Wayne Maki in an exhibition game.

The Rangers, as was always the case, had one or two good fighters and not much else. That year the cast included then heavyweight champion Orland Kurtenbach, as well as capable battler Ted Irvine and the pugnacious defenseman Brad Park, who loved pounding the Bruins.

Game One in Boston saw the Bruins win big, featuring five fights, including three in the last three minutes. Game Two was quiet, setting the stage for the big third game in Madison Square Garden. As is usually the case (or should I say was) in playoff series, the third game proved to be the wildest. One minute into the game, with a face-off in the Rangers' zone, Ranger goalie Ed Giacomin skated out to Sanderson and told him, "we're going to get you tonight." A few seconds later the puck went into the corner, and when Sanderson went after it, the Rangers jumped him and pounded him. The Bruins followed in and the brawl was on. That set the tone for the fight-filled game which the Rangers went on to win. The two teams accumulated what was then a league playoff record 174 penalty minutes.

The rest of the series was somewhat calmer with only a few fights, mostly being Tom Horton wrestling matches. The two teams did set a record for a playoff series with 375 penalty minutes, breaking the previous record set in the 1968 St. Louis-Philadelphia series. One of my recollections of the series was of the Bruins constantly hoping over the boards whenever there was an altercation. It was not uncommon to see nine or ten Bruins on the ice and only five or six Rangers. Thanks to the Bruins, in 1971 the NHL instituted rules ejecting the third man in as well as the first man off the bench. The Big Bad Bruins would win again in 1972 and then be dispersed, replaced by Don Cherry's Bruins who were legitimately tough with Terry O'Reilly, John Wensink and Stan Jonathan.

DECEMBER 2, 1973 CALIFORNIA AT PHILADELPHIA

It was early in December in 1973. The Philadelphia Flyers were in year three of the Fred Shero era and year two of the Broad Street Bully era. The previous season, the Flyers had brought to the NHL intimidation and fighting as a game strategy. While they were involved in quite a few brawls in 1972-73, it wasn't until the night of December 2, 1973 that they really established their reputation. The opponent that night was the California Golden Seals, a team whose muscle consisted of Bob Stewart, a semi-tough defenseman and Marv Edwards, the back-up goaltender. Among other players in the Seals lineup was Joey Johnston, who had gotten a taste of the Flyers two years earlier when he was jumped by Bob Kelly and Rick Foley in a game at the Spectrum.

The first period was uneventful. At the six minute mark of the second period, Bill Clement of the Flyers and Ray McKay of the Seals fought. Five and a half minutes later, Bobby Clarke, noted stickman, clipped Seals rookie Barry Cummins under the eye with his stick. Cummins then took a two-hander and whacked Clarke over the head, right in front of the Flyer bench. Bob Kelly led the charge from the bench and Bill Flett led the charge from the ice as Cummins tried to run, but there was no place to hide. The Seals also emptied their bench, but not before Cummins was buried under Flyer punches. Clarke needed 20 stitches to close the gash in his head and Cummins needed almost as many for his face. For receiving a match penalty, Cummins got a three-game suspension as well as a $3,000 fine.

Five minutes later, the benches were at it again. This time it started with Rick MacLeish and Ted McAneeley. Dave Schultz and Hillard Graves fought for about 10 minutes and Don Saleski led the charge from the bench as another brawl ensued. The badly overmatched Seals took a pounding and after hanging close with a 2-1 score after two periods, were blown out 5-1 in the third.

Afterwards, Cummins called Clarke at home to apologize for the incident. Coach Fred Shero said, "Something like this could happen in any sport where you give the players sticks." Seals coach Fred Glover vowed to bring more muscle to the lineup, but unfortunately for the team, it was never carried out.

APRIL-MAY 1974 NEW YORK RANGERS
AND PHILADELPHIA FLYERS

One of the 1974 Stanley Cup semi-finals matched up the Philadelphia Flyers and New York Rangers. The Flyers were in the second season of their "Broad Street Bullies" era and were coming off a four game sweep of the Atlanta Flames. The previous year the Flyers got as far as the semi finals before losing to Montreal in five games. The Rangers had defeated Montreal in the quarter-finals, the third straight year that they knocked off the defending Stanley Cup champions.

As described in *Sports Illustrated*, the matchup was the equivalent of George Foreman fighting a flyweight from Thailand. Philadelphia, *S.I.* explained, consisted of heavyweight king Dave Schultz, top contenders Bob Kelly and Moose Dupont, along with 17 other toughs. New York was countering with two fair heavyweights in Ron Harris and Ted Irvine, an overblown middleweight in Brad Park and 17 assorted paperweights.

The first two games were played in Philadelphia and Game One was quiet, as Philadelphia won an easy 4-0 game. At the start of Game Two, Bob Kelly jumped Jerry Butler in the corner and pounded him, 19 seconds into the game. That set the tone for the rest of the series as the Flyers started to run at the Rangers. Jimmy Watson and Pete Stemkowski also tangled in a fight during the game, and the Flyers came away with a 5-2 win and a 2-0 lead in games.

Game Three was in New York and proved to be the most exciting game of the series. Schultz ran Park along the boards early in the game and knocked him down, punched him a few shots in the stomach and then spit on him for good measure. That was all for the first two periods, but in period three, when the Flyers went down 5-3, the fun started. Steven Vickers, a fairly good fighter who rarely fought, got the best of Gary Dornhoefer. The Flyers then sent out Schultz, Kelly, Don Saleski, and Dupont. When Schultz tried to start with Rod Gilbert, Rangers' coach Emile Francis pulled Gilbert off the ice and sent on Ron Harris. Harris challenged Schultz but the linesman jumped in and when Dupont had something to say, Harris challenged him as well. After a lot of circling, nobody got to each other and Schultz and Dupont got misconducts. When play resumed, Rick MacLeish brought his stick up on Park and Park decked him with a punch. Also in that game, Harris hip-checked Kelly along the boards and put him out for the season.

The next three games were relatively quiet with only a couple of fights in each (Schultz pounding Stemkowski and Harris giving Dornhoefer his usual beating). The series came down to Game Seven and the fight everyone remembers (especially Ranger fans, who to this day have not gotten over it) Schultz grabbed Rolfe off to the side and started pounding him. It was about as one-sided a fight as there could be. Schultz landed about 15 punches and a pretty good headbutt. Rolfe staggered off dazed and bloodied and the Flyers went on to win the game, the series and the Stanley Cup. The Rangers were highly criticized for not jumping in and saving Rolfe. A look at the videotape, however, explains why they didn't. One the ice at the time for New York was their number one line — Jean Ratelle, Vic Hadfield and Rod Gilbert. The other defenseman was Brad Park, their top defenseman. None of them could afford to get thrown out. What they should have done was to send out Harris or Irvine on the next shift and take someone like Joe Watson and pound him. At least they could have gotten even that way.

Looking back on the amount of fights in the series does not really tell the whole story. The series was full of dirty, nasty, chippy play and many skirmishes that could have developed into something. Every game kept you on the edge of your seat.

One final thought on the subject is that while the Rangers could not match the Flyers in the muscle department, they could have made better use of the muscle they had. The Rangers two best fighters, Ted Irvine and Ron Harris had a combined one fight in the series. Had they done what they were capable of, who knows how the series would have turned out.

TORONTO AT DETROIT MARCH 31, 1976

The 1975-76 season was the last one before the NHL started putting in anti-fighting legislation. Toughness reigned supreme and many teams adopted the Flyers' physical style of play. While the Flyers were still kings of the hill with Schultz, Kelly, McIlhargey, Dupont, Bridgman, etc. Detroit had also put together a pretty impressive crew. Led by Dan Maloney, a good fighter although overrated by many writers, the Wings also featured a couple of 300 penalty minutes men in Dennis Polonich and Bryan Watson. Rounding out the lineup was veteran troublemaker Dennis Hextall and decent fighters in Rick Lapointe, Mike Bloom, Nick Libett and Jean Hamel. With the playoffs out of reach, the Wings went down swinging, getting involved in two bench-clearing brawls in the last week of the season. First, they took on the second year Washington Capitals, a team as sorry in fighting as in playing ability. Among the battles in the brawl were Dan Maloney vs. Rick Bragnalo, Bryan Watson vs. Mike Lampman and Dennis Polonich vs. Tony White. This, however, was just a warm-up for the following night against Toronto. The Maple Leafs were a bit more of a match for the Red Wings. Led by Tiger Williams and Pat Boutette, the Leafs had recently added two tough rookies in Kurt Walker and Scott Garland.

The game got off to a rough start with Polonich taking on Darryl Sittler at the 1:28 mark of the first period. Towards the end of the period, Tiger Williams tangled with Jean Hamel. This set the tone for the game, and when the second period started, it didn't take long for the brawl. Dennis Hextall took a run at Borje Salming and in came Darryl Sittler after Hextall and they started going at it. Then, big Kurt Walker came in, jumping Hextall from behind. Bryan Watson then jumped Walker, and Dennis Polonich led the charge from the Wings bench, cracking Walker in the back of the head with a flying butt-end. Unlike most bench-brawls where the fighting is usually limited to a few people, in this one practically everyone went. Williams and Hamel came out of the penalty boxes. Among the battles that took place were Williams and Polonich, Williams and Maloney, Polonich and Sittler, Watson and Walker. Pat Boutette had Red Wing rookie Mike Wong's sweater held so tightly around his neck that Wong passed out.

After the Detroit trainer came out and revived Wong, he got back up and went over and pounded Boutette. Maloney and Brian Glennie, who were involved in a court case over Maloney smashing Glennie's head into the ice, wound up paired off, but did not go at it. In all the game was delayed for 39 minutes. When the game resumed, there was a couple of more battles in the third period. Rick Lapointe took on Jack Valiquette and Al Cameron decked Jim McKenny. When Red Wing coach Alex Delvecchio was asked what was going on with his team, his comment was, "we're showing we can handle ourselves and we're showing team spirit."

Unfortunately the NHL tired of the brand of hockey being played and the following season began implementing more rules. An instigator rule, much like the current one, was put in, although it allowed the referee to assess either a minor, major or game misconduct. Also put in was the rule suspending players after accumulating three game misconducts. These rules led to the shocking trade of Dave Schultz to Los Angeles prior to the start of the next season. While a tough brand of hockey would continue to be played, 1976 was truly the last year when toughness was king in the NHL.

WORLD HOCKEY ASSOCIATION
CALGARY-QUEBEC APRIL 11, 1976

The year was 1976, the heyday of tough hockey, and the first round of the WHA playoffs featured one of the wildest brawls in hockey history. The Quebec Nordiques, led by WHA leading scorer Marc Tardif, finished with 104 points and were one of the top three teams in the league. The Nordiques had also taken over the mantle from the Minnesota Fighting Saints as the toughest team in the WHA. The Nordiques were led by former Fighting Saints Curt Brackenbury, league leader in penalty minutes, and Gordie Gallant. Additional muscle on the Nordiques was provided by Pierre Roy, Steve Sutherland, Bill Prentice, Bob Fitchner, Michel Dubois and Charles Constantin, the WHA version of Clark Gillies. In all, Quebec had four of the top ten penalty minute leaders in the league. If all that wasn't enough, for the playoffs they called up longtime EHL badman Gary Gresdal. Their first round opponents would be the Calgary Cowboys, a team which on paper was no match for the Nordiques in either talent or toughness. Calgary's top heavyweights were Peter Driscoll, Rick Jodzio and former Atlanta Flame Butch Deadmarsh. Beyond those three, the supporting cast featured Pat Westrum, Warren Miller and not much else.

Calgary took an uneventful game one, 3-1 on Quebec ice. That set the tone for a wild game two. As they had done many times, the Nordiques started it, two and a half minutes in when Gordie Gallant jumped Rick Jodzio from behind and pounded him. Pat Westrum had come in to save him. Three and a half minutes later, when Jodzio took his next shift, he decided to get even. Jodzio hopped over the boards and charged across the ice, taking an 80 foot run at Tardif. After blasting him and knocking him out cold, Jodzio jumped on Tardif and pounded away. As Jodzio was pummeling the mow unconscious Tardif, the Nordiques, led by Gresdal, charged onto the ice to get Jodzio. When the Nordiques got to him, they attacked Jodzio with fists and skates, punching and kicking him. As they attacked Jodzio, Tardif was accidentally kicked in the teeth by teammate Prentice, who was aiming for Jodzio. Now it was Jodzio who was in trouble and Cowboys goalie Don McLeod came to the rescue. McLeod came in, swinging his goalie stick like a shillelagh and stood over the fallen Jodzio, protecting him until he could be carried from the ice. Meanwhile, the brawl continued with both teams in an all out war. Unfortunately for Calgary, they had few weapons. Other than Driscoll, who did a number on Brackenbury, the Cowboys took a beating. Calgary's leading scorer, Danny Lawson was pounded by two Nordiques and had both his eyes swollen shut. Paul Terbenchie suffered a cut nose and a bruised eye. George Morrison, sustained a cut nose. The brawl was so wild that twenty Quebec City policemen had to come out on the ice and try to break it up. Ten players were ejected and the first period took two hours to play. When the dust settled, Calgary recorded an 8-4 win.

The next day Quebec was livid. The team sent a list of demands to the league saying that if they were not met, they would not fly to Calgary for game three. Quebec demanded Jodzio be suspended for life, Calgary coach, Joe Crozier be suspended for the year and WHA executive V.P. Bud Polie, who was the league representative at the game, be fired. The WHA agreed so that Quebec would finish the series, which they lost in five games. In addition Gordie Gallant was also suspended for the rest of the series, Danny Lawson and Quebec coach Jean-Guy Gendron were suspended for one game and both teams were fined $25,000.

Calgary coach Crozier was reinstated after the Quebec series and felt his team was not responsible. If Calgary was looking for trouble, Crozier said, they certainly would have had team penalty minute leader Deadmarsh dressed for the game. In addition, many of the Quebec players had come into the game with their hands taped.

The Nordiques, while they would remain a tough team, would never again put together the type of squad that they had that year. Marc Tardif would recover from his injuries, which included shock and a concussion, and in 1977-78 would surpass his 148 point total, scoring 156 points, the highest single season total in WHA history. Rick Jodzio would come back to Calgary the following year, but the effects of the brawl, as well as the many anti-fighting rules put in by the WHA, limited his effectiveness and he wound up in the minors. The next year he played with Colorado and Cleveland in the NHL, but was just a shell of his former self. With his toughness gone, Jodzio was soon out of the game.

EXHIBITION — BOSTON AT PHILADELPHIA OCTOBER 6, 1977

It started out as the Secret Life of Walter Mitty, but it ended up as The Wild Bunch. George Plimpton played goal for the Bruins in a special five minute exhibition prior to the main game. Once that was over, the real fun began. The Flyers had been eliminated in the semi-finals by Boston that spring. So revenge was in the air. Flyer rookie Dave Hoyda, the heir apparent to Dave Schultz, had been sent down a few days earlier. He dressed for the game anyway. That should give you an indication of the mood for the night.

In the first period, Paul Holmgren and Terry O'Reilly met and for the second straight time O'Reilly won the decision in a good fight. All was quiet until 4:56 of the second period when Jimmy Watson and Wayne Cashman started shoving in front of the net. They then started to swing sticks at each other. Holmgren came in and dropped his gloves and grabbed Cashman. They tied up quickly with Cashman reportedly trying to gouge Holmgren's bad eye. All three were thrown out of the game. Moments later the fight resumed in the runway beneath the stands. Cashman tried kicking Holmgren and when they began fighting both benches emptied and headed underneath the stands. With not a lot of room to do anything, it was more shoving and pushing than fighting. After it was broken up many of the Bruins needed to get their skates sharpened from walking on concrete. This would come into play as less than four minutes later the brawl moved onto the ice.

O'Reilly restarted it by cross-checking Orest Kindrachuk and going after him. While O'Reilly was pounding Kindrachuk, Mike Milbury sucker punched Flyer Don Saleski, and started to beat the daylights out of him. When the linesman left O'Reilly and Kindrachuk alone. O'Reilly started to pound him again. That was when Mel Bridgman led the Flyers off the bench, piling on top of O'Reilly. Stan Johnston grabbed Bob Kelly of the Flyers and pounded him. The Bruins were outnumbered and each player that came out of the runway was grabbed by a Flyer. Bridgman grabbed Peter McNab and got the surprise of his life. They went toe to toe with McNab getting the edge in punches. Dave Hoyda went for Bruin Bobby Schmautz but Bobby Clarke saved Schmautz from a beating by grabbing him first. Hoyda wound up with Mike Forbes and they went at it with Hoyda getting the edge. Referee Wally Harris separated them but he couldn't keep them apart and they went at it again, this time it was even. Gary Doak of the Bruins was paired off with Ross Lonsberry and after a lot of sweater tugging Doak threw a couple of punches. Lonsberry then beat the tar out of him. Bob Kelly wound up with Milbury and beat him in a fight. Bruin tough guy John Wensink was paired off with big Harvey Bennet and they did a lot of shirt pulling but that was all.

When the brawl finally ended, 15 players were thrown out bringing the total ejections for the evening to 18, an NHL record. Mr. Plimpton had something to write about.

1980 QUARTERFINAL BOSTON VS NEW YORK ISLANDERS

The 1980 Quarterfinal series between the New York Islanders and the Boston Bruins did not shape up as a particularly violent series. Although both teams possessed good, tough, physical hockey players, there was no history between the two teams that suggested anything might get out of hand. None of the games between the two teams had ever been very rough and you had to go back to 1974 to find a game with as many as five fights. So it came as no surprise when the first game contained only eight minor penalties. What did come as a surprise was when Game Two turned into a war. Just over two minutes into the game, Clark Gillies and Terry O'Reilly collided and dropped the gloves and in an upset, O'Reilly won a clear cut decision. Several minutes later, Gary Howatt blasted Dick Redmond into the boards and was pounced on by Wayne Cashman. However, Howatt regained his balance and decisioned Cashman. With about five minutes left in the period, John Wensink came out for his first shift and pretty soon started slugging it out with Bob Nystrom, whom he was not match for. Then with seven seconds left in the period, some pushing and shoving started Gillies and O'Reilly parted from the puck and squared off. This one went to Gillies as he knocked O'Reilly down early. Play resumed for the final seven seconds and then the action started again.

Mike Milbury and Duane Sutter, who had been jawing during the last fight, went to the corner and Milbury started swinging on Sutter. Meanwhile, Stan Jonathan grabbed Bob Lorimer, a non-fighter, and pummeled him. With the period over, the benches cleared and everyone paired off. Unfortunately, the two best fighters on each team, Nystrom, Gillies, Wensink and O'Reilly had been sent off after picking up majors in the final five minutes. Isles goalie Billy Smith, usually active in bench brawls, was contained by both Bruins goalies, Gerry Cheevers and Yves Belanger. Gary Howatt was trying to get at Jonathan, but was being held off by Cashman, who he was dragging around the ice. Al Secord was tied up with Gordie Lane and when he fell on top of Lane, he started swinging at him. They got back up and mostly wrestled. As the brawl moved out towards center ice, Jonathan grabbed Lorimer again and really let him have it, opening up a gash under his eye and knocking him down. Now Howatt really wanted Jonathan and came for him again. When Cashman got in the way again, Howatt drilled him with a right hand followed by about eight or nine more. Cashman then came back and returned fire with his left, taking the decision in a long battle. Finally, it was over, but only for this game.

The second period of Game Three saw Sutter and Milbury resume in a minor scrap. Then Gillies went after O'Reilly in the corner and knocked him down and dropped his gloves, winning his only clear decision. When they came out together later in the period they resumed again, with O'Reilly again coming out on top. When the linesman stepped in, Gillies got loose and landed a massive left to O'Reilly's nose, doing some damage. After that shot O'Reilly looked like he had gone through a windshield, and due to this, many people, then and now, mistakenly credited Gillies with a clear-cut edge in the fights. Objectively speaking, O'Reilly won two, Gillies won one and one was even. Even if you wanted to give a win to Gillies in the fight where they threw two punches each and fell, it would still be 2-2. Anyone who tells you Gillies won all four either has a faulty memory, or doesn't know fighting very well. In any event, with O'Reilly having two majors, Howatt came after him in the third period, picking a fight with him to get him out of the game.

Game four was relatively quiet, the only fight being Nystrom's pummeling of Brad McCrimmon. When the series shifted back to Boston for game five, Sutter and Milbury staged round three. While they were going, Secord popped Gillies with a sucker shot with his gloves on and they squared off. Secord went down quickly under a reign of blows. Later in the period, Ray Bourque beat Howatt to the punch and decisioned him. That would be all as the Islanders took the series four games to one.

For the Islanders it was sweet redemption from their quarterfinal series two years previously. That was when Toronto came at them from every direction with fists and sticks and even though they had the toughness to match them, they didn't, eventually losing in seven games. They had refused to play Toronto's game and it cost them, but the lesson was learned. When Boston tried the Toronto theory, the Islanders matched them punch for punch and won the series, then went on to win two more series and their first Stanley Cup.

THIRTY-SECOND
Third Degree

R ob Blake, Brent Severyn and Steve Konowalchuk are three diverse char-
acters with one common denominator: they play hard-nosed hockey and
will fight of the occasion demands fisticuffs.

Severyn saw his role change from a standard defenseman on the Devils
and Islanders to an enforcer with Colorado and Anaheim. Blake, captain of the
L.A. Kings and 1998 Norris Trophy winner, has gone in a different direction.
Although he failed to discuss fighting in detail, his observation are nonetheless
noteworthy. Konowalchuk, a forward, epitomizes the grit of the Capitals.

Each of the three participated in the following capsule interviews with Fischler
Hockey Service correspondents Lee Callans, Kevin Hubbard, Mark Losier and
Mary McCarthy, as well an NHL conducted forum, moderated by Dave Keon.

BRENT SEVERYN, MIGHTY DUCKS OF ANAHEIM

Lee Callans: Who are the toughest guys in the league.
Brent Severyn: Tony Twist is one of the hardest punchers. I consider him the
toughest guy in the league right now because he can hurt you. You've got to
be careful when you're fighting that guy. Chris Simon is a very good fighter
and a pretty good player. He does the job for his team. He's just a tough man.
Bob Probert is still up there and Marty McSorley.

LC: How about the younger guys in the league.
BS: I respect Darren Langdon because he's another who has had to work for
everything he got. Nobody has backed him up ever in his career. He started
from the East Coast League and worked his way up. I'm glad for the guy
because he's worked hard. He goes out there, does his job and he's not a dirty
player but will fight anybody. Guys like that you like to see succeed. He's not
a guy who is going to go out there and stick you in the face of hack you, but
he will fight you and that's what it is all about.

LC: What goes through your mind during a fight?
BS: I'm a very technical fighter. I do a lot of studying of what's going on and I
try to pick my spots when I'm fighting, waiting for the other fellow to open up.

LC: How do you train in the off-season:
BS: I've boxed for probably nine summers now and have taken Tae Kwan Do
and I do it more to stay in shape even though it is part of my job. I really enjoy
hitting the bag and going in there and working out and I lift weights and do
everything else to improve my game. Boxing though is part of the regimen in

the summer. When I'm fighting, I'm waiting for them to open up. Sooner or later, like when Holyfield was fighting Tyson, he was waiting for him to open up with that left hook and then he would come in and so that's what I would do to certain guys. I know their weaknesses and what they're trying to do and I try to read off them.

LC: Talk about picking you spots in the ice.
BS: The 1996-97 season was my first year really being an enforcer. There is a lot more to it from my perspective, but then again maybe I read into things a little more than I should. You really have to watch when to fight and when not to fight to help motivate the team. I you're up to four to nothing you don't want to be fighting the tough guy and giving them a bit of a spark. This job is all psychological as far as I'm concerned. It's tough on the head and you really have to be prepared every single game to fight. Before, I would go out and play and if a fight happened that wouldn't be a problem. Now (fighting) is strictly my role. When I was in Colorado, the Avalanche didn't want me for any other reason. What's funny is that now I'm stereotyped as that kind of a player after one year even though I have been playing for nine years. One year of being a goon and that's the kind of image I get.

LC: You've scored a few goals with a type of trick shot near the boards. Is there a story behind that?
BS: Yeah, the fake dumper. Robbie Ftorek showed me that one. I'll be coming down either side as close to the boards as I can and I fake like I'm going to dump the puck in just before the blue line. Most goalies are going to cheat and try to stop the puck as it is being rimmed around the boards. So as soon as I make the move to go to dump it in they are cheating, trying to go behind the net. They are off-balance or maybe even behind the net almost at that point when you direct the puck towards the net. Instead of dumping in the corner, I turn my body and shoot the puck into the net. Hopefully, the net is empty. I got half my NHL goals like that. My first goal in the NHL was a fake dumper. Robbie showed me this when we used to go out before practice. He used to do this move and I went out there and he showed me how to do it.

STEVE KONWALCHUK, WASHINGTON CAPITALS

Mary McCarthy: Even though you're not known as a person who drops his gloves at the drop of a hat, you certainly do have the reputation of someone who's willing to use his fists when provoked. When did you have your first fight in hockey.

Steve Konowalchuk: It was in hockey camp, and it was my brother. He started it. He didn't like that I stole the puck from him. The fight wound up being a draw.

MM: When do you fight in hockey? What makes you drop your gloves.
SK: Sometimes it's just the heat of the moment. You get frustrated with the other team. And maybe some guy has been getting under your skin for a few shifts. It's different on every team. Defenseman give me a whack with the stick. They get me mad. The way I play they understand that I'm just going to keep coming at them. And sometimes they think they can make me back off if they give me a whack. I get tired of that.

MM: Who are your models? Who did you admire as a kid?
SK: When I was in Junior, there was a quote from my coach on my card. He called me a "Dave Poulin-type player." And then when I started playing here, Dave Poulin was one of my very first roommates. It was neat. Also, Dale Hunter. He keeps telling me, "Be responsible." Hunt says if you're just always responsible and do your job well, you'll be there a long time. Some players come in here and they're flashy for a bit and then they're gone and sometimes you never hear from them again.

MM: What's it like to play against the stars in the NHL?
SK: It is distracting at first. I didn't play against Wayne Gretzky much when I first got here because he was playing in L.A. But we played against Mario Lemieux a lot. I wasn't responsible for covering him at first, because I was too knew. Mostly it was Kelly Miller's job. Later I would have to cover Mario for part of the game. He was such a presence on the ice.

MM: Who are the best fighters?
SK: Marty McSorley, Chris Simon, Darren McCarty.

MM: Who are the toughest forwards to play against?
SK: Just who you'd expect. Wayne Gretzky and Paul Kariya.

MM: Defensemen?
SK: Rob Blake. It's very tough to go to the net against him. Scott Stevens. Ulf Samuelsson.

MM: What do you think are the most important qualities in a coach.
SK: In the NHL, honesty and respect. The coach has to respect the players and the players have to respect the coach. Sometimes the coach will have the assistant coaches talk to you. But usually you can tell from how you're play-

ing, what line you're playing on and sort of the atmosphere on the bench, how you're doing.

MM: What do you see as your role on the team?
SK: To be responsible defensively. To create turnovers. To take the puck out of the corners. Go to the net.

MM: What's it like playing on Peter Bondra's line?
SK: It's so great playing with Bondra. He gives me a lot of room on the ice because everyone is always focusing on what he's doing. It's great playing with him.

MM: If you could give advise to kids, like yourself when you were playing minor hockey, what would you say?
SK: Have fun in hockey. It has to be fun. If you're not having fun, do something else. Play for the team. I'd tell them if it's not going to be hockey, then find something else and really like and stick with it. And they should realize that to be a good hockey player, to be successful, you don't have to always be scoring goals. There's too much emphasis on goal-scoring. It's become so important that people don't even notice assists any more. But there are lots of different roles on a team. Joe Reekie is a perfect example of that. He doesn't score goals but he plays a really important role on this team.

MM: What do you think of the way the NHL fools around with rules all the time? Right now it's the obstruction calls.
SK: The obstruction calls would be fine if they were consistent about it. But they're not. One rule I'd really like to see changed is the crease violation. They should go back to the old way. Just leave it up to the referee. If he thinks you're interfering with the goalie, then you get called. But this business of having your toe in and having a goal disallowed, when there was no way that toe bothered the goalie, that is not good.

MM: What rule changes would you like to see?
SK: If a goalie comes out of the net, he should get hit. They interfere with you anyway, so if they're going to be out, say a certain distance, then they should get hit.

LOUIE DEBRUSK — PHOENIX COYOTES

Mark Losier: Do you remember your first fight?
Louie DeBrusk: Yes, I remember it vividly. It was in the summer before I went

to play Junior B. I had started lifting weights that year, so I was a little stronger and I started to become more physical. I had gone to what I think is called "The Tournament of The Stars" in Ontario and I got picked up by a team that was being put together in Sound Port. We were playing an exhibition game against the Versaga Beach Team and I ended up getting into a fight behind the net. I didn't even drop my one glove. I threw punches and, at the end, I threw him down on the ice. I remember afterward — even during the whole ride home — I just had so much adrenaline in me. The fight really got me pumped up. It escalated from there. It just came very natural to me and, once I got used to it, I was pretty good at getting those helmets off and going at it.

ML: How did your parents feel about you fighting?
LD: Well my dad didn't seem to mind it too much. I think he liked the fact that I was getting my nails dirty and I was in there competing. He always believed that just because you are fighting doesn't mean you can't play, too. You don't have to go out there and fight all of the time. You make sure that you pick the right spots. I think it caught him a little off guard, though, because it was definitely not in his personality to do that. So to see me go out there and get into fights was a new thing. It was like "I don't know where you get it from." But if it is working for you, that's good It allowed me to jump up the ranks in hockey. I think he understood how it worked. My mother was a big, supportive fan but it took a little longer for her to understand that was my role. That was part of it for me and that was how I established myself on the team.

ML: What do you like better — scoring a goal or winning a fight?
LD: I would have to say scoring the goal, just because I don't do it as often. Scoring is the number one thing that the game is all about. Even for a tough player like myself, there is not a much better feeling than scoring goals. It's still great to go out there and do well in a fight, but I think to go out there and score or set up a really nice goal is the creme de la creme.

ML: During a game does a coach tell you to go out and fight or do you just know when?
LD: Well, I have had coaches tell me to go out and fight but Jacques — my coach now — has never told me to rough it up. He leaves that up to the players and realizes that, as professionals, we understand our role. He knows there are certain guys on the team who are willing to do that. I'm one of those guys. If there is a situation that comes up in a game, I can get into a fight maybe to spark things a little. Very rarely does a coach tell someone to fight, though.

ML: When you are lined up for a face-off is there any type of communication between you and the other player where you look at each other and just know?

LD: Those are situations that players like me are fairly familiar with. If a situation has come up prior to that that is going to result in an altercation then there is exchange of words sometimes. It's not uncommon for me to go out there and challenge a guy. Little things are said out there from time to time.

ML: Some players do not fight people they don't feel they can win against. Do you think some players pick and choose who they want to fight?
LD: Definitely there are some, but I don't think there is a lot of it that goes on only because it is so noticeable. That can turn into an advantage for the other team. It is better to fight and not do well than just not to fight. If you fight at least you are willing to show up and say "I don't care if you beat me, I am still going to run around and hit your players." Winning or losing a fight isn't everything — it's showing up. That's all it takes. That's the hardest part.

ML: Is there a technique fighting on the ice? It has been said before that you throw the first punch and it is actually detrimental.
LD: There are always strategies. Everyone has different styles. In boxing, they always say styles make fights. Some guys you might fight differently. If you know a guy has a dominant left hand, you might tie him up with your right and throw left hands as well. If you feel you have a stronger right hand than his left hand, then you'll throw rights against his left. It all depends on the situation. If you are fighting out of anger — maybe if somebody two-hands you in the back of the legs — your strategy is going to be a little different because you're not really thinking sensibly. It might sound contradictory to think you use sense in a fight. Most people think when you're fighting it's all crazed anger, but I'm actually a very strategical fighter. I think a lot when I fight, which is probably one of the reasons I do fairly well and don't get hit that often in a fight. I try to pick a spot where my opponent is a little weaker and I can get in there and get him without him getting me.

ML: Is a good hit as effective as a good fight to you?
LD: I've never really been a huge hitter, but I'm trying to work on it. For me when I get a hit like that it means a lot to me because it gets the crowd into it, your teammates into it. Obviously I don't want to see someone go out with an injury like that, but at the time we didn't know it was that severe. We just knew he was off the ice and they were down to five defensemen. I think a good hit is pretty equivalent to a good fight.

ROB BLAKE, LOS ANGELES KINGS

Q: Was there any point in the last couple of years where you looked at the Kings' situation and thought to yourself, "My god, were in so deep. It's just going to be impossible to get out of this hole?

Rob Blake: A point came in 1996-97. I had had been injured two years and wasn't really around the team. Then, I was around it and realized pretty quickly that things weren't going in the right direction. But bringing Dave Taylor in and bringing in some players like Jozef Stumpel, Luc Robitaille, Garry Galley, a couple of signings, you can see things turn around. But definitely there was a point in the season where I didn't think it could get any worse and I didn't know if I wanted to be around any more.

Q: You played on Canada's losing team at Nagano. What's wrong with the Canadian game?

RB: I don't think we should change at all. When you play a team like the Czech Republic and it comes down to a shootout they score one and we don't score any and that decides whether you go to a Gold Medal game or not, we're close enough. Nothing really has to be revamped. We were without Joe Sakic and Paul Kariya, two game-breakers and two guys who would have helped us down the stretch. Hockey is quite content in Canada. Obviously not having a medal throughout the whole Olympics hurt, but Canada is quite capable of once again being on top.

Q: What does it feel like to be healthy?

RB: Two years ago when I was sitting in rehab working on my knee, I didn't think I would get back to this level. There were tough stretches there. It was two solid years of injuries, beginning with half of a lockout. You know, it cut the seasons. It took a long time to come back. Now I can go out, make my decisions, be aggressive when I want to be and not have to hesitate. I makes a huge difference in the game.

Q: Do you feel like you're close to the level that that was expected of you when you came into the NHL?

RB: I'm up there and obviously, the Norris Trophy and Olympics helped with confidence. Being in that pressure hockey. That really gave me a key whether I was back to 100 percent.

Q: Much is being talked about the new rules, the obstruction rules, and the way the referees are calling the games. How do you think it's going to impact hockey? Is it the right way to handle these problems?

RB: The rules state you can't hook and you can't hold, that's obstruction and it has to be called. Obviously it's a dramatic change from before. It will take a little while for players to catch on, but in the long run, it's going to help. It's going to open up the game. It's going to let the players skate. You'll see more goals on rushes because you can't grab a guy and a hold him all the way to the pin.

Q: How will it affect your game?
RB: It's going to help everybody's game. It's nice that we have a goaltender that plays the puck and really helps our defensemen. You can't get the holdups and guys are on you so you need your goalie moving the puck. It also helps our team with aggressive fore-check and turnovers. Stephane Fiset had a stomach tear at the end of the season; we really missed him. He came back, making the big saves for us.

Q: How would you describe your system?
RB: It is a trap to a point. If we're not able to get in and get aggressive on a team, then we're going to force them up the wall. We have big players that get in the way and it's tough to move the puck through the neutral zone, but our key has been our forecheck. We've been able to cause turnovers. We don't have real offensive team. We've got guys who when there are turnovers will be able to score so definitely job is in place if we're not in an aggressive forecheck.

Q: As you mentioned, you don't have a lot of scoring like you used to have, you don't have the starters that the Kings had in the early 90's. Does it make it easier to play this kind of concept, there's not one person you know you can rely on to carry the team?
RB: Every club wishes it had a big-name player to lead every game, game in and game out. What's happening in L.A. is you're seeing guys who have been in other organizations who haven't really got chances to play. Guys like Jozef Stumpel. Definitely he's one of the key offensive guys in the league. Glen Murray is another. They're stepping up and they're going to make themselves a career out of it.

Q: What about the feeling of going through tough times and being part of something and building it back up to where you were a couple of years ago?
RB: I was pretty spoiled when I came in. I got to play with Wayne Gretzky, the greatest player in the world and our team was on top. We went to the Stanley Cup Finals and I was young. I thought that happened every year. I didn't know any better. Then you miss if for four years and you really see the struggles. Now to see it turning around and coming back up and the fans starting to come out again. I realize what winning is why it's so important for the organization.

Q: How has your game developed since you left Bowling Green?

RB: I was fortunate to go Bowling Green and practice five times a week and play tow games on the weekend and develop my skating and defensive ability. I came to the Kings and they had injury problems. I got to play right away at a young age and got to play with some experience with Larry Robinson and Gretzky. But my game evolved confidence-wise. Over the last few years, I began to focus on what we had to do to win, not just going out playing, but doing things to help the team get together to come closer together and win. That's basically been the difference from when I was younger to being a leader now.

Q: What did it mean to you playing in the Olympics?

RB: It was a highlight of my career. When you're young, you watch the Olympics, you look at the Olympics but at the time it was out of reach because you were in the NHL and you weren't allowed to go. Now the greatest players assemble for two and play. It's an experience I'll never forget.

Q: How does it feel to go up against super talented clubs like the Red Wings?

RB: When they put the lineups of Colorado, Dallas, Detroit on the board, guys would just look at them and put there heads down and say, "Let's get the 60 minutes over and go home." Now we can compete and we want to compete. That's the biggest difference. Talent-wise, we probably don't match up with those teams, but we want to be able to work hard and go out and compete.

Q: Do you like the idea of a shootout?

RB: I've been involved in two shootouts now, one where we won and one where we lost. I'm not a big favorite of the Shootout. But that's the international rule and we had to accept that going into the tournament. Whether you win or lose on that, it's but you do have to accept it.

DEAN MALKOC, BOSTON BRUINS

Kevin Hubbard: What makes you tick?

Dean Malkoc: I go out and play hard every night. I play the body and play a simple, obviously when I play hard I'm going to get in some battles and fights. That's a part of hockey. It's the way I have played since I played Junior. I wasn't going to change the way I play.

KH: What made you decide to be a hard hitting defenseman?

DM: In my first Junior game, we were playing a tough team. I didn't know what I could do in my first times scrapping, but I fought some guy and he was tough. I fought him and came back to the bench and the guys were loving it. The coach said, "We didn't know you could fight." I said, "I didn't know either!" But I won. It was my very first game, on one of the first shifts. I was thinking, "Holy smokes! This is Junior hockey. Wow, this is crazy." If I did some of that stuff in real life, I could have been charged with assault. So for me, playing tough started from the first game. It's a difficult way to play but it can be rewarding and fun.

KH: Have you been in two fights in one game?
DM: In my first or second year pro. It takes a lot out of you.

KH: How about the fate of fighting in hockey.
DM: They can't take fighting out of hockey. It has been a part of the game since it started and it should always be a part of the game. Knock on wood, most players don't get hurt in a fight. It is entertainment of for people.

KH: Does anything funny ever happen to tough guys?
DM: The Canucks once had a skills contest a couple of years ago. It was me, Tim Hunter, Alex Stojanov and Dana Murzyn. We were doing the hardest shot contest. We all took three shots and it came to Stojanov's turn and he came out with a brand new stick. The idea of it was to skate as hard as you could and shoot the puck in the net as hard as you can. So Alek skates up as hard as he can and is about to shoot the puck into the net when all of a sudden his stick breaks, juts like that. Everyone on the bench was laughing and the crowd was yelling, "He broke stick like a twig! Wow, he's strong." So he looks at his stick and sees it has been cut. Alek then goes to the bench and is thinking, "What the hell is going on here?" Now he gets three sticks out of the rack and brings the three with him. he skates to take another shot, breaks his stick again and the puck doesn't even move. Now everyone is laughing. Meanwhile, on the bench we're wondering, "Who pulled this off. This is pretty good." The crowd is going, "What with this guy!!??" Now Alek uses another stick and breaks THAT one, too. He finally realizes that all his stick have been cut. He wound up using a stick that's about two feet tall. Later we found out that Tim Hunter, who was also in the contest. did the cutting.

BLASTS FROM THE PAST

Bad Boys

The All-Dirtiest-Toughest Team

The difference between a dirty hockey player and a tough hockey player is about the same as the difference between sleet and snow. There is practically no difference.

What is dirty play to one viewer is nothing more than tough play to another. When Bobby Clarke of the Philadelphia Flyers skates against the Montreal Canadiens, the Montreal coach in- variably labels Clarke a dirty player.

"But," said a member of the Canadiens, "if Clarke was on our team, we wouldn't call him-dirty, we'd call him a good, tough player."

As a result, I make little distinction between the two unless a player such as a Jean Beliveau is so impeccably clean in spirit if not always in fact-that he can only be called tough, and rarely dirty.

My All-Dirtiest-Toughest Team covers every hockey era, but special emphasis is placed on the post-1930 era, since my information about pre-1930 ruffians was gathered by research and not first hand viewing. I'm not that old.

In evaluating the list, the reader must bear in mind that toughness and dirty play are relative to the era in which the players performed. There is absolutely no question in my mind that the contemporary players were pussy-cats compared with those who played in the pre-expansion post-World War II era. Likewise, I am convinced that those who skated in major leagues during the "prehistoric" era-1910-20 were the toughest and dirtiest players of all.

A man who played during that and subsequent eras, Frank Boucher, bears out this point. "Games were tougher," said Boucher, "and blood flowed even more freely then." Boucher recalled the night when Hall of Famer Jack Adams, playing for Toronto, was carved up by the Montreal Wanderers so freely that "he came out looking like the loser of a saber duel at Stuttgart."

Adams was taken to Montreal General Hospital, where his sister happened to be working as a nurse in the admitting room. "Jack;" said Boucher, "was so battered and bloodied that she didn't recognize her own brother until she recorded his name at the admitting desk.", Later, the wounded player dismissed suggestions that he was the victim of a wanton gang attack. "It wasn't an unusually tough game," said Adams. "When you got cut, you skated to the boards where the trainer sloshed off the blood with a sponge he kept in a bucket and patched you up with a slice of adhesive tape. That night most of my tape must have sweated off."

With that in mind, I present Fischler's All-Dirtiest-Toughest Team:

EDDIE SHORE (NHL, 1926-40)

No big-league hockey player came closer to killing an opponent in a game than Shore, a Boston Bruins defenseman who had 978 stitches laced over 80 wounds on his torso. Shore almost killed Toronto Maple Leafs forward Ace Bailey during a game at Boston Garden in 1933.

During a particularly bloody battle, Shore checked Bailey, a generally peaceful man, from behind. Bailey's head struck the ice, and he was carried off with a cerebral- concussion. For several days Bailey teetered between life and death in a Boston hospital. He eventually recovered but never played hockey again.

The fact that Shore wantonly charged a peaceful man like Bailey — apparently Shore mistook Bailey for another Leaf — while Bailey had his back turned and was totally unprepared for the blow, and damn near killed him, puts Shore at the top of the list. Shore eventually got his comeuppance years later when he started a fight with Phil Watson of the Rangers. Watson's teammate Murray Patrick intervened and flattened Shore for the count. Patrick had once been amateur heavyweight champion of Canada.

TED LINDSAY (NHL, 1944-65)

Lindsay was equally potent with his stick or his dukes, depending on the occasion. During a game between Boston and Lindsay's Detroit Red Wings in 1951. Lindsay and Bill Ezinicki of the Bruins dueled with their sticks and then exchanged punches. Ezinicki lost one tooth and needed nineteen stitches to close assorted wounds.

"It was a case of self-survival," said Lindsay. "He had hit me over the head after the whistle and cut me at the hairline, so I tapped him back. Then he dropped his stick and his gloves, so we ended up in a fight." Lindsay's flailing stick was used as often as an intimidating device as it-was for scoring. He is personally credited with running at least one player out of the NHL with his menacing tactics, some critics charged that Lindsay was tough only when his powerful line- mate Gordie Howe was around.

"I interpret toughness with ability to back up any situation which may arise," said former Montreal Canadiens manager Frank Selke, Sr. "I cannot place Lindsay in this category because he is mean and quick with his stick but cannot back it up with his dukes."

The majority opinion had it the 'other way. Before he died, former Toronto Maple Leafs president Stafford Smythe said of Lindsay: "He is tough because he is dirty!"

LEO LABINE (NHL, 1951-62)

As a member of the Boston Bruins, Labine made a policy of head-hunting the superstars, especially Maurice "Rocket" Richard. He nearly killed Richard one night, blindsiding him with a combination knee to the groin and cross-check to the head. Richard was carried unconscious from the ice but later returned to score the winning goal.

Labine could fight with his fists but like Lindsay was notorious for his quick stick, usually waved around an opponent's mouth. "I don't know any-body who likes to eat wood," said Labine, "unless he's a beaver."

Unlike many marauders Labine was as terrifying with his tongue as he was with his stick. One night a piqued Rocket Richard jammed the butt end of his stick into Labine's ribs. Leo barked: "Look, Rocket, you've got thirty-two teeth. Do you want to try for sixteen?" Labine had several bloody run-ins: parting the scalp of Chicago's Gus Mortson with his stick, trading punches with tough Tod Sloan, and fencing with Richard.

In his old age Labine mellowed. One night in Toronto Eric Nesterenko then of the Maple Leafs broke a hockey stick over Labine's head. "You shouldn't do such things," said Labine. "You'll get a penalty!"

GORDIE HOWE (NHL, 1946-71; . WHA, 1973-1980)

Dozens of players, coaches, and managers have branded Howe as the greatest and dirtiest player of all time. With surgical precision Howe has used his stick blade against the most formidable opponents.

Once, he nearly removed Ranger defenseman Lou Fontinato's ear. Another time he bashed in Fontinato's nose. "Howe," said Phil Watson, ex-Ranger coach, "gets away with murder. Cross-checks, high-sticks, the works. He's been doing it for years."

Former teammate Ted Lindsay was one of the few — besides Gordie him-self — to defend the Howe style. According to Lindsay it is less than fair to call Howe a dirty hockey player. "What is dirty?" said Lindsay. "If dirty means protecting yourself, Gordie is dirty. When you're the best, you can't let the other team take chunks of flesh out of you. In other words Gordie has been protecting himself."

When Gordie played in the NHL a poll among managers placed him at the top of the list among "toughest players in the league." More than a decade later, WHA bosses were saying, the same thing.

FERNIE FLAMAN (NHL, 1944-61)

A mean and highly competent defenseman, Flaman once nearly took Ranger

Andy Bathgate's eye out with a stick, and another time, almost skewered Camille Henry of the Rangers. "Flaman," said Henry, "was absolute murder to play against."

Although Flaman had a Milquetoast look about him, more than one NHL tough guy confided, "I wouldn't want to come face-to-face with him in a fight."

Flaman rarely lost his cool, but once former Red Wings coach Jimmy Skinner antagonized him from the bench. Flaman skated over to the Detroit bench and smacked Skinner in the face. One night in a play-off game against the Canadiens, Flaman lifted Henri Richard of Montreal off the ice with his two hands as Richard was in flight and then hurled the Canadien back on the ice in one motion "Flaman," wrote Jack Zanger in Sport magazine, "was the most dangerous Bruin to tangle with."

Former Washington Capitals manager Milt Schmidt, who once- coached Flaman in Boston, called him, 61 a solid body-checker who was at his best when things were rough."

EDOUARD "NEWSY' " LALONDE (NHL, 1917-22)

According to one veteran hockey writer, Lalonde "spilled enough corpuscles to gratify any blood bank on the continent." Prior to formation of the NHL, Lalonde played in various Canadian pro leagues. His clashes with "Bad" Joe Hall, who later became a teammate on the Canadiens, were studies in jungle brutality, but Newsy never reserved his venom for Hall.

Once, Newsy bashed Hall across the head with his stick, opening an eight-stitch wound. The next time they met, Hall crashed Lalonde so hard Newsy required ten stitches for his wounds. In another match Lalonde hit Odie Cleghorn viciously enough to inspire Odie's brother Sprague to charge rink and smash Newsy across the forehead. The blow just barely missed Lalonde's eye, and he required twelve stitches to close that gaping wound.'

"Without question," said Dick Beddoes of the Toronto Globe and Mail, "Lalonde could buckle a swash with any ruffian alive."

TONY LESWICK (NHL, 1945-58)

If you were to take the trouble to ask each NHL player during the late forties or early fifties for his opinion of little Tony Leswick, the reply would be "pest" or any number of synonyms thereof.

Ted Lindsay, who was Leswick's teammate after Tony was traded from the Rangers to the Red Wings in 1941, liked to greet Leswick with the observation, "You little toad!," Leswick was little (five feet, six inches; 160 pounds) and he was tough. He usually took on bigger men and frequently lost but always came back for more. Once, rugged Howie Meeker of the Maple Leafs grappled with

Leswick, lifted Tony about the waist, and dispatched him to the ice with a thud. The unconscious Ranger was taken to the infirmary, revived, and eventually returned to the game with a turbanlike bandage swathing his head.

"Tough Tony," as New York fans liked to call him, also was dirty, nasty, sneaky; you name it, that's what they called him. "He was the chippiest broke in the league," said former teammate Don Raleigh. Toronto defenseman Garth Boesch put it another way: "Leswick would get under your arms and between your legs. He'd annoy the life out of you." His style was similar to Leo Labine's. He'd use his tongue as effectively as his stick.

"Tony would get up close and laugh at his opponents," said former teammate Nick Mickoski. "He'd do anything to get under their skin. Once, when I played against him, we went into the corner and he winked at me, like we were good friends. I let up for a second and then, wham! He knocked me right out of the play."

Some of Leswick's more notable targets were Jean Beliveau, Bill Ezinicki, and Maurice "Rocket" Richard. The Rocket once bluntly summed up his feeling about Leswick's decorum this way: "I have nothing good to say about Tony Leswick."

CAROL "CULLY"' WILSON (NHL, 1919-2 7)

The post-World War I era produced a large number of brutalized skaters who would think nothing of shoving a stick down an enemy's throat and often tried it. Cully Wilson was one of them.

In 1925, when Wilson was playing for the Calgary Tigers, he cross-checked Dick Irvin's teeth into his tongue. When Irvin recovered he knocked Wilson cold, using his stick as a bludgeon. , Wilson's most memorable battle has long been regarded as hockey's most private fight and symbolized the ferocity of the old-time game.

It was 1917 and Wilson had been feuding with Cy Denneny, a star with the Ottawa Senators. Their run- running battle had extended through a whole season without noticeable result, and both players were thirsting for blood. They realized that a full-scale brawl during a regular season game might be damaging to their respective teams as well as bring suspensions upon themselves, so they waited until an exhibition All-Star game was to be played on non-NHL turf in Cleveland. "The two of them knew," said hockey historian Bill Roche, "that they would be free from fines and suspensions, since the NHL had no supervision over the game."

The match was played in Cleveland's old Elysium rink, and according to witnesses, it was one of the most vicious ever to take place on or off the ice. Hall of Famer Frank Nighbor, who was there at the time and who had played in hundreds of games, called it "the hardest and longest fight" he had seen.

"Neither the rink nor the city police were inclined -to interfere," said Roche. "The result was a draw in what was hockey's, most thoroughly private bout."

LOU FONTINATO (NHL, 1954-63)

Nicknamed "Leapin' Louie" because of his antics whenever a referee whistled him off the ice, Fontinato is more remembered for the bouts he lost — especially the decision to Gordie Howe — than those he won.

Muscular and fearless, Fontinato made the previously passive Rangers a respectable team in 1955 by beating up on the opposition large (Jean Beliveau) and small (Henri Richard). Louie knew every dirty trick in the book and once went public when a New York news- paper had him give photographic demonstrations of hockey's illegal play. Fontinato gladly complied. Louie's last NHL years were spent in Montreal.

His enemies were numerous. One of them, Bert Olmstead, once reportedly stabbed Fontinato with the point of his stick and sidelined the New York defenseman. When Louie returned to action he pursued Olmstead all over the ice and finally nailed him with a death-defying crosscheck that nearly severed Olmstead's bead from his neck. Another constant foe was Vic Stasiuk of the Bruins.

In March, 1958, they were sharing the penalty box at Boston Garden when several fans-friends of Stasiuk's taunted Fontinato until finally in a rage he took out after them. Boston police finally stopped the riot and pressed charges against Fontinato and some spectators. Stasiuk was a witness against Fontinato in the court proceedings. Louie never forgave Stasiuk for that.

Long after the episode the Bruins and Rangers embarked on a twenty four-game European exhibition tour. The games meant nothing but still Fontinato and Stasiuk kept at each other. "I remember one game," said a Ranger, "when Vic was playing with three sore ribs. Fontinato could have given him a break, under the circumstances, and eased up. He didn't, though." Fontinato's career as a Canadien was prematurely ended in 1963 when Vic Hadfield checked him into the end boards. Louie broke his neck and never regained proper use of it.

GEORGE "RED" SULLIVAN (NHL, 1949-61)

Never renowned as a fighter, the lightweight Sullivan was a forechecking specialist for the Bruins, Blackhawks, and later the Rangers, who used his stick in every possible manner. He completely disregarded the unwritten rule that goaltenders are off limits when it comes to mugging; and as a result, Sullivan frequently pursued and pummeled Montreal's wandering netminder, Jacques Plante.

Many of Sullivan's less-than-clean techniques were neatly subtle, except to the victim. Red was most notorious for his habit of "kicking skates," a method of dumping an opponent by allowing him to move in front of you in the corners, then kicking the back of his heel. The usual reaction is to fall on one's head. If the victim survives, as did defenseman Doug Harvey of the Canadiens, the assailant is in trouble, big trouble.

Harvey vividly remembered how Sullivan had nailed him. "It got so," said Harvey, "that there was no defense against it except spearing. I don't like it but I don't like to be taken either." - Harvey finally caught up to Sullivan on Madison Square Garden ice and nearly killed him with a plunge of his stick in Red's stomach.

"Sully was cutting for the goal," said teammate Andy Bathgate, "when Harvey shoved his stick in Red's gut. It looked like Harvey was using a fixed bayonet." Sullivan collapsed on the ice and was removed to the hospital, where an emergency operation was performed on a ruptured spleen. A Catholic priest administered last rites. The operation was successful and left Sullivan with a souvenir forty-five-inch sear across the stomach. "I thought I was going to die," said Sullivan.